Matthew Prior

Twayne's English Authors Series

George D. Economou, Editor
University of Oklahoma

TEAS 418

Matthew Prior's tomb in Poets' Corner, Westminster Abbey. *Photograph by Robert Harding. Reprinted by permission of Mr. Harding.*

Matthew Prior

By Frances Mayhew Rippy

Ball State University

Twayne Publishers • Boston

Matthew Prior

Frances Mayhew Rippy

Copyright © 1986 by G.K. Hall & Co.
All Rights Reserved
Published by Twayne Publishers
A Division of G. K. Hall & Co.
70 Lincoln Street
Boston, Massachusetts 02111

Copyediting supervised by Lewis DeSimone
Book production by Lyda E. Kuth
Book design by Barbara Anderson

Typeset in 11 pt. Garamond
by Modern Graphics, Weymouth, Massachusetts

Printed on permanent/durable acid-free paper
and bound in the United States of America

Library of Congress Cataloging in Publication Data

Rippy, Frances Mayhew.
  Matthew Prior.

  (Twayne's English authors series; TEAS 418)
  Bibliography: p. 154
  Includes index.
  1. Prior, Matthew, 1664–1721—Criticism and
interpretation. I. Title. II. Series.
PR3644.R57 1986   821'.5   85–14117
ISBN 0–8057–6902–1

*To Merrill
and to Felix, Conrad, and Marguerite,
who waited for supper
till I had completed one last paragraph*

Contents

About the Author
Preface
Chronology

> *Chapter One*
> Prior's Private and Political Life and His Poetry   1
>
> *Chapter Two*
> Prior's Laureate Verse   44
>
> *Chapter Three*
> The Variety of Prior's Shorter Poems   57
>
> *Chapter Four*
> Prior's Three Long Poems:
> *Henry and Emma, Solomon, Alma*   84
>
> *Chapter Five*
> Prior's Prose and Dramas   95
>
> *Chapter Six*
> The Major Impact of a Minor Poet   119

Notes and References   135
Selected Bibliography   154
Index   162

About the Author

Frances Mayhew Rippy is professor of English and director of Ph.D. Studies in English at Ball State University, Muncie, Indiana. Holding her A.B. degree from Texas Christian University, her A.M. and Ph.D. degrees from Vanderbilt University, she studied under Geoffrey Tillotson at Birkbeck College, University of London. She has taught at Vanderbilt University, Texas Christian University, and Lamar State University, and, as a visiting professor, at Sam Houston State University and the University of Puerto Rico. For over twenty years Dr. Rippy has edited the *Ball State University Forum*. She is senior advisor to the *Steinbeck Quarterly*. A specialist in Restoration and eighteenth-century British literature and in literary criticism, Dr. Rippy has written and published eleven articles or chapters and thirty-four reviews, which have appeared in *Non Solus: A Publication of the University of Illinois Library Friends at Urbana-Champaign; The Writer; Studies in Medieval, Renaissance, American Literature: A Festschrift* (Texas Christian University); *New Mexico Quarterly; Ball State Teachers College Forum; Beaumont Journal;* and *Descant: The Texas Christian University Literary Journal.* She has conducted workshops for the Midwest Writers Conference and for the Department of Arkansas Natural and Cultural Heritage, and has served as secretary-treasurer, vice president, and president of the Indiana College English Association. Dr. Rippy has held a Lilly Library Research Grant, a Danforth Summer Research Grant, and a Fulbright Scholarship to London. A member of the Literary Advisory Panel of the Indiana Commission for the Arts, she has served as a consultant-evaluator for the New England Association and for the North Central Association of Colleges and Schools. A Danforth Associate and a member of Phi Beta Kappa, Dr. Rippy is listed in *Who's Who in America* and was in 1973 named as one of the Outstanding Educators of America.

Preface

A single monument dominates its section of the Poets' Corner of Westminster Abbey. Two full-size female figures, Muses apparently, bearing a flute and a folio volume, flank a black sarcophagus, whose Latin inscription informs us that its occupant was thinking about writing a history of his times, when little by little a fever crept up on him and simultaneously broke off the thread of his work and his life, on 18 September 1721, at age fifty-seven. Atop the sarcophagus is a Coysevox bust of a clean-shaven man, youngish middle-aged, with pleasant, sensitive features, wearing a soft hat, his coat opened at the neck showing a shirt also opened, and looking with pleasant dignity to his left. Above the bust is a cherub's face and folded wings; on an eaved roof of marble still above recline two cherubic putti, one bearing an hour glass and the other a golden torch. A long double-columned Latin inscription at the base concludes by informing us that all things flowed forth spontaneously from him, as if from a perpetual spring, and that it was doubtful whether he was more refined as a writer or entertaining as a companion.

This sumptuous monument, largest and most impressive in the Poets' Corner, belongs not to Shakespeare or Milton, but to Matthew Prior. To sit for a few minutes near this tomb, softly illuminated by afternoon sunlight from an opposite door, is to watch the same scene repeated, with only minor variations. An American woman rushes up to the tomb, scans through the Latin for the proper name, and queries, in puzzled disappointment, "But who was Matthew Prior?" Her British guide murmurs reassuringly, "Some of these men were very important in their own day. . . ." She moves on to other monuments, not wholly satisfied. The tomb should have belonged to Dryden, who has a simple bust nearby, or to Spenser, who has no bust but a monument to Prior's right.

Her enthusiastic approach and disgruntled departure point up a critical problem to which there is no easy answer. Why is Prior, so important in his own day, so little known in ours? Or, to state the problem more generally, in what sense may a minor poet have a major significance, for his own day or our own?

MATTHEW PRIOR

There is an apparent solution that proves none at all. Matthew Prior left, by the terms of his will, £500 for "this last piece of human vanity"; this enormous sum in 1721 paid for a tomb designed by James Gibbs and monuments by John Michael Rysbrack, with a bust by Coysevox and a pompous Latin inscription by Dr. Robert Freind. But the problem is not solved. Not every man with £500 can be buried in the Poets' Corner. Prior did not buy the bust, furthermore; it was commissioned by Louis XIV, who presented it to him as a gift. The money that Prior left for the tomb, moreover, had been made by the issuing of his 1717 *Poems on Several Occasions,* one of the most successful literary ventures that England had seen. Thus the problem remains. If Prior's poetry could make a fortune for him in England 265 years ago, then why is it so little remembered today?

When we designate a man as a minor poet, we are saying about him one or more of several things. We may be saying that poetry was his avocation while he pursued a nonliterary vocation. Or we may be saying that he served as an official or unofficial laureate to his own times, expressing their peculiar enthusiasms and limitations so exactly that he is hopelessly dated in times other than his own. More charitably, we may be saying that he excelled in one narrow genre, probably some form of brief verse, but could not move beyond this area of excellence to other types of brief verse or to the long poem. Similarly, we may be saying that he lacked range and variety, that he wrote well in one verse-form but in no other. Finally, and most gently, we may be saying that, whatever his merits as a poet, he was more important in his influence upon others than in his poems in their own right.

This book will examine Matthew Prior on these several grounds, trying to determine the senses in which he is a major or minor poet. It will explore the biographical question of poetry and his vocation. It will look at his "laureate verse" written to celebrate affairs of state, at his shorter pieces, at his prose and dramas, at his three long poems. It will touch upon his experiments with various prosodic forms and his relationship to and influence upon the three major literary figures of the eighteenth century: Swift, Pope, Johnson. An examination of all these facets of Prior's life and writing will reveal that there are several senses in which he may be said to be a minor poet with a major significance.

Preface

Like anyone who has worked with Matthew Prior during the past quarter century, I am deeply indebted to the edition of *The Literary Works of Matthew Prior* edited by Professors H. Bunker Wright and Monroe K. Spears. I am especially grateful to Professors Wright and Spears for their permission to quote selections from Prior from their edition.

In the preparation of this manuscript I have had the assistance of a number of grants—of released time and of funding—without which its completion would have been much delayed. I acknowledge with gratitude the aid of Dr. James McClintock, for the McClintock Award for summer research; of Ball State University, for a faculty research grant, a summer research grant, and a special leave to work on portions of this project in the British Library and in the Miriam Lutcher Stark Library of the University of Texas; and of a Lilly Library Small Research Grant to work at Indiana University.

My special thanks go also to my husband and children, who suffered inconveniences uncomplainingly in order that this manuscript might be completed.

Frances Mayhew Rippy

Ball State University

Chronology

1664	July 21 or 23, Matthew Prior born in Westminster, London, to Elizabeth and George Prior, a London joiner (carpenter).
c. 1672	Enters Westminster School.
c. 1675	George Prior dies; Matthew is withdrawn from Westminster School and placed to work keeping accounts in his uncle Arthur Prior's Rhenish Tavern.
1676	Charles Sackville, sixth Earl of Dorset, discovers Prior reading Horace behind his uncle's bar and eventually pays Prior's tuition to return to Westminster School.
1681	Becomes a King's Scholar at Westminster School.
1683	April 3, receives a scholarship to St. John's College, Cambridge.
1687	February, is graduated from Cambridge University. July, Prior and Charles Montagu win instant public acclaim with *The Hind and the Panther Transvers'd*.
1688	April 3, enters as a Keyton Fellow at St. John's College.
1688–1689	Acts as tutor to the two sons of the Earl of Exeter.
1690–1697	Serves as secretary to Lord Dursley, the English ambassador to The Hague, in negotiating Treaty of Ryswick (signed 20–21 September 1697).
1690–1706	Flanders Jane ("Jinny") serves as Prior's mistress and housekeeper in The Hague, London, and Paris.
1692	February, Motteux praises and publishes in the *Gentleman's Journal* Prior's "To the Honourable Charles Montague, Esq;". August, Tonson publishes Prior's first military panegyric, "An Ode in Imitation of the Second Ode of the Third Book of Horace."
1697	December, appointed secretary to the reopened British embassy in Paris.
1698	c. 23 March, elected fellow of the Royal Society.

Chronology

1699	May, returns to London as under-secretary of state to the Earl of Jersey.
1700	By 19 January, becomes a member of the Whig Kit-Cats. Spring, Cambridge University awards Prior the M.A. degree.
1700–1702	Serves William III as peripatetic diplomatic agent.
1700–1707	Serves as commissioner of the Board of Trade and Plantations, succeeding John Locke (28 June 1700–22 April 1707).
1701	February–June, serves as a member of Parliament from East Grinstead in Sussex.
1703–1704	Winter, the fifth part of Tonson's *Miscellanies* appears, containing eighteen of Prior's poems. Casually courts the poet Elizabeth Singer.
1706–1710	Is assigned Linacre Lectureship at St. John's College.
1707	January, Edmund Curll publishes a pirated edition of Prior's *Poems on Several Occasions*.
1709	Tonson prints authorized edition of Prior's *Poems on Several Occasions*; second edition appears in same year.
1709–1715	(or 1718). Anne Durham ("Cloe") is Prior's mistress.
1710	Writes for—and perhaps is in general charge of—the Tory *Examiner*, a political newspaper. Joins Swift, Arbuthnot, Erasmus Lewis, and various Tory politicians as members of the Brothers Club.
1711	Another authorized edition of Prior's *Poems on Several Occasions*.
1711–1713	Beginning on 12 July 1711, Prior, Gaultier, Mesnager, Bolingbroke carry on secret negotiations culminating on 11 April 1713, in the signing of the Treaty of Utrecht ("Matt's Peace"), ending the War of the Spanish Succession.
1712–1714	Serves as commissioner of the customs (January 1712–late 1714).
1712	Late September, is appointed minister plenipotentiary to France.
1713	Another authorized edition of Prior's *Poems on Several Occasions*.

1713–1714	Serves as acting ambassador in Paris (August 1713–August 1714).
1715	Relieved of his duties as ambassador to France (January) and returns to London (late March).
1715–1716	Arrested (9 June 1715) and confined at house of sergeant-at-arms till 26 June 1716. Writes *Alma: or, The Progress of the Mind* while confined.
1716–1721	Elizabeth Cox ("Lisetta") becomes Prior's mistress.
1717	Another authorized edition of *Poems on Several Occasions*.
1719	Mid-March, Tonson and Barber's subscription edition of Prior's expanded *Poems on Several Occasions* appears, including all of the poems in the 1709 edition and adding a number of key poems, notably *Solomon* and *Alma*.
1720	First half, Prior and Edward Harley jointly purchase Down Hall, a country estate in Essex, about which Prior writes "Down-Hall; A Ballad."
1721	While guest of the Edward Harleys at Wimpole, suffers a week-long attack of "cholera morbus," dies 18 September and is buried in Poets' Corner, Westminster Abbey, 25 September.

Chapter One
Prior's Private and Political Life and His Poetry

Birth, Childhood, Westminster School (1664–83)

The baptismal register at St. Margaret's, Westminster, records the baptism on 2 August, 1664 of "Matthew Pryor s. to Geo. by Eliz."[1] Matthew, whose birthday was either 21 July or 23 July 1664, was the fifth of six children and apparently the only one to survive early childhood. His father, a carpenter, had left Dorset to practice his trade in London, where his brother Arthur already owned the Rhenish Tavern on Channel Row and another brother, Samuel, kept the Rummer Tavern between Whitehall and Charing Cross.[2] Prior's mother may have been Elizabeth Pennefather; she appears to have come from a good family and married below her rank.[3]

Young Matthew lived comfortably enough. Stephen's Alley, Westminster, his birthplace, was a handsome if busy street. His uncle Arthur's Rhenish Tavern flourished, and his father's business as joiner seems to have been a responsible and reasonably lucrative one. From his early childhood, moreover, he had the pleasure of making verses. He was later to write in his "Heads for a Treatise upon Learning" that "I would advise no Man to attempt [poetry] except he cannot help it, and if he cannot it is in vain to disswade him from it. . . . As to my own Part I found this Impulse very soon, and shall continue to feel it as long as I can Think; I remember nothing further in life than that I made Verses, I chose Guy of Warwick for my first Hero and killed Colborn the Gyant before I was big enough for Westminster Schole."[4] Noting the literary bent of his only surviving child, his father sent him to nearby Westminster School, ruled rigidly by Dr. Busby to emphasize strict discipline, the traditional classical curriculum, extemporaneous composition in both prose and verse, and oratory. Even before Busby,

Westminster could boast of Ben Jonson and Abraham Cowley as alumni, but Busby's reputation was such that he could attract sons of the leading families in England away from their private tutors or private academies—Cavendishes, Russells, Montagus, Legges, Sackvilles—while simultaneously drawing upon sons of country gentlemen, professional men, and even—as in Matthew's case—London tradesmen. The older generation of Busby's graduates included two lord chancellors, an archbishop of York, "the whole bench of bishops" (as Busby himself boasted), John Locke, Christopher Wren, and John Dryden—the leading philosopher, architect, and poet-dramatist of their day. The younger generation included Prior, Nicholas Rowe, and Francis Atterbury.[5] Prior later praised the training that he had received at the school: "I think . . . Nicety of Judgement particularly eminent in those bred at Westminster Schole, and gained probably from their being used very Young to what Dr. Sprat calls *the Genius of that Place,* which is to Verses made Extempore, and Declamations composed in very few hours. . . ."[6]

About 1675, when Prior was around eleven, his father died and his widowed mother, unable to pay his school fees, withdrew him from Westminster and placed him to work keeping the accounts in his uncle Arthur's Rhenish Tavern. There he formed a very close attachment with his cousin Katharine, two years his senior, who was later to marry George Villiers and, after Villiers's death, George Harrison. Prior later wrote poems to celebrate her first marriage, to sympathize with her upon her first husband's untimely death, and to observe several less notable occasions. In his last London house, he lived next door to Katharine and her second husband, and he left her £100 when he died.[7]

His uncle Arthur's Rhenish Tavern brought Prior something even more immediately valuable than the love and friendship of his cousin Katharine: the patronage of Charles Sackville, sixth Earl of Dorset, who had come into the Rhenish Tavern in search of his friend, Fleetwood Shepherd. Having found the twelve-year-old Prior behind the bar reading Horace, Dorset asked him first to construe a passage or two and then to turn an ode into English verse. Prior performed these scholarly tasks so admirably that in later visits Dorset and his noble friends often asked the young boy to translate Horatian odes or Ovidian verses into English. Not long after, Dorset offered to pay Prior's tuition to return to Westminster School, with his uncle

Arthur continuing to provide his clothing and other necessities. The Priors gratefully accepted. Lord Dorset's sponsorship of Prior was not at all an unusual act for him, for he was also friend and patron to Dryden, Congreve, Shadwell, Lee, Otway, Etherege, and a number of less important literary men.[8]

About this same time (in 1676) Prior was to form still another fortunate friendship because of his uncle's Rhenish Tavern. The Honourable George Montagu moved into Manchester House, a palatial home across the street from the tavern, and the Montagu boys, Charles and James, entered Westminster School and became two of Matthew's closest friends.

In 1679 Charles Montagu, three years older than Prior and James, finished at Westminster and entered Trinity College, Cambridge. In 1681 Prior became a King's Scholar at Westminster, an honor that Charles had previously held. This important award, based upon a distinguished command of classical languages, exempted the student from fees at the college (both for tuition and for residence), gave him an allowance for his dress and for various festive expenses, and conferred upon him certain rights and privileges, both ceremonial and practical.

Study at St. John's College, Cambridge (1683–87)

It was customary for the Westminister King's Scholars to go to Christ Church, Oxford, and Lord Dorset wished Prior to follow this tradition. George Stepney, another of Prior's close Westminster friends, had, however, joined Charles Montagu at Trinity College, Cambridge, in 1682, and James Montagu planned to join them there in 1684. The eighteen-year-old Prior did not wish to go up to Oxford while his three closest friends were at Cambridge; instead, he defied the wishes of both Lord Dorset and Dr. Busby by applying in the spring of 1683 for one of the five scholarships just established at St. John's College, Cambridge, by the Duchess of Somerset. He received a scholarship and enrolled in St. John's College on 3 April 1683.

As one of the first five holders of the Somerset scholarships, Prior was in an enviable position, even if he had briefly alienated his previous sponsors. By the terms of the scholarship, he would be exempted from paying all tuition and would receive an allowance of five shillings a week for living expenses, a bedroom to be shared with four other boys, and a private room for studying. His tutor at St. John's was a Mr. Billers.[9]

During his four years at St. John's, Prior followed a curriculum still heavy in logic and divinity, one that he was to feel in later years had turned him away from poetry and toward prose and politics: ". . . I had two Accidents in Youth which hindred me from being quite possest with the Muse: I was bred in a Colledge where prose was more in fashion than Verse. . . ." ("Heads for a Treatise upon Learning," *LW*, 1:583.) Yet from these four college years we have an impressive body of Prior's poetry in both Latin and English and chiefly pastoral or Pindaric in form. There are still extant over thirty Latin pieces (*LW*, 2:723-53) and a dozen poems in English (*LW*, 1:1-27). None of them would have made Prior's literary reputation, but his careful retention of them is an indication of the seriousness with which he took them. Almost all of these poems are occasional. Some were called forth by notable events in the royal family or the Earl of Dorset's family. Several are addressed to churchmen—two to the Right Reverend Francis Lord Bishop of Ely—and suggest that at this time Prior may have been seriously contemplating taking holy orders, one of the careers open to the Cambridge graduate. Two other poems were addressed to his cousin, Katharine Prior. Another *(A Satyr on the modern Translators)* he steadfastly refused to acknowledge as his in later life, striking out as it does in a direction that he seldom later took.

These college exercises assumed certain forms recognizable in Prior's later, more finished efforts. He tends to be an occasional poet, looking to the events of royalty and nobility for his topics. He enjoys manipulating pastoral and mythological machinery, and does so with considerable skill. He can use the poem as a highly successful instrument to win over those whom he may formerly have antagonized—the Earl of Dorset by refusing to attend Christ Church, Oxford; Katharine Prior by not answering her letters; or Dr. Humphrey Gower, master of the college, for a breach of discipline that had caused Prior to be confined to his room on a sharply limited diet. In every case the result of the poem was precisely what Prior wished—the Earl of Dorset and his family became his patrons once more and continued so for the rest of his life; Katharine Prior remained his closest family friend; Dr. Gower promptly reinstated him with full dining hall privileges. Thus the young Prior had learned a lesson that he would never forget: that a winning poem, reflecting the writer's penitence and the recipient's merits, was a powerful diplomatic instrument. Furthermore, though these early poems, written while Prior was between the ages of nineteen and twenty-three, are not significant whole poems, they do contain effective groups of lines that show him to be a young poet of skill if not of consistency.

On 9 February 1687, Prior was graduated from Cambridge University with a bachelor of arts degree, eleventh in the *Orde Senioritatis* for that year. For the occasion he produced a Latin hexameter poem of thirty-four lines, "Fuit justum et injustum ante Leges Civiles," arguing that, despite Hobbes's contention in the *Leviathan,* justice and injustice did exist before civil laws were written down or judicial courts established.

Years in London, Cambridge, and Burleigh (1687–90)

Shortly after his graduation Prior returned to London, perhaps because of the last illness of his uncle Arthur, who died there in May 1687, leaving Prior £100 in his will—a much larger sum than he bequeathed to any other relative except the members of his immediate family. Still without a settled career, Prior turned to a continuation of the satires upon literary figures that he had begun at St. John's with *A Satyr on the modern Translators.* Early in May 1687, he wrote *Satyr on the Poets: In Imitation of the Seventh Satyr of Juvenal,* in which he adapted the first one hundred lines of Juvenal's poem to satirize the literary figures of his own age. The theme of Prior's poem is that poetry was not a paying profession in late seventeenth-century England, a consideration that must have impressed the young Prior at this decisive point in his life, when he had soon to commit himself to a career. If the later piece lacks some of the sharply individualized satiric portraits of the earlier one, it compensates by striking at moments some of the first clear tones of a complex melody which we shall hear again in Prior's poetry at its best—a witty, cynical, realistic melancholy.

Within two months of the composition of *Satyr on the Poets,* Prior brought out, in collaboration with his old friend, Charles Montagu, *The Hind and the Panther Transvers'd,* a satire that was to be decisive in making the careers of both men. Dryden, whom Prior had already attacked in his two other satires, had just brought out, on 27 May 1687, *The Hind and the Panther,* an allegorical beast-epic in which he defended the Roman Catholicism to which he had been a recent convert. The poem became the target for a number of Anglican and Dissenting satires, though only Montagu and Prior's is still read.

Joseph Spence quotes Dr. Lockier as having recalled that "Dryden was most touched with the Hind and the Panther transverst. I have heard him say, 'For two young fellows that I have always been so civil to, to use an old man in so cruel a manner.' And he wept as he said it."[10] But Spence's account is somewhat suspect. We have no evidence that Prior had ever met Dryden, much less had been civilly treated by him. Dryden was scarcely "an old man" when the burlesque appeared: he was fifty-seven. Dr. Johnson repeats a portion of the anecdote but wisely cautions: "Dryden had been more accustomed to hostilities than that such enemies should break his quiet, and if we can suppose him vexed it would be hard to deny him sense enough to conceal his uneasiness."[11] However Dryden may have reacted to the burlesque, it was an instant and meteoric success.

Prior wrote one more poem in 1687, "Epistle, to Lord ----." The poem and an accompanying letter were written in the summer to the Earl of Dorset, apparently in answer to Lord Dorset's praise of Prior's wit in *The Hind and the Panther Transvers'd* and his order that Prior should write more poetry. The poem begins with a customary but graceful praise of the Earl himself, but its main point becomes a theme that Prior will repeat throughout much of his mature poetry—that although every man has some talent, most men suffer from an illogical urge to attempt tasks for which they have no talent at all. Prior gives a series of lively examples of men who ruin their lives in such attempts and, as he was frequently to do later in his mature poetry, he turns the final jest on himself. Prior suggests to the Earl of Dorset that, despite his patronage, he may seek a career outside the world of poetry, for which he may have no particular talents.

Despite the summer success of *The Hind and the Panther Transvers'd* and his growing conviction that poetry was not the career for him, Prior had found no other profession in 1687 and remained for the next fifteen months a young man knocking about London and writing a few occasional poems. When Charles Montagu married, in

February 1688, Prior wrote him a fulsome congratulatory poem containing lines suggesting not a marriage but a translation to glory.

At about the same time (1688) Prior wrote ninety-four lines of "A Session of the Poets," dealing with the question of who should succeed John Dryden as poet laureate, if he indeed was to be replaced. The genre, and even the title, as Professors Wright and Spears have commented, were established by Suckling and most recently attempted by Rochester.[12] Prior's fragment breaks off before Apollo reaches a decision; presumably the reward was to be given to someone ridiculous, because Prior has already rejected, on grounds that he considers patently foolish, the three applicants whom he believes to have real talent: Waller, Sedley, and Wycherley. Though no aspirant receives the coveted laureateship, the poem shows Prior's high regard for Waller, Sedley, and Wycherley, and his contempt for the bad poets of his time. Only on Dryden does his judgment differ sharply from ours.

On 3 April 1688, Prior was entered as a Keyton Fellow at St. John's. He had shown his usual politic deviousness in winning the position. Both of the fellowships at St. John's from Middlesex were filled, but a Keyton fellowship, intended for a chorister from Southwell Minster, was vacant. Prior became a member of the Southwell Choir on 1 February, after due examination, and was appointed a Keyton Fellow at St. John's College only two months later. In April 1688, he moved into the Fellows' quarters of St. John's. He was assigned to one of the two medical fellowships and was later required to lecture on Galen as Linacre Lecturer (1706–10). Although both the choral and the medical aspects of his fellowship seem surprising to us now, he was not ill-qualified for either position. Westminster boys received careful musical training for their choir work in the Abbey. Moreover, often ill throughout his fifty-eight years, thin and coughing, Prior had ample reason to be sharply interested in medicine and related subjects.[13] Prior's *Alma* is filled with anatomical detail—technical descriptions of the brain, nerves in the eyes, fingers, toes, ears, and mouth, and various other parts of the body.[14]

Sometime in the same year, perhaps mid-October, Prior wrote as an exercise for St. John's College an irregular ode in the style of Abraham Cowley, another Westminster Scholar turned poet and diplomat a generation earlier. This ode "On Exodus iii.14" was apparently a favorite of Prior's, for he was later to use it as the lead poem in both of his own collections of his verse. It may also be

considered his first mature effort, for the attitude toward religion
that it expressed persisted in Prior's serious work throughout his
life. In lines indebted to Dryden's *Religio Laici* as well as to Cowley's
odes, Prior elaborates upon the scriptural passage that gave his poem
its title, concluding that finite and fallible man is presumptuous in
asking to name God, whose existence alone is sufficient for man's
limited knowledge. Prior's exploration of man's limits in understanding himself, the physical world, and the nature and attributes
of God, was later to find echoes in Pope's *Essay on Man,* and some
of his strongest lines to date are contained in the descriptions of the
folly of man's intellectual pride, and of the mysteries of the un-
fathomable universe. Prior concludes the poem by advocating the
"Immortal Perspective" of Faith, rather than "Reason's glimmering
Light," maintaining that no philosopher has ever invented "So pol-
itick an Instrument" for reaching heaven as the ladder that Jacob's
faith gave to him in his dream. "On Exodus iii. 14" is an uneven
poem; there are still weak stanzas, unfortunate word-choices, jum-
bled metaphors. But Prior, still young, has struck a solemn and
reverberating note on a lyre often to be treated by modern critics
as if it played only light songs. The Exodus ode stands squarely
within the Augustan tradition of serious philosophical poetry, as a
link between the earlier poems of Dryden and the later poems of
Pope.

During this same two-year period, when Prior was graduated
from St. John's but had not yet found employment outside the
college, he also wrote four Latin pieces directly related to specific
occasions at either Westminster School or St. John's College and
reflecting his respect for both institutions, especially for Dr. Humphrey Gower of St. John's. In a fifth Latin piece of the same period,
"Ad Magistrum," Prior expressed his gratitude to a past master for
encouraging his studies, shaping his character, and, most recently,
obtaining for him a new and benevolent patron. Professors Spears
and Wright conjecture convincingly that this Latin piece, like several others by Prior, was addressed to Dr. Humphrey Gower, thanking him for having obtained for Prior his first position outside the
college, that of tutor to the sons of the Earl of Exeter, at Burleigh.[15]
Evidence in this Latin poem and one that followed it ("Epistola ad
Magistrum") makes clear that Prior accepted the position of tutor
at Burleigh about the middle of the year 1688 and held it at least
until August 1689.

Prior's poems during this year as tutor indicate his widely varied interests at Burleigh. A broadside, "The Orange," written in the politically crucial month of December 1688, ironically advises the English public to "Throw the Orange away" (reject William of Orange) while it really attacks James II, his newborn son, and their supporters. A similar political message is conveyed in late April of the next year (1689) in "To Mr: K----s Tune of the Prince's march," a song urging William, now in control of the English throne, to declare war upon James, just landed in Ireland. The two poems are interesting chiefly as first expressions of a fierce affection that would inform many of Prior's poems for the next fourteen years: his warm loyalty to William.[16] Three other poems concern the Earl of Exeter's family,[17] and another three show Prior sharply aware of the fine paintings that surrounded him at Burleigh.[18] Three more were exercises in honor of Lady Margaret Beaufort, mother of Henry VII and foundress of St. John's College.[19]

The most interesting grouping consists of four poems written to Fleetwood Shepherd, the wit and poet who served as intermediary between the Earl of Dorset and the many young men whose patron he became. One, the mock-heroic "On Fleet: Shepheards takeing away a childs bread and butter," tells of the trivial incident in high-flown phrases suited to an encounter between classical heroes. In another, "On Mr: F. S. Killing the French K . . . ," Prior twits Shepherd, a notorious liar, by pretending mock-heroically to believe that Shepherd has indeed killed Louis XIV. The two most revealing of the Shepherd poems of this period are not mock-heroic but are familiar verse epistles, which exhibit a facet of Prior's versifying not fully seen before: his ability to write easy, informal verse-letters, which present a winning portrait of himself in the seemingly artless manner that conceals much art. "To Mr. Fleetwood Shepherd" and "An Epistle to Fleetwood Shepherd, Esq; Burleigh, May 14, 1689" are mines of biographical information about Prior's childhood and youth: his tavern-keeping uncle; his nonconformist country grandmother; Dorset's early patronage of Prior, making a poet of the tavern-boy; his friendship with Charles Montagu and their joint writing of *The Hind and the Panther Transvers'd*. More important, the poems show Prior's mature strength in informal light verse—lively, easy, charming. The first poem is essentially an appeal to Shepherd to intercede on Prior's behalf with the Earl of Dorset, who had become lord chamberlain on 14 February 1689, the day after

William and Mary formally took the English throne, and hence had many appointments at his disposal. The other, dated poem is even more significant as the first clear instance in which Prior attempted a subject that was to interest him for all his life: the folly of mankind as shown in the strange customs of other nations, which would find England's equally irrational and odd. In its ludicrous feminine rhymes as well as its subject matter, the "Epistle to Fleetwood Shepherd" foreshadows *Alma,* as its ending, expressing Prior's restlessness in his retired country seat, anticipates his "laureate" verse to come.

A fifth poem from this period, "Journey to Copt-Hall," describes a thirty-six mile journey from Cambridge to Copt-Hall, where Fleetwood Shepherd was superintendent and where Lord Dorset lived retired during most of James II's reign. Not published until 1907, the poem, though metrically rough, reveals at several points Prior's close acquaintance with Samuel Butler's *Hudibras,* probably the strongest shaping force in his use of the burlesque octosyllabic. In its joggingly informal account of a journey in all its minutiae—its cost and its discomfort, the precise mode of travel and the conversation at the dinner upon arrival—it also anticipates one of Prior's best poems, written thirty years later: "Down-Hall; A Ballad."

That Prior was still at Burleigh on 1 August 1689, is established by the Latin poem "The Crest of the Arms of the Earl of Exeter a Wheatsheaf supported by Two Lyons," which is given that date both in the Longleat Calendar (28) and in the 1740 edition of Prior's poems. But his occupation throughout the next fourteen months is uncertain. Most plausibly it has been suggested either that he remained as tutor to the boys for an additional year or that he returned to live as a fellow at St. John's College. In either case, his various epistles to Fleetwood Shepherd show that he, finding the retired life too dull, was pleading with Lord Dorset for a livelier and more public existence.

Years at the Hague (1690–97)

Prior's opportunity came on 16 October 1690, when Charles Montagu wrote to George Stepney about the third of the Westminster triumvirate of friends: "We are endeavoring to get Mr. Prior to be secretary to Lord Dursley in the room of Dr. Aglionby."[20] By the first of November the appointment was made, and Prior arrived at The Hague to serve Lord Dursley, the English ambassador, as secretary, a post that he was to hold for the next seven years. Prior's first appointment, like those that followed, had greater responsibilities than his title would indicate. Partly because of his low birth and partly because of his lack of funds, Prior throughout his lifetime was to perform diplomatic functions for which superiors were to receive most of the acclaim—and often most of the money as well.

The Hague was an important listening post and relay station in the War of the Grand Alliance (The War of the League of Augsburg), which had already been going on for two years when Prior's appointment was made and was to continue for almost another seven. In this war, whose basic issue was the balance of power between the Bourbons and the Hapsburgs, Louis XIV and France were pitted against England, the Netherlands, Spain, Savoy, and the Holy Roman Empire.

Prior's post included duties that we would expect of a vice consul or a cultural attaché in the modern American foreign service. He issued or refused passports, forwarded newspapers with details relevant to England, sent on with his own comments newsletters arriving from various important towns in the League of Augsburg, and reported details of battles in the war and of local diplomatic gossip. The recipient of all these communications was Daniel Finch, Earl of Nottingham, the senior secretary of state.

Prior was physically much the same figure at twenty-six that he would be thirty years later: thin, wooden-faced, with red cheeks characteristic of his country relatives in East Dorset, and already somewhat easy prey to the recurrent lung and intestinal disorders that were to mark his remaining thirty years and finally claim his life. Furthermore, by 1690 he had apparently established an intimate relationship with a woman known today only as Jane or Flanders Jane or Jinny, the first of the three women who would successively become his mistresses during his bachelor life. It appears that Jane was a widow; she was Prior's mistress and housekeeper for the next sixteen years, in The Hague, Paris, and London, and became the subject of one of his most effective poems, "Jinny the Just."

Along with his diplomatic correspondence, Prior continued his writing of poetry during these seven years at The Hague, but his verse took a more distinctly laureate tone. He had written poems before on affairs of state; now they became a major item in his production. It was no accident that his arrival in Holland coincided with the production of "A Pindarique on His Majesties Birth-Day. Sung before Their Majesties at Whitehall, The Fourth of November 1690." This millennial panegyric is not the best that Prior was to write, but it is the first that he would produce as an official government spokesman.

In addition to his occasional panegyrics, Prior during the next two years continued to write upon other topics which he had already explored in his earlier years: six love poems and songs, two religious poems on Scriptural themes, a classical paraphrase, an epithalamium, a bit of medical scatology.

The year 1692, moreover, was to see the composition of two of Prior's most finished and successful poetic efforts up to that point. In February, Motteux published in his *Gentleman's Journal* a Prior poem, prefacing it by remarking: "Whilst things like the following Stanza's made by Mr. *Prior,* shall be given or sent me, you may believe I shall be prouder of making them publick than my own."[21] "To the Honourable Charles Montague, Esq;" was, in fact, Prior's first flawless success. Mature, balanced, mellow, it never falters, expressing a recurring theme of Prior in conversational quatrains of deceptive ease. Writing to his old friend, Prior comments that it is well that mankind is permitted to fight against real cares by imagined pleasures, for the truth, if seen clearly, is bleak and painful.

> Our Hopes, like tow'ring Falcons, aim
> At Objects in an airy height:
> The little Pleasure of the Game
> Is from afar to view the Flight. . . .
>
> If We see right, We see our Woes:
> Then what avails it to have Eyes?
> From Ignorance our Comfort flows:
> The only Wretched are the Wise.
>   (ll. 21–24, 33–36, *LW,* 1:109)

The tone of wittily rueful melancholy is one of Prior's truest tones; the poem has been frequently anthologized and deservedly included in almost every selection of Prior's best poetry.

Prior achieved a second notable poetic success in August of the same year, when Jacob Tonson published "An Ode in Imitation of the Second Ode of the Third Book of Horace," celebrating the English naval victory at La Hogue, 24 May 1692. The ode was

Prior's first panegyric on an English military victory over foreign troops and his most highly praised poem on affairs of state to that time.

It was not Prior's poetry, however, not even the panegyrics, that brought him to King William's attention. Rather, it was the skill, diligence, and good sense that he displayed in his diplomatic post. Prior's efforts in his new position were such that when Lord Dursley went home to England on sick leave in November 1692, two years after Prior's arrival at The Hague, William suggested, only half jestingly, that Prior should be left at The Hague as "secrétaire du Roy." On 16 March 1693, Prior was appointed by King William a Gentleman of the King's Bedchamber and was granted by Queen Mary a pension of one hundred pounds per year. With Lord Dursley absent from The Hague for eleven months before he finally resigned his office, Prior fulfilled the duties of a minister and dealt directly with the principal secretaries in London. After Lord Dursley resigned, Antony Carye, Viscount Falkland, was appointed to succeed him but died of smallpox before he could assume the office, and his successor, Edward, Lord Villiers, did not assume office until September 1695.

During these three years in which he was acting as chief minister while receiving the pay of a secretary,[22] Prior still found time to write other things than his frequent letters begging for an increase in salary: "Hymn to the Sun. Set by Dr. Purcel, and Sung before their Majesties on New-Years-Day, 1694," "On the taking of Huy" (1694), "An Ode. Presented to the King, on his Majesty's Arrival in Holland, After the Queen's Death. 1695," "An English Ballad, On the Taking of Namur by the King of Great Britain, 1695." In this last poem Prior achieved his greatest and most widely acclaimed success in panegyric verse. He also wrote during this same period three brief poems more personally connected with the royal family and four others concerned with his noble patrons. One of the latter ("A Prologue made for Lord Buckhurst to Speak at Westminster at Christmas 1695") was a prologue to Dryden's *Cleomenes,* which may have been acted in honor of Dryden (also an alumnus of Westminster) and suggests a softening of Prior's feeling for the aging Dryden. Yet another poem grew from Prior's school connections, complimentary verses in Latin addressed to Samuel Shaw, a Cambridge contemporary of Prior who was defending his M.D. thesis on jaundice at the University of Leyden. Prior also produced his first

"Enigma," which, like Prior's later verse-riddles, sounds military and political in nature, although its solution, as given by Motteux, was "The Knave of Clubs, or *Pam* at Lantrelu."

The appointment of Edward, Lord Villiers, to the Dutch post was a fortunate one for Prior, because the men had two strong bonds in common. Both were alumni of St. John's College; and Prior's favorite cousin, Katharine, had married Colonel George Villiers, cousin to Edward. It is thus not surprising that Lord Villiers recommended emphatically that Prior remain at The Hague; King William seconded the request and—perhaps even more to Prior's liking—doubled his salary.

His position at The Hague at last settled for a time, Prior took a house and prepared to remain there until the end of the War of the Grand Alliance. By 1696 there were persistent rumors of peace, for the English were turning the tide of battle against France, and both nations were finding the war expensive and increasingly unpopular. Prior wished strongly to be made Secretary to the Embassy if a treaty of peace was to be made. On 1 September 1696, Lord Shrewsbury wrote to Prior from Whitehall: "I have your letter of the 4th, n.s., and shall by this post desire Mr. Blaithwayt to lay before his Majesty your pretension to be Secretary of the Embassy, in case of a Treaty of Peace; and shall add my opinion of the justice of your request, and hope the King upon this occasion will give proof of his confidence and kindness to one who, having served him long and faithfully, is so well qualified for this employment."[23] True to his word, Shrewsbury wrote to Blaithwayt on that same day, and Prior received the appointment, made official when he visited London and returned with his privy seal as secretary to the Embassy beginning 10 March 1697.

The negotiations for peace were complicated and wearing. The first meeting of the Congress at Ryswick took place on 9 May 1697; the papers were signed on 20 and 21 September of the same year, with Prior's function to check the French and Latin versions. Once more, his facility with languages had stood him in good stead. He was immediately sent from Ryswick to London bearing the official message that England, Holland, and Spain had signed the treaty with France and ended the War of the Grand Alliance; on 24 September he arrived in London, on an occasion of great rejoicing. Narcissus Luttrell wrote on that day that "Just now Mr. Prior, secretary to the embassy, came to Whitehall, being sent expresse of the signing the peace as aforesaid, upon which the guns at the Tower were discharged, the flagg displayed, bells ringing, bonefires, and other demonstrations of joy are preparing."[24] Prior left Holland for the last time in November 1697, precisely seven years after he had gone there. He had made no fortune, but he had attained diplomatic experience and skill, made important political connections, and convinced his superiors—even King William himself—of his diplomatic talents.

During this critical period leading to the Treaty of Ryswick, Prior understandably did not write many poems, and two of those that he did write were of a political nature: "Presented to the King, at his Arrival in Holland, after the Discovery of the Conspiracy 1696" and "A New Answer to An Argument against a Standing Army" (1697). He also produced three brief and informal poems; though none is a serious or sustained performance, all three are of unusual merit. "In a Window in Lord V......s house 1696" is a single quatrain that evinces Prior's skill as a writer of the amorous epigram.

The poem " 'Who would,' says Dryden, 'Drink this draught of Life' " (1697) is a graceful compliment paid in a letter to Charles, second viscount Townshend. Not published until the twentieth century, it is a wryly melancholy variation on the observation that Prior had made before in his "To the Honourable Charles Montague, Esq;" and would make again in *Alma* and *Solomon:* that man is mercifully constituted so that small pleasures (imagined or real) can blot out momentarily the recollection of large and undeniably real pains and woes. The poem is significant not only in itself but as another indication that Prior now felt only companionable respect for the aging Dryden, whom he had often attacked when a college boy.

The third poem in the group is the most interesting biographically, for in describing the pleasures of his free Saturday evenings and Sundays at The Hague, Prior by indirection suggests the typical activities of the six other days of the week. "Written in the Year 1696," often—but never by Prior—titled "The Secretary," exhibits many of the traits of his best colloquial verse. In this poem he shows his easy command of classical learning while shrugging it off as scarcely relevant to his modern state, forces humorous multiple-worded feminine rhymes, and deprecates himself and his work while making both seem attractive and significant. He rides out on Saturday night in his little Dutch chaise, with Horace on his left and a nymph on his right. He has "No Memoire to compose and no Post-boy to move. . ." (l. 5, *LW*, 1:158); his companion can relinquish her week of tea parties and formal visits. Prior rejects the classical analogies to this procession. Anacreon and Sappho give way to the present:

> When good *Vandergoos* and his provident Vrough
> As they gaze on my Triumph do freely allow
> That search all the province you'l find no Man there is
> So blest as the *Englishen Heer* SECRETARIS.
> (ll. 23–26, *LW*, 1:158)

The negotiations for the Treaty of Ryswick had brought Prior other triumphs than political reputation and three excellent short poems. During the negotiations themselves, on 17 May 1697, he had been named chief secretary to the Lords Justices of Ireland. Even more important (especially to the ultimate publication of many of his poems) he had met at the Congress of Ryswick Adrian Drift, later to become his friend, amanuensis, transcriber, and preserver of his manuscript poems after his death. Drift, like Prior, was London born, and was taken to the Congress of Ryswick in the Earl of Jersey's service.

First Years in Paris (1697–99)

Upon his return to England in November 1697, Prior expected to be sent to Dublin to assume his duties as secretary to the Lords Justices. Instead he was appointed secretary of the reopened British Embassy in Paris, to work again under Lord Portland, its new Ambassador Extraordinary. Prior's appointment was announced by 11 December 1697; and he and Portland left for Paris one month later, on 21 January 1698. During this brief period in England, he was proposed as a fellow of the Royal Society, but before the election took place he had left to take up his duties in Paris. Nevertheless, he was elected to membership, possibly on 23 March 1698.[25]

Meanwhile, in Paris Prior had had his first private audience with Louis XIV on 4 February 1698; in mid-August of the same year he saw the exiled James II and his queen; still later he glimpsed the young Stuart prince. Official duties for Prior at this time were few; his chief responsibility seems to have been reporting on those in power in France and on the activities of English Jacobites there.

When the Earl of Portland left France in June 1698, the Earl of Jersey was appointed to succeed him and arrived in September of that year. Although Prior remained at the embassy for nineteen months, Paris, with its opportunities for cultural and literary contacts, did not immediately stimulate his poetical output. It seems, in fact, to have had the contrary effect, for not a single Prior poem dates from this period. It is nevertheless likely that these months added another dimension to Prior's view of the world.

However attractive culturally, Prior's Parisian stay was destroying him financially. Always short of cash, he punctuated his correspondence of this period with pleas for more money to be spent on entertainment or for an appointment that would remove him from his expensive Parisian post. In April 1699, the Earl of Jersey was appointed Secretary of State for the Southern Department, replacing the Duke of Shrewsbury, who had resigned. When the Earl of Manchester (cousin and son-in-law to Charles Montagu) was appointed to replace the Earl of Jersey in Paris, Prior, at his own request, was sent back to London as Under-Secretary of State. He left Paris on 27 August 1699. Though he had produced no literary work during his nineteen months there, he had formed warm ties with such literary figures as Boileau, Dacier, and Fontenelle, and had attracted the favorable attention of such political figures as the duc de Villeroy, the marquis de Torcy, and Louis XIV.

Further London Years (1699–1711)

From Paris Prior went to Loo in Holland to report to William III, who helped him to resolve a problem about the position of chief secretary to the Lords Justices of Ireland, which he had held officially for over two years without being able to go to Ireland to fulfill his duties. Through William's intercession, Prior was permitted to keep his Irish post, in absentia, and was given an allowance of £600 per year as well, to continue until he received a new government post. From Loo Prior journeyed to The Hague and returned from there to London with William III and the Earl of Jersey.

Prior's tasks for the two remaining years of William's life were those of a peripatetic diplomatic agent. He went on repeated journeys to Paris and Marly, in secret negotiations with Louis XIV on the Second Partition Treaty. On 28 June 1700, he was appointed a commissioner of the Board of Trade and Plantations to succeed

John Locke, who had resigned because of ill health. The work of the Board of Trade and Plantations was important and diversified, for it oversaw the governing of all the American colonies and supervised all international English trade, including that of the powerful trading companies.

Though Prior was frequently ill during this period of roving ambassadorship, he found time for vigorous social as well as business and political activities. In a letter to Abraham Stanyan, 19 January 1700, he tells of his membership in the Kit-Cats. His is the earliest extant reference to that gathering of Whig aristocrats and the young writers whom they patronized, although Ned Ward was to declare that the group had existed years earlier and that *The Hind and the Panther Transvers'd* had grown from Kit-Cat meetings.[26] The club derived its name from the Cat and the Fiddle, where the Whig lords and wits met weekly under the sponsorship of Jacob Tonson. Prior's old patron, the Earl of Dorset, was an important figure in the club, as was Prior's childhood friend Charles Montagu, who was to become the Earl of Halifax in this same year. Besides Prior, its literary members included Addison and Steele, Congreve and Rowe.

Despite his membership in the Kit-Cats, Prior was becoming less and less a Whig during these last years of William's life and more and more a Tory, a change probably hastened by his parliamentary experience. When he decided to stand for Parliament in 1700 as representative from Cambridge, he ran neither as Whig or Tory but simply as a "Moderate." By fall it became apparent that he had no chance of victory without waging an active campaign, for which he had neither the time nor the inclination. Instead, he withdrew from the race and accepted, from the Earl of Dorset, the pocket borough of East Grinstead in Sussex. He thus became a Member of Parliament from February to June 1701. During these months his shift from Whig to Tory became open and complete.

If Prior was moving to the right politically, in the belief that England needed a strong king like William unhampered by a majority opposition in Parliament, so had the Whig party moved to the left, in increasing fear that William or Anne, whose last surviving child had just died, might be succeeded on the throne by the son of James II. The Whigs wished to limit William's powers still further and to strengthen the position of the Low Churches, even of Dissenters; Prior opposed such moves. The issue came to a climax during Prior's brief term in Parliament in a vote of censure on the Partition Treaty, which, unpopular in England and never signed by the Austrian emperor, was later repudiated by Louis XIV. Although he himself had had some share in drawing up the treaty, Prior voted impeachments against the four leading Whigs involved in it: Baron Somers and the Earls of Orford, Portland, and Halifax (Prior's childhood friend, Charles Montagu). Although Prior and Montagu had still been on sufficiently friendly terms in 1700 for Prior to compose the Latin "Preamble to Baron Halifax's Patent" when Montagu was awarded this honor, Prior explained that to vote against the impeachments was to hold William himself, rather than his agents, responsible for the unpopular treaty, and that he had to vote as he did to ward off a direct attack on William. Whatever his motives, he had cut himself off from any hope of further Whig patronage. The Earl of Dorset, whose Whig friends Prior had voted to impeach, did not award him the pocket-borough seat in Parliament again; the Earl of Portland and Charles Montagu were no longer his patrons or his friends; and his membership in the Kit-Cat Club was abruptly terminated.

Yet, despite his shift in party, Prior seems to have avoided much of the bitterness often attendant upon political change. He later patched up his friendship with the Montagus; and Horace Walpole, the son of the greatest Whig of the eighteenth century, was to write that "Prior is much a favourite with me, *though a Tory,* nor did I ever hear anything ill of him. He left his party, but not his friends, and seems to me to have been very amiable."[27]

Even during this period of relative prosperity Prior sometimes found himself in financial discomfort. He was not paid his salary as one of the commissioners of Trade and Plantations from 29 September 1700, to 8 March 1702. The total unpaid salary (£1446. 16s. ½d.) was written off at Prior's death twenty years later as "An Arrear of Salary Due From King William To Matthew Prior . . . ."[28] Yet his expenses were increased by his purchase in 1700 of his Westminster house on the west side of Duke Street, with its rear overlooking St. James's Park. A source of great pleasure to Prior, although expensive to maintain, "Matt's Palace" was to be his chief place of residence for the remaining twenty years of his life.[29]

Using his Duke Street "palace" as base of operations, Prior continued to serve the king as William played a decisive role in shaping the Grand Alliance between England, Austria, and Holland as a force for containing or defeating Louis XIV. But William, already in failing health, was thrown from his horse and injured in a hunting accident on 21 February 1702, and he died on 8 March of the same year. He was succeeded on 23 April 1702, by his sister-in-law, Anne, who like Prior himself was thirty-seven, ailing, and now childless.

During the last three years of William's life, when Prior was serving as his London-based agent, Prior's poetical output was both extensive and interesting. His formal public verse shows him hopefully aware of William's potentialities and promise as a patriot king, for his most elegantly contrived Pindaric poem, "Carmen Seculare, For the Year 1700. To the King," is an almost 600-line vision of the bright future of England under William, as it stood on the threshold of the new century. Three much briefer and more private poems by Prior, produced after "Carmen Seculare," show Prior's increasing despair that William will ever achieve his promise, for if William is a great man and a great leader, he is also beset by the opposing factions. In handling these parties weakly, assert these poems, he is destroying his own chance for greatness. "A Fable" ("IN AEsop's Tales an honest Wretch we find") asserts that William is like a henpecked bigamist, permitting his young wife to pluck out his grey hairs and his old wife, the black, till the observers, seeing him quite bald, "thought he wanted Brains as well as Hair" (1. 8, *LW*, 1:182). A second poem from this period, "Ballad" ("THE factions that Each other claw"), adds to this same theme a sharp lament for the popular military hero turned unpopular politician:

> Whilst those upon thy faults discants
> Harlay and Mountagu shall joyn
> Not one but roars at Irish Grants
> But all forgett you past the Boyne.
> (ll. 5–8, *LW*, 1:182)

The latest and most despairing of these political poems is another "Ballad" ("THE Crown once again"), in which Prior mocks William's demand (and his own, while in Parliament) that the English should act with vigor. Prior feels that either party, acting vigorously, can only bring England closer to defeat—the Whigs will not support William's efforts to prepare for another war against Louis XIV; the Tories will bring back the Roman Catholic Stuarts and the Prince of Wales.

Prior's increasing conviction that William had frittered away his possibilities of greatness by dealing weakly with political factions provoked perhaps the strongest attack on Prior himself ever written by a figure of major importance. In the second part of his "Reformation of Manners, A Satyr," Daniel Defoe devoted over twenty lines to a violent attack upon Prior, chiefly on the grounds of his tavern origin and of his writing both panegyrics and satires upon William.

Prior's less controversial and nonpolitical poetry of this same three-year period (spring 1699, through spring 1702) shows an impressive range and power. There are two love songs, deftly and delicately polished—"A Song" ("IN vain You tell your parting Lover") and "Les Estreines," a New Year's gift. Prior's first ribald tale in verse, "Hans Carvel," is a free adaptation of La Fontaine, who in turn had taken the account from Rabelais. Still another new venture for Prior became probably the most famous of all his poems for and about children, "To a Child of Quality of Five Years Old, the Author suppos'd Forty," in which Miss Mary (Lady Mary Villiers, daughter to Edward Villiers, first Earl of Jersey) makes beds for her silk-worms and has her hair rolled up in the love poetry that Prior has been writing her. Adding four years to his real age, Prior intensifies his contention that both he and the child are trapped in time:

> For as our diff'rent Ages move,
> 'Tis so ordain'd wou'd Fate but mend it,
> That I shall be past making Love,
> When she begins to comprehend it.
> (ll. 25–28, *LW*, 1:190)

Finally, this period produced two more of the colloquially Horatian poetic requests for the simple life. In "Written at Paris, 1700. In the Beginning of Robe's Geography," Prior apostrophizes Rhea with simple, bucolic requests. In a related classical fashion, the six lines of "Song. Sett by Mr: Abell" praise friendship above learning, love, wealth, or mere conviviality.

Although the accession of Queen Anne strengthened the power of the Tory party, it lessened Prior's scope. Anne's own preference for persons of high extraction and for politicians who supported the Marlboroughs excluded Prior. His family were country folk or tavern keepers, and Sarah Churchill, Duchess of Marlborough, hated him thoroughly, convinced that he had written a lampoon upon her—or at least that any political figure as witty as Prior was dangerously likely to satirize her sooner or later. Moreover, although Prior had written one of his strongest panegyrics, "A Letter to Monsieur Boileau Despreaux; Occasion'd by the Victory at Blenheim, 1704," in honor of Marlborough's great victory, Sarah always believed him responsible for attacks in verse upon the Duke.[30]

Neither did affairs go well in Prior's private life. On 10 November 1703, Colonel George Villiers, first cousin to the Earl of Jersey, husband of Katharine Prior, and Prior's nearest Duke Street neighbor, was drowned in the Piave River in Italy. For the occasion Prior wrote one of his most moving laments, in heroic couplets. In May of the next year Jersey himself was removed from the position of Lord Chamberlain because of his opposition to Marlborough. The chief cheerful note for Prior in these first few years of Queen Anne's reign was poetical, not political: his reputation as a poet was growing steadily. The fifth part of Tonson's *Miscellanies,* published early in 1704, contained eighteen of Prior's poems, along with poems by Addison, Congreve, and Dorset.

For several months Prior also carried on a lively correspondence with Elizabeth Singer, a twenty-nine year old pastoral poet whom he met at Longleat, the country seat of Viscount Weymouth, in the autumn of 1703. Nine letters extant from Prior to Miss Singer display a mannered and teasing courtship. Though Prior was attracted to Miss Singer and professed to be pursuing her in these letters and in two poems—"To the Author of Love and Friendship: A Pastoral" and "To a Lady: She refusing to continue a Dispute with me, and leaving me in the Argument"—he never seemed to pursue her very seriously in real life.[31] After 1704, even the epistolary and poetical phase of the courtship ceased, though Miss Singer was later to praise in verse Prior's accomplishments in *Solomon.* In 1710 she was married to Thomas Rowe, an ailing young man thirteen years her junior.

During this lightly taken courtship Prior continued to maintain Flanders Jane as his mistress and housekeeper, but between 1706 and 1708 she was replaced in his affections by Anne Durham, his second mistress. Anne was to go with him to Paris when he returned there, and remained his mistress, perhaps until 1718, when she was at least twenty-six. Almost certainly she is the subject of three of his poems and probably of nine others. Prior would later set her up in business, probably as the proprietress of a small shop, and would leave her £300 in his will. Less demanding than his other two mistresses, she seemed sincerely grieved at his death and satisfied with her legacy.[32]

John Macky, who performed secret services during the reigns of William, Anne, and George I, described Prior during this period as "one of the best Poets in *England,* but very factious in Conversation; a thin hollow-looked Man, turned of forty years old." Twelve or more years afterwards, Swift wrote under this statement in his copy of Macky: "This is near the truth."[33]

Prior's position as a Moderate—neither High Tory nor Whig— and his close friendship with his patron the Earl of Jersey, now out of favor at court, kept him from receiving any political appointments during these years. Indeed, on 22 April 1707, he even lost his position as member of the Board of Trade and Plantations. The appointment, however, had not been congenial to Prior's talents or his interests, which still lay in poetry and politics. During 1708 he busied himself with the first of these interests, putting together the first authorized edition of his poems. Edmund Curll had published a pirated edition the year before, as *Poems on Several Occasions;*[34] Prior used the same title for his authorized edition, which was published by Jacob Tonson in 1709, went into a second edition the same year, and was further reprinted in 1711, 1713, and 1717. The 1709 edition was dedicated to the Earl of Dorset and contains a preface valuable for showing Prior's picture of himself as a writer of *"Public Panegyrics, Amorous Odes, Serious Reflections, or idle Tales . . ."* (*LW,* 1:247).

Not all of the poems that Prior wrote from mid-1702 through late 1708 were published in *Poems on Several Occasions.* Some did not appear until the much more famous edition of his work nine years later; others were to come out independently between 1709 and 1718; still others appeared only posthumously, one of the best not until the twentieth century. Nevertheless, Prior's four categories for his work are useful in analyzing his rich variety of poetical composition during these years of enforced diplomatic semiretirement.

"Public panegyrics" included a number of short poems and two longer state panegyrics: "A Letter to Monsieur Boileau Despreaux; Occasion'd by the Victory at Blenheim, 1704" and "An Ode, Humbly Inscrib'd to the Queen. On the Glorious Success of Her Majesty's

Arms, 1706." In these two poems Prior's enthusiasm is plainly not as unified as in his eulogies of William, the last English ruler to be both monarch and general. The monarch whom Prior must now praise is Anne, who was contemptuous of his "mean extraction"; and the general whom he lauds is Marlborough, whose Duchess hates and suspects Prior and whose own continuance of the war is increasingly in opposition to the wishes of the Tories whom Prior most respects. In a somewhat earlier and more peaceable panegyric, Prior praises Anne and her policies. "Prologue, Spoken at Court before the Queen, on Her Majesty's Birth-Day, 1704." Two much briefer pieces of political-military eulogy are "Seeing the Duke of Ormond's Picture, at Sir Godfrey Kneller's" and "For the Plan of a Fountain . . . ," four lines of English verse followed by four lines of Latin equivalent.

Eighteen of Prior's poems during the period 1702–08 might be classified as "Amorous Odes," if we restrict this term to poems that treat love seriously, generally within the modes and conventions of the pastoral. Eleven are openly mythological or pastoral; the others borrow an occasional name or term—Celia, Damon, Nymph—and the tone of formal elegance. The second group, in eliminating mythology, gives Prior a chance to sound more clearly one of his most convincing notes: the mutability of love. The members of the uneasy triangle in "The Merchant, to secure his treasure," performing patterned social functions while only half concealing lust, jealousy, or embarrassment, would not have found themselves out of place a century and a half later in George Meredith's *Modern Love*. Two other poems, already mentioned, which could be called, by some extension of the term, "amorous odes," are those written by Prior to Elizabeth Singer during his pleasant courtship of her.

A different and much more cynical treatment of the amorous theme is given in Prior's three "Idle Tales" of this period. In each there is a couple whose pastorally ideal days of love-making are long over, if indeed they ever existed. In "To a Young Gentleman in Love. A Tale" (1702) Celia and Celadon are lovers, not spouses; thus they still speak to each other in terms of sugared endearments. Yet their vows are mere hypocrisy, for each is thinking more of another object of his affection: Celadon, of a place at court; Celia, of Thyrsis, hiding under the bed. In "The Ladle," written one year later, Prior reworks Ovid's story of Baucis and Philemon. Finally, "Paulo Purganti and His Wife: An Honest, but a Simple Pair," written in 1708, deals with another unsatisfactory marriage, in which the aging husband succeeds in outwitting the aging wife whom he can no longer satisfy.

Prior's fourth category is "Serious Reflections," most of which season their meditations with bits of grim humor. The 1702 "Epitaph" ("NOBLES, and Heralds by Your leave"), the first in a series of self-epitaphs, reflected his view of himself in his society. In the next year came "Adriani Morientis ad Animam Suam. Imitated," a poem that would tempt the young Pope into two competing poetical productions. In the same year Prior wrote "Charity. A Paraphrase on the Thirteenth Chapter of the First Epistle to the Corinthians," a sixty-line elaboration upon the same New Testament passage that he had treated at equal length twelve years earlier in "Charity never faileth." "An Ode. Inscribed to the Memory of the Honble Col. George Villiers, Drowned in the River Piava, in the Country of Friuli. 1703," already mentioned, was a lament for his dead cousin. Among other serious reflections, Prior by 1708 had expanded six lines written a decade earlier into a poem four times that long, "Written in the Beginning of Mezeray's History of France," which Sir Walter Scott was to recite from memory and apply to himself over a century later. During this same period Prior produced three other "Serious Reflections" as well, two of them classical translations.

Some important poems of this period do not fit easily within any of these four categories. Admittedly, it might be possible to classify "Henry and Emma" as an "Amorous Ode," but its nearly 800 lines are narrative and dialogue, not lyric. *Solomon,* 2600 lines long, is too nearly narrative to be classified merely as a "Serious Reflection," though it has strong affinities with the poems in this category. Similarly, two highly successful shorter poems, "An English Padlock" and "Jinny the Just," have something of the nature of three categories (Amorous Odes, Serious Reflections, Idle Tales) without fitting neatly into any. The first deals with the best way of keeping a faithful wife; the second, with the virtues and foibles of a fallibly attractive housewife. Wittily cynical reflections upon human nature are embodied by Prior during this period in a figure of speech— "A Simile" ("DEAR THOMAS, didst Thou never pop. . . .") (1707) and "The Chameleon" (1708); in a reaction to a foreign book just read—"Written in the Nouveaux Interests des Princes de l'Europe" (1708); and in an elaboration upon a foreign epigram—"A

Dutch Proverb" (1708). Prior even turned out an ingratiatingly comic epilogue to a highly serious tragedy, "Epilogue to Phaedra. Spoken by Mrs. Oldfield, who acted Ismena" (1707), in which he teases the audience into not being shocked by its incestuous overtones. His only Latin piece of the period was "Epitaphium Joannis Comitis Exoniae" (1704), an epitaph for John Cecil, fifth Earl of Exeter.

With the publication of the 1709 edition of *Poems on Several Occasions,* Prior's fortunes took an encouraging upswing. The collection attracted attention to Prior as a poet, just as his career as a diplomat was being tentatively reopened by the downfall of his implacable enemies—the Godolphin ministry, which fell on 8 August 1710, and the Duchess of Marlborough. His entry into published journalism came when the new ministry, composed of Moderates, began, on 3 August 1710, to publish the Tory *Examiner,* a political newspaper for which Prior wrote one poem ("A Fable"— *"THE Fox an Actor's Vizard found. . . .")* and at least one number (no. 6—31 August 1710). The essay, which ridicules by close examination Samuel Garth's poem eulogizing the fallen Earl of Godolphin, stung the Whigs sufficiently for Joseph Addison to reply to it two weeks later in the first issue of the *Whig-Examiner,* and a month still later in the *Tatler,* no. 239. On 30 November of the same year, Prior collaborated with Swift and Rowe in another letter to the *Tatler,* attacking a bit of Whig-British chauvinism on the part of Richard Steele. John Gay wrote in 1711 that the *Examiner* was "look'd on as a sort of publick Notice which way (some Great Persons who sit at the helm of Affairs) are steering us," and he named Swift as its "reputed Author," "with the assistance, sometimes" of Atterbury and Prior.[35] Though he may have written little for the *Examiner,* Prior was by this time notable enough for the Whigs to persist in believing that he had a large share in its writing. Swift himself stated that some of the *Examiner* papers were written by Prior with "much spirit and sharpness" and "published with great applause."[36]

Prior's ventures into Tory journalism were related to one of the most fruitful associations of his life, his friendship with Swift and the other members of the Tory Brothers Club. It is largely through Swift's *Journal to Stella* that we view Prior among this club of Tory friends, ranging in number from seventeen to twenty-two and meeting weekly during the last years of Anne's reign. The *Journal to*

Stella records at least thirteen occasions when Prior was dining with Swift, often with all the brothers, but sometimes with only two or three. The two men were warm friends by 18 November 1710, when Swift recorded that "To-day I dined with [Erasmus] Lewis and Prior at an eating-house, but with Lewis's wine. Lewis went away, and Prior and I sat on, where we complimented one another for an hour or two upon our mutual wit and poetry." Not all their dinners together went gastronomically well. Less than a month later, Swift wrote Stella of a dinner at Prior's Duke Street house: "then made a debauch after nine at Prior's house, and have eaten cold pye, and I hate the thoughts of it, and I am full, and I don't like it. . . ." On 16 January 1711, Swift wrote that Prior had given him a fine Plautus; on 21 February of the same year he noted that they often took walks around St. James's Park together, though for opposite reasons: "This walking is a strange remedy; Mr. Prior walks to make himself fat, and I to bring myself down; he has generally a cough, which he only calls a cold: we often round the Park together." On 21 April, Swift was again to refer to "Prior's lean carcase." Pleased with Prior's ready wit, Swift wrote Stella that "Prior puns very well," though Prior had sworn seven months earlier that a pun of Swift's was the worst he had ever heard. By 30 March Prior was showing Swift a copy of "To Mr. Harley. Wounded by Guiscard" before his poem was published, just as Prior was later to see Swift's *Proposal for Correcting . . . the English Tongue,* lent him by Oxford, while it was still in manuscript form. Swift's political writings were often attributed to Prior; Swift finally had to declare in number twenty-six of the *Examiner* that Prior was no longer writing *Examiner* essays. Similarly, Swift records in the *Journal to Stella* that his *Rod of Sid Hamet* and his *Conduct of the Allies* were both thought by some to have been written by Prior: "They think no-body but Prior or I could write them." By 28 November, 1711, the two Tory writers were so closely associated in the public mind that Swift wrote to Stella: "Prior and I are called the two Sosias in a Whig newspaper."[37]

Negotiations with France (1712–15)

Just as the last two years of Queen Anne's reign brought Prior his first published collection of poetry, a new mistress, and new friends, so they brought him political recovery and advancement.

Secretly, he was reestablished as a diplomat and negotiator, attempting to arrange the peace with France. He was a logical choice because of his talents and experience in commerce, diplomacy, and languages, and because of his popularity at the French court. Swift, writing in his *History of the Four Last Years of the Queen,* praises the selection of Prior to carry out this delicate and important mission, describing him as "a Person of great Distinction, not only on account of his Wit, but for his Abilities in the management of Affairs. . . ."[38] Trevelyan, writing of the same negotiations two centuries later, agreed with Swift: "A Better choice could not have been made. Prior was not only a man about town with a reputation as a wit and a writer of society verse; he was also an experienced diplomatist, skilled in the French language and in the arts and courtesies that paved a man's way at Versailles."[39]

During the latter part of June 1711, Robert Harley, now Earl of Oxford and Lord Treasurer, asked that Prior be sent to France along with Abbe François Gaultier, the French priest who was serving similarly as a secret negotiator but for the opposite side. On 12 July 1711, Prior and Gaultier left London and eventually crossed the Channel incognito (with Prior named in his passport as Jeremy Matthews) and journeyed to Fontainebleau. There Prior entered into negotiations with Jean Baptiste Colbert, Marquis de Torcy, his friendly acquaintance from his previous mission in Paris over a decade before. After ten days of negotiations and an audience with Louis XIV, Prior set out once more for England, accompanied by Gaultier and by Nicholas Mesnager, who was empowered to carry out further negotiations in England. When the returning travelers reached Deal, they were stopped by John Macky, an overzealous customs official. Prior, still traveling under a false passport, was recognized and briefly jailed, and the news of the secret negotiations was out, for Prior's secret return from France under a false passport could mean nothing else. To direct aroused public interest to the Tory cause, Swift quickly wrote what purported to be an inside account of these negotiations, under the pseudonym of the Sieur de Baudrier, supposedly Prior's confidential secretary: *A New Journey to Paris: Together with some Secret Transactions Between the Fr---h K--g, and an Eng---- Gentleman.*[40] Swift's satiric spoof operates on two levels, both of them advantageous to the Tories. For the sophisticated, it ridicules all such speculative revelations as fabricated and fanciful, thus dictating a need for patience until the government of the Queen should reveal the fruits of such negotiations. For the more gullible, who would take Swift's account seriously, there is a very favorable portrait of Prior as negotiator at Bologne and Paris, proudly insisting on "tout ou rien" in defiant negotiations with Louis XIV and Mme de Maintenon. Prior nonetheless was annoyed by the pamphlet, for Swift's "pure inventions" came uncomfortably close at several points to the fiercely guarded truth. When the Earl of Nottingham attacked Prior in Parliament for his efforts at peacemaking, Swift wrote as rebuttal "An Excellent New Song, Being the Intended Speech of a famous Orator against Peace," concluding "He has vamp't an old Speech, and the Court to their sorrow, / Shall hear Him harangue against PRIOR to Morrow."[41]

Peace negotiations continued during August and September 1711, often at Prior's Duke Street house, where Mesnager was sequestered. On 8 October three documents were signed as preliminary treaties between England and France. Prior's share in the drawing up of these documents, to become the basis of the Treaty of Utrecht, was so conspicuous that the Whigs derisively called the final treaty "Matt's Peace."

Yet Prior was not to have the public glory of being a plenipotentiary at the signing of the final Treaty of Utrecht. The English government had wished to name Prior as plenipotentiary to look after England's commercial interests, as Mesnager would protect those of France. Queen Anne grudgingly agreed, but wrote to the Earl of Oxford on 19 November 1711: "I have no objection to Mr. Prior then what I mentioned in my last, for I always thought it very wrong to send people abroad of meane extraction; but since you think Mr. Prior will be very usefull at this time, I will comply with your desire."[42] The next day Swift wrote to Stella, already expressing fears for Prior's appointment:

I hear Prior's commission is passed to be ambassador extraordinary and plenipotentiary for the Peace; my lord privy-seal, who you know is bishop of Bristol, is the other; and lord Strafford, already ambassador at the Hague, the third . . . Lord Strafford is as proud as hell, and how he will bear one of Prior's mean birth on an equal character with him, I know not.[43]

Swift's fears were well-grounded, for Lord Strafford flatly refused to serve with Prior. Without the formal appointment, Prior continued to work behind the scenes, particularly in his negotiations with the

Marquis de Torcy, in efforts to convey the preliminary peace treaty into a formal and final one.

In a year of such political activity, Prior found time to write and publish only a single poem, this one on a topic of immediate political interest: "To Mr. Harley, Wounded by Guiscard. 1711." (*LW*, 1:398–99) The incident with which the poem dealt had occurred on 8 March 1711, when Antoine de Guiscard, a French double agent, was being questioned by a committee of the Privy Council. Guiscard suddenly stabbed Harley with a penknife, inflicting wounds from which he did not recover for six weeks. In his eulogy Prior assures Harley that "the sharp Point of cruel GUISCARD's Knife, / In Brass and Marble carves Thy deathless Name" (ll. 15–16, *LW*, 1:398). Public sympathy for Harley and his faction did indeed run high after the stabbing, and he recovered to be named soon thereafter Earl of Oxford and Mortimer.

On 25 January 1712, immediately after it had become plain that Prior would not be appointed to serve as plenipotentiary, he was appointed commissioner of customs, a post that he complained of to Swift as spoiling his wit, so that he dreamed of nothing but "Cockets, & Dockets and Drawbacks, and other Jargon words of the Custom house."[44] During this time in London Prior continued to live in his Duke Street "palace" and to attend the Thursday meetings of the Brothers Club, held together by its members' common Tory principles and the magnetism of Swift. One of Prior's few poems of 1712 is his "An Extempore Invitation to the Earl of Oxford, Lord High Treasurer. 1712" to attend a meeting of the club at Prior's Duke Street house. During this time Prior probably also wrote "Erle Robert's Mice. In Chaucer's Stile," a poem that describes a meeting at Robert Harley's house in which Prior makes a witty but unsuccessful plea to be given a sinecure such as teller of the Exchequer.[45]

During the spring and early summer of 1712, Prior continued his correspondence with the Marquis de Torcy. Then, on 17 August 1712, Prior arrived once more in Paris, having accompanied Henry St. John, now Viscount Bolingbroke. There he met with Torcy, concluded an agreement for a four-months' armistice, and was received in private audience by Louis XIV on 21 August. Prior also became involved with Mlle Claudine Alexandrine Guérin, later Mme de Tencin, who had just run away from the Convent of Montfleuri and was attempting to have her vows as a nun annulled. Mlle

Claudine figures heavily in gossip concerning Prior's amorous escapades during this period. Bolingbroke and the others in the party departed for London on 4 September 1712, while Prior remained in Paris, but without official position, and suffering from an attack of cholera morbus followed by dysentery.

By the end of September papers arrived in France naming Prior as minister plenipotentiary. At the desire of Torcy and Bolingbroke, he journeyed to London by 5 November, to deliver to Queen Anne a long letter from Louis XIV, praising peace, Anne, and Prior, but specifically defending the claims made by the elector of Bavaria. Three days later, Swift wrote in his *Journal to Stella,* ". . . Prior is just come over from France for a few days; I suppose, upon some important affair. I saw him last night, but had no private talk with him. Stocks rise upon his coming."[46] After some delays, Prior departed again for Paris on 12 December, having assisted in settling two key points interfering with the making of the final treaty: the fate of Tournai and of the elector of Bavaria. He returned to Paris to work with the Duke of Shrewsbury, just named ambassador to France.

Finally, on 11 April 1713, the Treaty of Utrecht was signed between England, Holland, Portugal, Prussia, Savoy, and France, ending the War of the Spanish Succession for these nations. The Duke of Shrewsbury wrote to the Earl of Oxford, 8 March 1713, of Prior's role in the Treaty of Utrecht: ". . . I think I may congratulate your Lordship that the peace is made, in which if by good fortune I have any share, I must do Mr. Prior the justice to inform you, that I have been in so particular a manner assisted by his zeal, diligence and ability that I hope he will be immediately encouraged and countenanced by some mark of your Lordship's favour."[47]

In the celebrations that followed the signing of the treaty, Prior once again fell ill of cholera morbus, complicated this time by pleurisy as well. Though he remained in Paris, his commission had really expired with the signing of the treaty, and he was troubled about his physical and financial present and his political future. He served in the absence of the Duke of Shrewsbury as an acting ambassador to France and stayed at Fontainebleau during September and October of 1713 at the particular request of King Louis XIV. His main role during this period, at Bolingbroke's behest, was to draw France into a closer military, political, and commercial alliance with England. During these last years of Queen Anne's life, Prior, like his master Bolingbroke, was frequently moving through centers of Jacobite intrigue though he never became a Jacobite.

Prior wrote few poems during this period of increasing political turmoil; but three of these, for different reasons, are of considerable interest. "Frederic &ca: From Boccace," though left unfinished, is significant as a reworking of La Fontaine in blank verse. "For His Own Epitaph," the fullest and most detailed of his three self-epitaphs, sums up in eight four-line stanzas his view of himself at the half-century mark. Finally, "True Statesmen" reflects cynically upon the quarrel between Oxford and Bolingbroke at a time when there was still some hope that "common Int'rest" might still make "em Friends" (l. 10, *LW*, 1:411). It closes with witty and practical advice, Polonius-like, on moderation and probity:

> Be not the Bully of the Nation
> Nor foam at mouth for Moderation.
> Take not thy Sentiments on trust
> Nor be by others Notions just.
> (ll. 27–30, *LW*, 1:411)

In *Henry Esmond*, Thackeray writes of Prior that "he was the earthen pot swimming with the pots of brass down the stream, and always and justly frightened lest he should break in the voyage . . . thinking about his plate and his place, and what on earth should become of him should his party go out."[48] But Prior's concern was more than that; not only his place and his plate but his life might hinge on the settling of the quarrel between Oxford and Bolingbroke or upon the survival of Queen Anne.

At home in England, the quarrel between Oxford and Bolingbroke became increasingly bitter. Swift believed that Prior could have reconciled the two angry ministers if he had been in England at this critical juncture,[49] but he was absent in France, and the quarrel climaxed by Oxford's being forced out of office. Two days later, on 1 August 1714, Queen Anne died, and the Stuarts no longer ruled England. Marlborough had landed; Shrewsbury was appointed lord treasurer; the elector of Hanover was proclaimed the legitimate successor to the throne; the Whigs had triumphed. Prior's last poem to Anne, "An Epistle, Desiring the Queen's Picture," some thirty-four lines in length, lies unfinished, bearing the somber subtitle: "Written at Paris, 1714. But left unfinish'd, by the sudden News of Her Majesty's Death" (*LW*, 1:408-9). Instead, Prior, acting ambassador in Paris since Shrewsbury's departure in August 1713, went to Versailles on 20 August 1714, to make the formal announcement of the death of Anne and of the accession to the British throne of George I.

Arrest and Confinement in London (1715-16)

Upon the Hanoverian succession to the throne, Prior found himself still forced to act as ambassador in Paris without official appointment or sufficient allowance, negotiating with Louis XIV about the destruction of Dunkirk while worrying about the £5000 debt he had incurred, distrusted and ill-supported by the new Whig government. He was removed from his post of commissioner of customs. In January of 1715, John Dalrymple, Earl of Stair, came to serve as ambassador to France and relieve Prior of his duties. The Whig ministry finally agreed to pay off Prior's ambassadorial debts in France, chiefly, it seems, so that he might be questioned and examined in England. By late March 1715 the debts were paid and Prior left Paris for London, where he arrived early in April. He had counted upon the good offices of his childhood friend, Charles Montagu, Earl of Halifax, but Halifax died of pneumonia late in May 1715, and Prior was left without a strong sponsor among the Whigs. After the House of Commons set up a secret committee to investigate corruption and treason in the previous ministry, especially concerning the Treaty of Utrecht, Prior and Thomas Harley were arrested and confined in their own homes in Duke Street on 9 June, and a week later, Prior was summoned to testify before the committee. As he later noted in his *History of His Own Time*,[50] the committee intended to support charges of treason against the Earl of Oxford by having Prior verify that the Earl had been present at a meeting at Prior's Duke Street house with Mesnager and Gaultier. Prior replied, however, that either the Duke of Shrewsbury or the Earl of Oxford had been present, with the other absent, but that he could not recollect, four years later, which man had attended—an answer, Prior recorded, that "had this Effect, that it was the same Thing as if they were both absent, since they could not determine which of them was present."[51] Despite repeated questioning, Prior kept to his story. Although he was confined in the home of the sergeant-at-arms of the House of Commons for more than a year thereafter, he had managed to protect his Tory friends while saving his own neck, the most delicate diplomatic maneuvering of his whole political career.

Yet during the spring months in London in 1715, when his life and those of his friends hung in the balance, Prior was able to write one of his most successful poems in domesticating the myth, "Daphne and Apollo," which begins with Apollo wooing Daphne in courtly terms borrowed from Ovid. Daphne, replying in terms strictly Prior's own—mocking, human, and homely—points out how ill the graces and virtues of the classical god suit the cares and concerns of the mortal Augustan maid, who prefers to remain in England's wholesome air and be courted by a suitor who will read the newspaper with her father, pull off his hat in the presence of servants to inquire as to her health, bring home trifles from his journeys, and become a faithful husband. The same period produced Prior's "Observations on Homer: A Letter," brief, shrewd comments upon the strengths and weaknesses of the *Iliad*.

One of the surprising aspects of Prior's art is his ability to produce during such a troubled period pieces entirely detached and nonpolitical in nature; plainly, the classics provided him with a refuge from the political turmoils of England. Much more predictable was his writing, shortly after his appearance before the secret committee, "The Viceroy. A Ballad," which Professors Spears and Wright call "Of all P[rior]'s ballads . . . closest to the street-ballads in style."[52] "The Viceroy" attacks Coningsby in the typical ballad fourteener meter for his dishonesty, greed, maladministration, and cruelty in Ireland, particularly for having Gafney executed without a trial. It devotes thirteen quatrains to praise of the late Queen Anne (against whom Coningsby is shown as satanically ungrateful), and closes with the threat that Coningsby will eventually find justice, either from heaven and hell or at the hands of a mob.

No charges were preferred against Prior, yet he was confined, unable to receive guests except by permission of the speaker of the House of Commons, or to write or receive letters from friends. On 27 August 1715, he wrote to the speaker to protest his imprisonment; three weeks later, Walpole replied that Prior had lied to the secret committee and was being held as a material witness against others. Prior was not released until 26 June 1716, when Parliament was prorogued. Even a year later, his name, along with Thomas Harley's and the Earl of Oxford's, was omitted from the list of those pardoned by the Royal Act of Grace, July 1717. The injustice of the whole episode rankled with many Tories; Prior's name became synonymous with undeserved ill-treatment. After Prior's death Swift was to write "To Charles Ford Esq. on his Birth-day January 31st for the Year 1722-3,"

> Your Foes, triumphant o'er the Laws,
> Who hate Your Person, and Your Cause,
> If once they get you on the Spot
> You must be guilty of the Plot,
> For, true or false, they'll ne'er enquire,
> But use You ten times worse than Pri'r.[53]

At some time during his year of confinement, Prior wrote the first draft of one of his most successful longer poems, *Alma: or, The Progress of the Mind*. Prior at first deprecated the poem, telling Pope (who had praised it as a masterpiece) that he had merely written it "to relieve the tedious hours of my imprisonment, while in the messenger's hand."[54] Likewise, he told Lord Bathurst that it was "a trifle . . . that I wrote in three weeks, not worthy of your attention."[55] But the opinions of Pope, Bathurst, and others convinced Prior of its merits; extant manuscripts in Prior's hand and in Drift's show that Prior revised the poem extensively after his release from confinement, adding, deleting, and altering numerous passages.

Last Years in London and Essex and Death (1716-21)

After his release, Prior returned to his Duke Street house, his political career irrevocably ended. His most pressing problem was financial. To assist him, Bathurst and Lord Edward Harley conceived the scheme of bringing out his poems in a subscription edition. Details of the plan were worked out at a meeting in January 1717, at which Bathurst, Harley, Prior, Pope, Gay, Arbuthnot, and Erasmus Lewis were present. Lewis wrote to Swift in Ireland of the plan, asking his assistance there:

Our friend, Prior, not having had the vicissitude of human things before his eyes, is likely to end his days in as forlorn a state as any poet before him if his friends do not take better care of him than he has done himself.

Therefore to prevent the evil which we see is coming very fast, we have a project of printing his *Solomon,* and other poetical works by subscription; one guinea to be paid in hand and the other at the delivery of the book.[56]

Jacob Tonson, who was much experienced in subscription publication, was to be the publisher of the edition, and Pope, who had himself just brought out his *Iliad* translation in a very successful subscription, would be a valuable adviser on the effort. When the volume finally appeared in mid-March 1719, it was a large, handsome folio, a foot across and three feet tall, 500 pages long, with a list of 1,445 persons who subscribed for 1,786 books. The subscription, as Lewis had written Swift, called for the payment of one guinea in advance and the second upon delivery. In addition, as noted by Harry Ransom, "Prior assigned to Jacob Tonson, 'his heirs and assigns forever,' all rights in the edition. The poet was to receive 1,000 copies of the work. For all remaining copies of the edition Prior agreed to pay Tonson £900 and to give the bookseller £80 for corrections."[57] The book reprinted and rearranged all of the poems from the 1709 edition of *Poems on Several Occasions* and added a number of poems written since that time, notably *Solomon* and *Alma*.

None of Prior's friends was more indefatigable in collecting the promised money for the subscription than Jonathan Swift in Ireland; his letters were punctuated for months before and years after the publication with his efforts to raise money from laggard subscribers. Almost three years after Prior's death, Swift was still concerned with payments into Prior's estate of money collected and with returning thirty copies that subscribers had not called for.

Despite the continuing difficulties of collecting the second guinea, a chief advantage of the subscription method of publishing his works was that it enabled Prior to collect a portion of the money (the first guinea of each subscription) for his publication months before its appearance. The commonly cited profit that Prior is assumed to have made from its publication was 4000 guineas. Though Prior probably did not make this large a profit,[58] he undeniably made a small fortune by the publication and found himself comfortably well off for the rest of his life.

Though barred from public office, Prior was, for the first time, independently wealthy and no longer dependent upon repayments from a remiss and recalcitrant government. He thus found himself suddenly free to devote himself to his chief interests beyond public life: women, collecting, friends, a country estate, and writing.

The nineteenth-century John Dennis wrote of Prior, "His faults were the faults of Tom Jones, not the faults of Blifil,"[59] to which might be added that, like Captain Booth, Prior continued these indiscretions well into his maturity. Anne Durham, Prior's mistress of almost a decade, is almost certainly the subject of three of his poems, and probably of nine others. By 1715 or 1716 Prior had met Elizabeth Cox, the wife of John Cox, a tavern keeper in Long Acre, and by 1718 Betty had apparently supplanted Anne Durham as Prior's mistress. A number of his better lyrics are attempts to reassure Anne Durham ("Cloe") of his abiding love in the face of his growing interest in Elizabeth Cox ("Lisetta"). Prior died a month after John Cox, and Dr. Arbuthnot believed that "PRIOR has had a narrow escape by dying; for, if he had lived, he had married a brimstone bitch, one Bessy Cox, that keeps an alehouse in Long Acre. Her husband died about a month ago. . . ."[60]

The behavior of the two mistresses at the time of Prior's death affords an interesting contrast. Prior had set Anne Durham up in a small shop, but he also left her £300 in his will. She seemed sincerely grieved at his death and satisfied with her legacy. On the other hand, Elizabeth Cox proved greedy, boastful, ungrieved, suspicious, and very troublesome after Prior's death, though she received from the will an annuity of £100 from Harley and £1500 besides.[61] Dr. William Stratford wrote to Harley on 6 November 1721:

> I find by my letters that poor Prior's will makes a noise in town much to his disadvantage. Some malicious fellows have had the curiosity to go and enquire of the ale house woman what sort of conversation Prior had with her. The ungrateful strumpet is very free of telling it, and gives such accounts as afford much diversion. You know I suspected such things.[62]

Prior's new wealth enabled him to collect more than mistresses. A virtuoso, he filled his Duke Street house with treasures until it became known as "Matt's Palace." He collected coins and medals, jewels and trinkets, antique bronzes, prints, and drawings. Most important, he collected paintings, sculpture, and books. Almost a hundred pictures covered the walls of his drawing room and its adjacent "closet." H. Bunker Wright and Henry C. Montgomery, who studied records of Prior's art collection, describe it thus:

> Prior's collection had breadth and variety. The Dutch-Flemish school of painting was most adequately represented. The Italian school came next, and then the French and the English, with a sprinkling of others. There was every type of subject: still life, genre, architecture, landscapes, seascapes, historical subjects, religious and mythological subjects, and portraits. The pictures in the last two categories were the most numerous. About a fourth of the collection had religious and mythological subjects, and more than a third consisted of portraits.[63]

Prior's book collection, equally impressive, consisted of several thousand volumes. W. Roberts, studying "Prior as a Book Collector," concludes that the library was "a thoroughly representative collection. . . . Mr. Prior was . . . a genuine book-lover who liked to have good editions of the best books, and the excellence of the judgment which he displayed in forming his library is unquestionable."[64]

Prior also maintained and expanded his friendships during these last years, by visits and by correspondence. He had been a gifted and winning public letter-writer when abroad; he displayed the same abilities as a private correspondent at home in retirement. Through his correspondence he kept up his friendship with Jonathan Swift in Dublin, whom he was never to see again. He strengthened his longstanding friendship with Adrian Drift, who moved into the Duke Street house at the latest by the end of 1717, to serve as amanuensis and as companion and friend. Drift wrote after Prior's death that Prior had honored him with "Esteem and Affection full Five & Twenty Years, without One harsh word ever falling from his Tongue."[65] When Drift died in 1737, he was buried in Westminster Abbey near Prior.[66]

The brightest new friendship which Prior was to make in this final period of his life was that with Edward Harley, son of the Earl of Oxford, his wife, Lady Harriett, and daughter, Margaret. Prior's testimony before the secret committee had probably saved the life of the Earl of Oxford, but it had cost Prior the wrath of Coningsby and a year's confinement. The Harleys and Prior became close friends; three solemn poems of Prior's last years are responses to the parents in the family.[67] More important, Prior wrote a charming poem directed to young Peggy Harley, in an age that showed in general little interest in children's poems: "My noble, lovely, little Peggy," advice on the occasion of her sixth birthday.[68] He also addressed the coda of his long "The Turtle and the Sparrow" to her, "O DEAREST Daughter of Two dearest Friends. . . ." In writing these appealing poems to a young girl, Prior was once again taking up the strain he had played so well in 1700, with his "To a Child of Quality of Five Years Old, the Author suppos'd Forty" (*LW*, 1:190). When Lady Margaret was old—by then the dowager-Duchess of Portland—she still spoke of Prior with affection, saying that "he made himself beloved by every living thing in the house,—master, child, and servant, human creature or animal."[69]

It was partly through Harley that Prior was able to realize his wish to own a country estate—Down Hall in Essex. Harley provided Prior with half the amount necessary for its purchase, in return for an agreement that the property should revert to Harley at Prior's death. Prior wrote to Harley on 2 July 1720, describing his impressions of the beauty of the location and the mathematical imprecision of the house: "It is impossible to tell you how beautiful a situation Down is, and how fine the wood may be made; but for the house, as all the cross unmathematical devils upon earth first put it together, all the thought and contrivance of man cannot make a window to be looked out of, or a door to be shut."[70] Down Hall was "Plaister, and Lath," but Prior engaged James Gibbs to draw up plans and specifications for a new house[71] and Charles Bridgeman to plan its gardens.[72] The plans were never put into effect, however, for Prior's death cut them short. According to H. Bunker Wright,

> Prior did not live long enough to see Down become the comfortable, luxurious seat he had envisaged. At time of his death the repairs were incomplete and the furnishings very scanty. Four of the rooms had beds; a closet contained tools, clothing, and harness; and in the pantry were the essential utensils for cooking and for serving food and drink. In all the house there were only five chairs, and for decoration there was nothing except a few pieces of landscape tapestry and a few maps.[73]

At Prior's death, the house reverted to Harley. Pope spent part of the Christmas season of 1725 there, comfortable enough, hoped to visit it again, and advised Harley against making any changes. "For my own part I declare, I liked my Lodging so well (both the Apartment above, & the closet below) that I am utterly against

Gibbs, & all his Adherents for Demolition."[74] Finally, in 1780 the house was replaced with brick and mortar.[75] After passing through various hands, it became Downham girls' school in 1932.[76] Located three miles southwest of Hatfield Broad Oak Church, the estate still boasts of having on its grounds "a famous avenue of hornbeams, planted by Matthew Prior."[77]

The greatest significance of Down Hall to Prior was not as a realized dream of a luxurious country estate but as the subject of his last important poem, "Down-Hall; A Ballad," in which he joins his talent for sounding like a balladeer (the poem is "To the Tune of King John and the Abbot of Canterbury"[78]) and his ability to mock himself and the world about him gently, while looking with friendly, detached interest at both, in verse which seems easy and effortless. Disclaiming any identity with those classical wanderers of old—Jason, Aeneas, Ulysses—Prior and Harley's land-jobber, John Morley, set out to find the estate desired by Prior. They hire a chariot and drive to an inn in Hodsdon (Hoddesdon), where Prior has visited eight years before. He inquires by name about all those whom he formerly met here, and receives the usual account of some prosperity and more woe. At Harlow the next day, they are given a similar sad accounting. Their guide, moreover, cannot find the estate, and when Prior finally sees it, he wishes that he had not. But Morley rebukes Prior for his impossible dreams of grandeur, and the two men part friends, with Prior presumably chastened. "Thus ends the First Part of the Ballad of DOWN" (l. 176, *LW,* 1:557), wrote Prior, who makes full use of the felicitous circumstance of the ballad nonsense refrain's coinciding with the name of the hall (hey derry DOWN). There was never to be a second part.

Although Harley is frequently treated as Prior's benefactor and was certainly his friend, Prior's unexpectedly early death meant that Harley profited heavily from all their financial transactions. Down Hall, with a number of improvements already made, reverted to him, a year after its purchase, with his having paid only half its selling price. Prior furthermore had set up with Harley two financial arrangements that were rather like life insurance policies in reverse, with Prior paying a lump sum to begin with and Harley then paying Prior an annuity every year that Prior lived. Prior would have had to live ten years to break even on these arrangements, not counting interest. He lived only four years after the first and two years after the second.[79] Harley, as Drift wrote, "was a Gainer by Mr. Prior's Death" by the sum of £2058. 6s. 8d."[80]

Prior spent these last years writing poems and prose as well as planning his country estate. The problem of determining what he actually wrote during those years is a complicated one, because, particularly after the success of the 1718 *Poems on Several Occasions,* every obscene Grub Street production seems to bear on its title-page the name of Prior, Pope, or Swift. Richard Savage's Iscariot Hackney in *An Author To be Lett* confesses that ". . . I was employed by *Curll* to write a merry Tale, the Wit of which was its Obscenity. This we agreed to palm upon the World for a posthumous Piece of Mr. *Prior.*"[81] In addition to those poems already cited, however, Prior unquestionably also wrote a number of other pieces during these last years, some of which will be considered in a later chapter but three of which deserve special attention here.

The first of these, "The Conversation. A Tale" (1720), was shown by Prior to the young Pope for his comments and advice.[82] In this light tetrameter poem, a vain and aging Damon begins by praising modesty and truth, then violates both by telling the assembled company how directly and helpfully he often advised Matthew Prior, in politics and in poetry, not realizing till much too late that "The Man You talk with is MAT. PRIOR" (l. 86, *LW,* 1:525). The poem ends with a graceful compliment and dedication to Lionel Cranfield Sackville, Duke of Dorset, son of Prior's original benefactor.

The second of this trio of significant poems is "The Turtle and the Sparrow" (1720), already mentioned because of its dedicatory close to young Lady Margaret Cavendish Harley. The close urges Lady Peggy to emulate the fidelity of the turtledove, not the licentiousness of the sparrow, but in the poem itself the debate comes out a draw. The turtledove grieves for her dead mate, Columbo; the sparrow endeavors to comfort (or corrupt) her, urging upon her the speedy taking of a second mate by telling her of his own series of domestic misadventures. Having gone the Wife of Bath one better, he has had six wives, has outlasted and outlived them all, and is eager to marry again as soon as his year of mourning is past. He quotes a wise man, who observed that the two happy hours that a married man sees are the first and the last of his marriage. It is questionable what moral the six-year-old Lady Margaret might have drawn from this, her birthday poem.

The last of the three poems, consisting of fragments totaling almost 300 lines, dates from the year of Prior's death (1721). It is the serious "Predestination, A Poem," Prior's renewed attempt to grapple with some of the theological questions that had most interested him in *Solomon* and elsewhere—free will and predestination, the existence of evil in a world ruled by an omnipotent, omniscient God, the balance of God's mercy and God's justice. The poem exists in manuscript in ten "brouillons," so numbered by Drift, who transcribed the fragments after Prior's death.[83] Prior's conclusion is fideistic; he accepts on faith what he cannot know by reason or observation, refusing to choose even between predestination and free will. Pope read the poem in 1725, punctuated it, and worked toward its publication, though the publication did not take place. Parts of the poem are echoed in his *Essay on Man*.

In August 1721, Prior went to Wimpole as a guest of the Harleys. On 11 September he fell violently ill of cholera morbus, recurring fits of vomiting to which he had been subject all his mature life. On 13 September he seemed somewhat better, but the attacks resumed that evening, and Prior died at one in the afternoon on 18 September 1721. What his "cholera morbus" represents in modern medical terms is uncertain, but the symptoms that Prior described resemble those of recurring attacks of appendicitis, climaxed by a ruptured appendix on the day when he felt temporarily better, with death resulting from peritonitis. The cause should not have been food poisoning—none of the Harleys fell ill—but if it was not appendicitis, Prior may have been unusually susceptible to some gastroenteritic infection.

On Friday, 22 September 1721, Prior's body was carried to Westminster Abbey in a hearse accompanied by a mourning coach, each drawn by six horses and escorted by an outrider. The body lay in state in the historic Jerusalem Chamber for three days. The funeral, held on 25 September was attended, among others, by Richard Shelton, probably Prior's closest personal friend, Dr. Arbuthnot, Erasmus Lewis, forty King's Scholars from Westminster School, carrying white tapers, seventy men in mourning with branchlights, and a dozen almsmen with torches.[84]

A few weeks after the funeral, all those who had been present and forty-two persons who had not, received gold mourning rings engraved "M. Prior. Ob: 18. Sep: 1721 AEtat 57."[85] James Gibbs, who had drawn up the plans for Prior's new country estate at Down Hall, instead designed his "stately Monument."[86]

Despite sizable losses when the South Sea Bubble burst,[87] Prior died a wealthy man. After all funeral expenses, debts, appraisers' fees, and other expenses of administration of the estate had been paid, £9875. 17s. 6d. remained on 7 April 1722, to pay the legacies.[88] H. Bunker Wright calculates that £15,000 had passed through Prior's hands, "Practically all of it—except for the amount represented by the Duke Street house and some indeterminable part of its furnishings—during the period which followed his confinement."[89] He had amassed almost all of this fortune not from his political posts but from his poetry, and thus became one of the earliest examples of a writer supported handsomely by the reading public rather than by wealthy patrons.

Chapter Two
Prior's Laureate Verse

The poet laureateship fell vacant twice within four years in England, when Prior was in his twenties: when it was taken away from Dryden because of his political and religious position in 1688, and when Thomas Shadwell died in 1692. Brice Harris is probably correct in believing that the Earl of Dorset would have selected Prior as poet laureate in 1692 had Prior been better known at that time.[1] Nahum Tate was chosen laureate instead, however; by the time of Tate's death in 1715, Prior had himself, like Dryden before him, become persona non grata with the king and party in power. The appointment was given instead to Nicholas Rowe. Nevertheless, throughout the reigns of King William III and Queen Anne, Prior served as an unofficial poet laureate. On the great occasions of state, he was expected to produce a suitable poem. Like Abraham Cowley before him, he became an active diplomat celebrating in poetry political events in which he had himself participated. One of the most revealing aspects of Prior's poetical career is his development as a poet on occasions of state.[2]

For James II

Even while he was a student in St. John's College, Cambridge, Prior wrote two poems that show his inclination to celebrate national events in verse. When he was twenty he wrote his first extant poem, "On the Coronation of the Most August Monarch K. James II, and Queen Mary. The 23rd. of April, 1685," an ode in irregularly rhymed stanzas, most notable for its closing two lines. These lines manage the touchy business of referring to the death of Charles II immediately past, and the coming death of James II by implying that just as James has been long awaited on the British throne, so is he being awaited with the same wistful anticipation in heaven, a bliss that he is postponing only for the good of the English people: "Late He Possest, long may he fill the Throne, / And for the Nations Bliss, defer his own."[3] In this, his first "laureate" verse, Prior is already displaying his gift of a felicitous close to an otherwise commonplace poem.

Just as he turned twenty-one, Prior wrote a second poem, of a very different type, on a national political topic, "Advice to the Painter. On the happy defeat of the Rebels in the West, and the Execution of the late Duke of Monmouth." Although this lively satire in heroic couplets on the Duke of Monmouth has justly been eclipsed by Dryden's more famous "Absalom and Achitophel" from which it borrowed much, including its allegorical names, it contains some effective couplets directed against the fickle British people, especially those who directly support the invading forces of Monmouth. "Advice to the Painter" differs from Dryden's poem in Prior's finality. By the time of his writing, the young Duke, having made one last desperate gamble for power, has been defeated once more, and, not finding in his uncle the clemency that he found in his father, has been executed. Prior is writing about a finished and closed episode; Dryden described one whose outcome was still in abeyance. Thus, Prior could see his poem not so much as an imitation of Dryden's as a sequel to it.

For William and Mary

After Prior had been graduated from St. John's College, he made his first real literary reputation with his satirizing of Dryden in *The Hind and the Panther Transvers'd to the Story of The Country Mouse and the City Mouse*. Part of Prior's motivation in the satire is again national and political, just as part of it is theological and part aesthetic.

During the year that Prior served as tutor to the two sons of the Earl of Exeter (mid-1688 to August 1689) he wrote his first two poems on William III, whom Prior was to love and revere in life and even after William's death.[4] In December 1688, at the height of the political turmoil in England, Prior wrote the broadside, "The Orange," to be sung to the old tune, "A Pudding," ironically advising the English public to "Throw the Orange away" (reject William of Orange) while in reality violently attacking James II, his newborn son, and their supporters—Catholic, Anglican, and Quaker. The poem is a very effective broadside—rowdy, insulting, acerbic—playing a number of variations upon the fruit figure (orange, medlar, pippin). In the following April Prior produced a more dignified song on a related topic, in "To Mr.: K----s Tune of the Prince's march," a song urging William, now in control of the English throne, to declare war upon James, just landed in Ireland. The poem is a short homostrophic (therefore Horatian) ode, in three stanzas, in strong, short, martial lines. On strikingly different levels, both poems were strongly supportive of William's cause and may have helped Prior obtain his first political appointment, when on 1 November 1690, he arrived at The Hague to serve Lord Dursley, the English ambassador, as secretary, a post that he was to hold for the next seven years, the first step toward his helping to make the history which he had formerly only celebrated. From this point on, his verse was to take a more distinctly laureate tone. Poems on affairs of state were to become a major item in his literary production, expected and even demanded of him.

Prior's arrival in Holland coincided with the production of "A Pindarique on His Majesties Birth-Day. Sung before Their Majesties at Whitehall, the Fourth of November 1690." The date that the poem celebrated in song was more than William's birthday; it was also his wedding anniversary, and a single day before the anniversary of his landing in England and of Guy Fawkes Day. The poem is a Pindaric ode, in the loose sense in which the seventeenth century used the term—a lofty, patriotic poem in long stanzas, irregularly rhymed. This millennial panegyric is not the best that Prior was to write, but it is the first that he would produce as an official government spokesman. It is an interesting revelation of the hopes and aspirations that Prior held for William, England's last warrior king, whom he by implication equates with that other William who came across the Channel to conquer and remake England.

Eighteen months later, in 1692, Prior wrote his first panegyric verse in celebration of an English military victory over foreign forces, "An Ode in Imitation of the Second Ode of the Third Book of Horace," a 243-line celebration of the defeat and burning of the Comte de Tourville's fleet by the British fleet commanded by Edward Russell, Earl of Orford, in the battle of La Hogue, 19–24 May 1692. The naval victory, which took place in full view of the French army assembled in Normandy, was the one successful British venture in a year of failures, and Prior took full advantage of it to urge the British, in Horatian terminology, to rouse themselves from their apathy and concentrate their full energies upon defeating the French. Though largely a celebration of William's courage and wisdom and a forecasting of a glorious British victory and a reign of peace to follow, the poem contains blacker shadows too: England is lethargic, lulled asleep, dangerous; deeds dark and impious are yet to be punished; "Merit has lain confus'd with Crimes. . . ." The poem is also interesting because, as the Longleat 29 manuscript points out, Prior is at least at two points in his poem mocking an earlier poem by Boileau, celebrating Louis XIV and a French victory, by pointing out that Louis XIV, unlike the wounded William III, is a discreet coward. It is this awareness of Boileau as his opposite number in France, celebrating those numerous French victories about which Prior must keep silent, that will later animate two of Prior's best and most effective poems on affairs of state. Even here, in a rousing and lively effort, Horace has stood Prior once again in good stead, for the poem did much to make Prior's reputation as a poet. It was the first of his poems to be printed by Jacob Tonson, the most discriminating of the London publishers, and it won high praise from Peter Motteux in the *Gentleman's Journal,* August 1692, as being "an Original deserving the Admiration of the greatest Judges."[5]

Over a year later, in 1693, Prior produced his next piece of laureate verse, "An Epitaph on True, her Majesty's Dog." The poem is noteworthy for several reasons. In an age rarely writing about animals or children, Prior was beginning to show that he could write gently yet unsentimentally about either, preserving his wit in situations that tempt the maudlin. This particular tribute to Queen Mary's pet dog stresses its prudence, wit, and gratitude because these qualities are infrequently found in men. The point turns from the faithfulness of the dog to the infidelity of men, and the epitaph gains a satiric bite.

On New Year's Day, 1694, there was performed before William and Mary Prior's new "hymn to the Sun," "Set by Dr. Purcel." Though for the most part a conventional tribute to William and Mary in the light of the seasons to come, expressed in irregularly rhymed stanzas, the poem once again is strongest in its close, in which the double powers of the Apollo-Sun (poetry and illumination) are equated with the inexhaustible riches of the reign of William and Mary.

Late in the same year Prior wrote a brief celebration of the Allied retaking of Huy, September 1694. The victory, though not a major one, was the only significant English military success of that year, and hence important to English morale. Prior's four heroic couplets celebrating the victory are significant only because here for the first time he is openly taunting Boileau, clearly seeing him as the enemy poet laureate, and throwing his deification of Louis XIV back in his teeth. Prior's most successful laureate verse would be an elaboration of precisely this technique.

On 28 December 1694, Queen Mary died of smallpox. Six months earlier (22 June 1694), Prior had called himself a "professed panegyric poet"[6]; that his public saw him in the same light is shown by the rebukes he received when he produced no immediate elegiac verse on Mary's death. For some reason, Prior, who was usually so quick and apt with his occasional poems, procrastinated on this one. He wrote to Lord and Lady Lexington from The Hague on 1 March 1695: "I am as yet so afflicted for the death of our dear mistress, that I cannot express it in bad verse, as all the world here does; all that I have done was to-day on Scheveling Sands, with the point of my sword:—

> Number the sands extended here;
> So many Mary's virtues were:
> Number the drops that yonder roll;
> So many griefs press William's soul."[7]

In a letter to the Earl of Dorset, 18 March 1694, Prior wrote, "We have had nothing new here for some months but volumes of bad poetry upon a blessed Queen. I have not put my mite into this treasury of nonsense, having been too truly affected by the subject to say anything upon it. . . ."[8] In a Latin epigram, "Inter Emblemata et Carmina," whose full title is as long as the poem, Prior ridicules poems written in French by De Vrigny on the death of Mary (*LW*, 2:763). Prior designed a medal to commemorate the occasion of the queen's death, but the act was considered an insufficient performance. Nowhere is his role as unofficial laureate more clearly shown than in James Vernon's response to receipt of the medal: "if you think this will acquit you from the expectations people have of a poem from you, you will be mistaken, for they say you are not to come off with a posey and a shred of Horace; and they further desire, if you write anything in memory of the Queen, that you will take a little more notice of her than you do in your stamp. . . ."[9] Prior's reluctance to write a poem upon the occasion of the queen's death is intriguing, because this was the first such occasion of state when he did not seem eager to write. The reasons he gives—his own sincere grief and the volumes of bad poetry already produced on the occasion—-may have been part of his motive. His strong affection, moreover, always seems to have been with William, the warrior king, not with the gentler virtues of the Stuart queens under whom he served. To young girls and women he could be playful, witty, charming; they found him an easy man to love. But in his winning, informal courting of them, there is always a comfortable superiority. He is the man of the world, explaining the ways of the world to them. This is his most successful note in dealing with women, yet it is plainly not a proper tone to strike in tribute to one's dead queen. Grieved, unwilling to add to the volume of bad verse already produced on the topic, asked to strike an uncharacteristically unwitty tone of reverence for a dead lady, Prior hesitated. Although he delayed almost three months in producing the poem, William had delayed an almost equal length of time in holding the funeral, which did not take place until 5 March 1695, two and a half months after Mary's death.

When he did find a workable approach for his own feelings and talents, Prior not surprisingly directed the poem as much to William as to Mary, urging him to further military victories in the name and cause of Mary. In "An Ode. Presented to the King, on his Majesty's Arrival in Holland, After the Queen's Death. 1695," Prior eschews the complicated stanza form of Horatian or Pindaric odes and writes instead in simple tetrameter rhymed quatrains. Prior's friend George Stepney reproached him harshly for the simplicity of these stanzas and the starkness of the sentiment. The meter was "neither proper for Heroick nor Elegy . . . You have thrown away all your Classick Learning, and have not imitated any Roman Poet."[10] To modern ears, however, the simplicity is a pleasing innovation, an improvement over the baroque Pindaric patterns which appear in most of Prior's earlier panegyrics and in those of his contemporaries. His message is simple. Mary, though admirable, is dead; William must not allow his grief for her death to interfere with his military campaigns, lest he lose in his middle years all the victories won in his youth. The poem offers its advice plainly yet tactfully, in repeatedly shifting figures. Stepney had also objected to Prior that there was in the whole piece "no design, allegory, or pretty Poeticall fiction or History to enliven the Composition. . . ."[11]

And he was right. There are small metaphors within single quatrains, and brief classical allusions, but there is not a single classical deity or place-name in the whole poem, and no classical mythologizing. Prior has decided, as Johnson would afterwards, that "Where there is leisure for fiction, there is not much grief." The poem is a bare and simple statement of a bare and simple grief, with its attendant political and military problems. It now seems for that very reason perhaps the most satisfactory of all of Prior's completely serious laureate poems.

Later the same year Prior was to produce the poem, not entirely serious in tone, that has received the most acclaim of all his laureate verse, "An English Ballad, On the Taking of Namur by the King of Great Britain, 1695."[12] The French had taken the city of Namur in 1692; Boileau had written a high-flown ode upon the occasion, exalting Louis XIV as a divine hero, even greater than the legendary heroes of Greece. In August 1695, the English recaptured the city, and turned the tide of battle in their favor in the War of the Grand Alliance. Prior then wrote a burlesque of Boileau's poem, stanza by stanza, and sent it to Tonson, 23 September 1695, with a letter instructing that it be printed with Boileau's poem on one side of the page and Prior's on the facing side, but anonymously: "A secretary at 30 is hardly allowed the privelege of burlesque."[13] The poem falls welcome upon modern ears partly because of its wit; it is as much an antipanegyric as a panegyric, deflating Boileau as fiercely and wittily as it praises William.

For several years Prior had come to see himself more and more as Boileau's opponent, the English laureate combating the French. He had taken that position by implication in "An Ode in Imitation of the Second Ode of the Third Book of Horace" in 1692; he had countered Boileau and a Boileau ode specifically and by name in the brief "On the Taking of Huy" in 1694. Now he burlesqued the claims of Boileau's "Ode Sur la Prise de Namur, Par les Armes du Roy, L'Annee 1692," in a stanza by stanza refutation. Boileau had declared that Pindar extending his wings had soared like an audacious eagle in his immortal songs, and that Boileau, in the ardor that inspired him, hoped that his faithful lyre could survive his transports. Prior replies that Boileau more closely resembles a handsomely paid vulture. Boileau tells that Namur is guarded by ten thousand valiant Herculeses, opening a sepulcher to whoever dares advance; Prior increases the number and deflates the casualty list.

Boileau had pointed to the feather of Louis XIV, which like a star attracted all looks and led his men to victory (plainly remembering that famous white plume of Henri IV); Prior retorts that it was more like a short-lived meteor. Prior's poem consists of sixteen stanzas, of eight, twelve, or sixteen lines each, rhyming alternate lines, often with humorous feminine rhymes. Despite its difference from Prior's earlier poem of the same year, "An Ode. Presented to the King, on his Majesty's Arrival in Holland," the two poems have in common a single element that explains their superiority to their fellows for modern ears. In very different fashions, both poems demythologize. "An Ode. Presented to the King" does so by stark simplicity, by the absence of myth where it was expected; "An English Ballad, On the Taking of Namur" does so by turning Boileau's classic and mythological weapons upon himself.

On 23 February 1696, the English public learned of an assassination plot to murder King William, invade England from France, and restore James II to the throne. Prior wrote on the subject by May of that year an ode, "Presented to the King, at his Arrival in Holland, after the Discovery of the Conspiracy 1696." The poem, though not as notable as Prior's recent laureate poems, like them eschews the earlier Pindaric form. Its irregular stanzas are in heroic couplets (with one triplet and one alexandrine); Christian guardian angels have replaced the mythological machinery. Once again in this poem Prior is praising William as military leader as well as king.

On 20 September 1697, the Treaty of Ryswick was signed, ending the War of the Grand Alliance. Later that same year, Prior wrote the broadside "A New Answer to An Argument against a Standing Army," in which he argues the need for a standing army to counteract Louis XIV's warlike intentions. Otherwise, England might once more find itself ruled either by James II or as a commonwealth. The broadside consists of seven groups of rhyming triplets, each followed by the refrain "This is the time."

Two years later, in 1699, Prior wrote the last lofty and serious panegyric that he was to produce for William, the "Carmen Seculare, For the Year 1700. To the King." It is a long poem (565 lines), with irregular Pindaric rhymed stanzas and frequent classical allusions and references. It stands at the threshold of a new century, looking backward to the bright past of England under William and forward to its anticipated brighter future. In it Prior, through the eyes of Janus, sums up William's political and military career. The poem, popular in its own day, was set to music for its performance before the king and translated into Latin by Thomas Dibben. Today its seems merely a reversion to Prior's earlier style, unsmiling and stiff with classical ornament.

In two other poems of the year 1700—"A Fable" ("In Aesop's Tales") and "Ballad" ("The factions that Each other claw")—Prior expressed his first real disappointment in William as politican, unable to control either party and victimized by both. The same theme is taken up again at more length the next year in "Ballad" ("The Crown once Again"), Prior's least complimentary poem about William. William had asked the Parliament, of which Prior was then a member, to act with vigor on the succession question; Prior replies that William has allowed the parties in Parliament to make him so impotent that vigor is no longer possible. They are lost either way. If the Whigs succeed, the king will find himself deprived of all power; if the Tories get the upper hand, they will bring in the Old Pretender. Prior's reverence for William as military leader and as statesman abroad could not extend to William's political dealings at home, as seen by a member of Parliament. When William died on 8 March 1702, Prior wrote no elegy for him. He had lost in William the properest subject for his panegyric poetry, a military hero as well as king. But he also, in William's last year, had seen in him the spectacle of a great man made powerless by shrewder politicians. It was a lesson he would not soon forget.

For Anne and the Duke of Marlborough

If Prior wrote no poem memorializing William, neither did he write one honoring Anne on her coronation. If he had no expression of public grief on William's death, neither did he have congratulations for his successor. Two years later, however, Marlborough's victory at Blenheim roused him once more to laureate verse. He begins "A Letter to Monsieur Boileau Despreaux: Occasion'd by the Victory at Blenheim, 1704" by taunting Boileau once again upon the occasion, as a paid panegyrist who will have difficulty finding anything laudatory to say in these circumstances. By this time, however, Boileau had become Prior's friend—and a very complimentary friend—in France, and Prior, though proud of Marlborough's victory, was also aware that the poetical problems faced by

Boileau on this occasion have also been his own in the past and may be so again. The panegyric becomes subtly transposed to something else; praise of Marlborough is interspersed with praise of Boileau's poetic abilities, though never of his master's military prowess; accounts of Marlborough's exploits are punctuated by complaints on the difficulties of writing panegyrics. Boileau's task and Prior's are the same, writes Prior, and Boileau has more talent for it; it is simply an accident of fate that finds them on opposite sides. His trouble, Prior writes, is that the spoils of the Blenheim victory are so vast and numerous that they will not fit into verse. He praises Anne in her choice of a general and Marlborough in his victory, hoping that Marlborough will be to England what the dead William once was. He should write a panegyric for Marlborough and the English victory, says Prior, as Virgil once wrote for Rome and her victories, but he will not because he cannot:

> But We must change the Style.—Just now I said,
> I ne'er was Master of the tuneful Trade.
> Or the small Genius which my Youth could boast
> In Prose and Business lies extinct and lost.
> Bless'd, if I may some younger Muse excite;
> Point out the Game, and animate the Flight.
> (ll. 182–87, *LW*, 1:226)

Thus this is laureate verse in which Prior, amidst praise of Anne and of Marlborough, declines to be a laureate. He states that the task is an uncongenial one, for which he no longer has the talent, and leaves the role to somebody younger. He was himself by no means an old man—he had just turned forty—but he is implying that panegyric verse, seeing the world in terms of black and white, evil and good, is the business of younger men, with less knowledge of the world as it is. The poem is, in a sense, his resignation from laureate verse.

Although he wrote other shorter, wittier pieces on political questions, Prior's only other major piece of laureate verse was written two years later, on 5 July 1706. Marlborough had won the victory at Ramillies on 23 May; Prior had shown no immediate inclination to eulogize it. An anonymous poet, however, apparently expressing a general public attitude, had demanded in "A Letter to Mr. Prior" that Prior sing the conquest.[14] Even an unofficial laureateship, once accepted, is not easily laid down. Prior complied, and produced "An Ode, Humbly Inscrib'd to the Queen. On the Glorious Success of Her Majesty's Arms, 1706." The poem is unremarkable in content, though it is as usual with Prior strongest in its close, with its mixed praise of Anne and Marlborough (whom the poem once more sees as the successor to William), deprecation of Prior's panegyric talents, and hope for peace growing out of war. The remarkable aspect of the poem is the verse form that Prior chose for it and which he defended in his preface: a modified form of the Spenserian stanza, with a simpler rhyme scheme in the first eight lines and a rhyming alexandrine couplet at the end. By the use of this verse form and of occasional archaic terms, Prior hoped to instigate a Spenserian revival, and there is considerable evidence that he did just that.[15]

Prior was never again to write full-blown laureate verse. He would express his worries as to his country's impending fate ("Florimel," 1708), write an *Examiner* essay and poems on political topics (1710), and compose a brief poem "To Mr. Harley. Wounded by Guiscard. 1711," on the occasion of an attempted assassination of Robert Harley. Sometime during the latter years of Anne's reign he wrote the informally tetrameter "True Statesmen," contrasting his own political philosophy and integrity with the time-serving politicians that he found about him, and drawing the moral:

> Be not the Bully of the Nation
> Nor foam at mouth for Moderation.
> Take not thy Sentiments on trust
> Nor be by others Notions just.
> To Church and Queen and Laws be hearty
> But hate a Trick and scorn a Party. . . .
> Vote Right tho certain to be blam'd
> And rather Starve than be asham'd.
>   (ll. 27–32, 36–37, *LW,* 1:411–12)

At Anne's death on 1 August 1714, Prior left unfinished "An Epistle, Desiring the Queen's Picture," which in its fragmentary form mingles heroic couplet praises of the queen with an implicit reminder that he has had no reward from her for his efforts in drawing up the Treaty of Utrecht and for his other diplomatic services.

Once the Hanoverians were in power, Prior had no need of panegyric. Rather, he needed his poetical powers to sway public opinion in street ballads and to save his own reputation—and his neck. It was for these motives that he wrote "The Viceroy. A Ballad" in 1715, attacking Coningsby and defending the dead Anne against Coningsby's "reviling." With this last street ballad, to be sung "To the Tune of the Lady Isabella's Tragedy: Or: The Step-Mother's Cruelty," Prior's career of verse on topics of national interest came to a close.[16]

To study the course of Prior's poems on affairs of state is to see a striking variety of forms and attitudes. Even in his college days, Prior was writing political poems in satiric couplets as well as in solemn irregular Pindarics. By the time he was twenty-four, he had added the street-ballad form as another string to his political bow; these broadside forms alternated with the lofty Pindarics for all his mature writing during his diplomatic career. Before he was thirty, he could make a satiric political point in a dog's epitaph while almost simultaneously producing an ode to be set to music by Henry Purcell. In 1695 in his ode on the death of Queen Mary, he employed a bare, unadorned quatrain form, without mythological ornamentation. Almost simultaneously, he struck one of his most winning panegyric notes, in mocking Boileau's ode on the taking of Namur with a corresponding English treatment of its retaking, paralleling the two poems stanza by stanza. In late 1699 he wrote "Carmen Seculare," celebrating the incoming century and the king's exploits in impeccable English Pindaric, ornate and heavily mythological; yet he produced almost at the same time three short, informal, witty, irreverent poems on William's political ineptitude. When Anne (and Marlborough) came to power, he twice wrote poems celebrating Marlborough's victories, at Blenheim and Ramillies. The Blenheim poem is really a poem about the writing of panegyrics, in which Prior treats in couplets the difficulties that both he and Boileau ("old Friend, old Foe") face in writing laudatory verse about the military exploits of their respective countries—he further declares that long years in prose and business have made him unfit for such an occupation, which he will leave instead to younger men with more talent for versifying. In the Ramillies poem he attempted an interesting Spenserian imitation, and his final shorter poems, generally satiric, close with his bitterly incisive attack on Coningsby, in street-ballad style.

Thus, no one generalization will fit all of Prior's laureate verse. Some of it is highly conventional. Because it no longer seems possible that a single great man might free Europe and bring in a millennium of peace, Prior's serious Pindarics seem peculiarly dated. Yet even these formal panegyrics are remarkable for being so rarely sycophantic. Maynard Mack, who in general disapproves of these laureate efforts as mere "exercises of piety," admits of Prior that "he has few illusions about himself; in an age of attitudinizing, he strikes few poses."[17] It is this refusal to pose that gives special interest to the two pieces addressed directly to Boileau, in which Prior tells of the perils and pitfalls of panegyric writing.

Chapter Three
The Variety of Prior's Shorter Poems

In the nineteenth century Prior's literary reputation began to depend heavily upon his shorter poems, and it is for them that he is almost exclusively known in the twentieth. Part of their attraction has been their prosodical variety, in a century that is often treated as if all of its poetry were written in heroic couplets. These poems are varied, moreover, not only in their metrical types but also in their content, style, and subject matter. Most of Prior's short poems fall into one of eight general groups. They are epigrams, epitaphs, songs, prologues and epilogues, serious philosophical poems (often nonpolitical odes), satires, tales, and light verse *(vers de société).*

Epigrams

To excel as an epigrammatist, Prior needed not only certain traits of his own—wit, precision, balance, a sharp eye and a quick thrust of words—but also an audience that, attuned to these qualities, agreed on what was ridiculous and what was not, and could follow the quick wit and laugh at its object without having the standards of ridicule spelled out for it. Like *vers de société,* of which the epigram may be simply one brief form, it required a large body of educated persons who agreed on social norms and social ideals, on what was proper and valuable in society and what was not.

A Victorian who heartily disliked Prior's epigrams, Henry Philip Dodd, wrote of them, "Perhaps no English poet was guilty of plagiarism to such an extent as Prior. . . ."[1] Dodd is both right and wrong. Some ten of Prior's epigrams are direct translations from the Latin or Greek; more than ten more have much less familiar French sources. But by far the greatest number of them have no classical or French sources at all. Some are titled; some are simply called "Epigram" or "Another"; some are called "Simile" or "Enigma" or "Riddle," but with their answers are still essentially epigrams.

In the epigrams taken from familiar sources—from Meleager or Moschus or the *Greek Anthology* or Martial—Prior's audience had the pleasure of watching a remolded epigram two thousand years old illuminate a modern instance of folly, ingratitude, or vanity. In those taken from less familiar sources, such as contemporary French epigrammatists, and in the many original epigrams, Prior's audience had the opposite pleasure of encountering a new turn of wit.

It is revealing to note the similarities among these three types of epigrams. Three of his classical-based epigrams—"The Lady who offers her Looking-Glass to Venus," "Written in Imitation of a Greek Epigram," and "Democritus and Heraclitus"—treat three recurring subjects: female vanity, the professions, and the troubled brevity of life.

Two of the French epigrams reflect much the same technique and play of wit as those based on Latin sources. The first of these, "Another" ("To John I ow'd great Obligation. . . ."), is a translation of an epigram by one of Prior's favorite French sources, Jean Ogier de Gombauld, on a boastful benefactor. A second, "A Reasonable Affliction," is based on an epigram by Antoine Le Brun and concerns the hypocrisy and antagonisms of marriage.

Prior's original epigrams also use the same techniques and consider the same topics as those from the Greek, Latin, or French. Two of the most interesting accomplish in a single couplet a graceful compliment to a learned patron—"FAME counting Thy Books, my dear Harley, shall tell / No Man had so many, who knew them so well"[2] or an Eliot-like comment on the futility of human existence—"WHAT trifling coil do we poor mortals keep; / Wake, eat, and drink, evacuate, and sleep" ("Human Life," *LW*, 1:687). Others are, like the translations, comments upon human folly and vanity or upon the incompetence and venality of the professions. An example of female vanity is Prior's Celia, who has the same zeugmatic difficulties as Pope's Belinda:

> HER time with equal prudence Celia shares,
> First writes her billet doux then says her prayrs
> Her Mass and Toylet, Vespres and the Play;
> Thus God and Astoroth divide the day. . . .
> (ll. 1–4, *LW*, 1:542)

Just as foolish is Roger, who neglects to seize the day until there is no day left to seize:

> STIL craving yet stil Roger cry'd
> I'll live to-Morrow but to-Night he dy'd.
> Strange the delusion of his hopes and fears
> While that he Starv'd Himself to cram his Heirs.
> (*LW*, 1:559)

Not all folly is personal; some is professional. Just as prevalent as personal foolishness, and as proper a subject for epigram, is the dishonesty and foolishness of office, whether in state or church. A preacher may harangue against temptations to which he has already succumbed:

> LUKE Preach-ill admires what we Laymen can mean
>   That thus by our Profit and pleasure are Sway'd.
> He has but Three Livings, and wou'd be a Dean,
>   His Wife dy'd this Year, He has Marri'd his Maid.
>
> To suppress all his Carnal desires in their Birth
>   At all Hours a lusty young Hussy is near;
> And to take off his thought from the things of this Earth
>   He can be Content with Two Thousand a Year.
>   ("Epigram," *LW*, 1:684)

One of his similes observes that the numerous fools in politics, as in all of life, make it possible for the occasional knave to prosper and grow powerful:

> THE worthless Cypher when Alone
> Is in himself much less than One
> But plac't behind more cunning Men
> Exalts Each figure up to Ten
> And when two thoughtless Noughts have blunder'd
> The Knave before becomes a hundred.
>
> So by the aid of worthless fools
> The Man who knows to use his tools.
>   (*LW*, 1:716)

All of these epigrams depend upon an educated and unsentimental audience that agrees on the definition of folly, vanity, moderation, and honesty, can respond quickly to a brief suggestion of improper learning, priestly chicanery, or marital antagonism, and likes the quickness and obliqueness of wit, without explanation or overt moralizing.

Epitaphs

Prior spent a good deal of his literary effort on works commemorating the specific dead; short pieces and long ones, in Latin and English prose and verse, both comic and serious, on queens and on their dogs, including three epitaphs on himself.

There are at least fifteen of these epitaphs, four of them written in Latin. David's lament upon Saul and Jonathan, Prior as a young man expanded into an irregular Latin ode, "Lamentatio Davidis super Saulum & Jonathanem," taking suggestions from the Biblical account in 2 Samuel but going far beyond it in details. His other three Latin epitaphs all commemorated the death of public figures and were inscribed upon the appropriate tombstones. The first was the long prose epitaph in 1704 for John Cecil, fifth Earl of Exeter, "Epitaphium Joannis Comitis Exoniae," carved on his monument in St. Martin's Church, Stambord, Lincolnshire. The second, "Epitaph. H. S. E. Georgius Churchill," 1710, is for the Westminster Abbey monument to Admiral George Churchill, younger brother of the Duke of Marlborough, "Invictissimi Ducis Marlburij / Frater non indignus" (ll. 6–7, LW, 2:766). His last Latin epitaph was written in 1719, on Charles Montagu, Lord Halifax, his childhood friend, at the request of James, Charles's younger brother, and also appears on his monument in Westminister Abbey. The Latin epitaphs are long—Charles Montagu's exceeds sixty lines—showing another aspect of Prior's laureate position.

The most interesting epitaphs are the eleven in English. Three of these serve the same purpose as the Latin epitaphs. They are formal and polished solemn commemorations of the life and death of a man, either a private friend or a public figure. When his cousin Katharine's husband, George Villiers, was drowned in Italy in 1703, Prior wrote an ode, a Horatian imitation, to commemorate his death: "An Ode. Inscribed to the Memory of the Honble Col. George Villiers. . . ." It is a strong, melancholy poem, particularly in its passages on predestined death.

> In vain We think that free-will'd Man has Pow'r
> To hasten or protract th'appointed Hour.
> Our Term of Life depends not on our Deed:
> Before our Birth our Funeral was decreed.
> Not aw'd by Foresight, nor mis-led by Chance,
> Imperious Death directs His Ebon Lance;
> Peoples great HENRY's Tombs, and leads up HOLBEN's Dance.
> (ll. 16–22, *LW,* 1:217–18)

Though not an epitaph in the narrower sense—the poem is ninety-six lines long and was not intended for a monument—it is a moving poem probing the meaning of life and death as seen in terms of a single death. In some ways it is reminiscent of *Lycidas,* though without the pastoral machinery.

Prior's treatment of the death of Queen Mary in "An Ode. Presented to the King, on his Majesty's Arrival in Holland, After the Queen's Death. 1695," has already been discussed.[3] Like Prior's poem on Villiers, it was not intended for a monument but was rather a meditation on the circumstances and significance of life and death. Twenty-five years later, Prior wrote in English prose the forty-six line "Epitaph for Sir Thomas Powys," which now appears on Powys's monument in the Church of St. John the Baptist, Achurch, Northamptonshire. Perhaps the best summation of this epitaph came in a letter from Ambrose Powys, his third son, to Prior, thanking him for "transmitting the character of my Father in the most elegant manner to his Posterity, from which I hope we shall learn to be wise and be instructed" (*LW,* 2:984).

The other eight of Prior's epitaphs are all to some degree comic—layered with wit and not intended for a monument. We have already considered Prior's poem on True, Queen Mary's dog, a poem that compares many men unfavorably to this dog.[4] Two of the other epitaphs deal, before his death, with Francis Atterbury, bishop of Rochester and dean of Westminster, and his lively litigiousness: "Epitaph" and "The Epitaph upon Gilbert Glanvill Bishop of Rochester, as written in Rochester Cathedral. Translated."[5]

One of the remaining English epitaphs is the highly successful "Jinny the Just," written for Flanders Jane, perhaps Jane Ansley, Prior's housekeeper and mistress from 1690 to 1706. If Flanders Jane is indeed Jane Ansley, the epitaph is one of several of Prior's written while the person was still alive. Though not published until the twentieth century, the epitaph was highly regarded by Swift and Pope, the latter writing to the Earl of Oxford (unsuccessfully) on 26 December 1727, asking him to permit them to print it in their *Miscellanies*.[6] "Jinny the Just" is a long tribute, in anapaestic triplets, to an earthy and warm-blooded woman, unlearned yet shrewdly adaptable, wrapped up in her own world of butcher and baker, footman and landlord, following her own will, charitable and uncensorious, concerned with household matters:

> So Nations and modes she referr'd to the Scholes
> And in matters of Conscience adher'd to two rules
> To advise with no biggots and jeast with no fools. . . .
>
> While she read and accounted and pay'd and abated
> Eat and drank, play'd and workt, laught and cry'd, lov'd and hated
> As answer'd the End of her being created. . . .
> 			(ll. 73–75, 85–87, *LW*, 1:303)

"Jinny the Just" presents a revealing comparison and contrast with another of Prior's humorous epitaphs, the grouped couplet stanzas of "An Epitaph" to "Saunt'ring JACK, and Idle JOAN." On first glance, this couple seems to resemble Jinny. Like her, they enjoy the bodily processes of eating and sleeping, keep their virtues within bounds, give their aid when asked, do not probe into matters political or theological. But whereas Prior heartily approves of Jinny, he disapproves of Jack and Joan, who lack her saving quality of caring a great deal about things within her own sphere. Jack and Joan care about nothing; having lost four children, they do not bother to try for more. Neither praising nor blaming, they have slatternly servants, no enemies, and no friends. They use Christmas to add up their year's accounts, church for slumbering.

> Nor Good, nor Bad, nor Fools, nor Wise;
> They wou'd not learn, nor cou'd advise;
> Without Love, Hatred, Joy or Fear,
> They led—a kind of—as it were;
> Nor Wish'd, nor Car'd, nor Laugh'd, nor Cry'd;
> And so They liv'd; and so They dy'd.
> 			(ll. 57–62, *LW*, 1:462)

They are like the souls whom Dante meets in the Vestibule of the Inferno, damned by heaven and rejected by hell for having lived indecisive neutral lives of no blame and no praise.

Three times in his life Prior wrote mocking epitaphs on himself, though he wished none of them used on his Westminster Abbey monument; having composed elegant Latin inscriptions for the Abbey monuments, he expected a like one for his own. Two of these epitaphs are very brief, mere funeral epigrams. The first, probably written in 1702, concerns Prior's low birth, which repeatedly blocked his rise in diplomatic circles, and rephrases a similar epigram in many languages:

> NOBLES, and Heralds by Your leave,
> Here lyes what Once was MATTHEW PRIOR,
> The Son of ADAM and of EVE,
> Can STUART, or NASSAW go higher.
> (*LW*, 1:195)

The last, "For my own Tomb-stone," written in 1718, is an even briefer triplet epigram on death as the inevitable leveler: "TO Me 'twas giv'n to die: to Thee 'tis giv'n / To live: Alas! one moment sets us ev'n / Mark! how impartial is the Will of Heav'n?" (*LW*, 1:466).

The most interesting of the three is "For His Own Epitaph," written in 1714, in which Prior, at the age of fifty and at the end of his long political career, sums up his life in alternately rhyming quatrains. He begins by confessing that he is writing his own epitaph for fear that his heir (nonexistent in fact) will fail to do so. He assures the reader that the sculptor of the monument has been paid but warns him to mistrust the inscription, "For we flatter our Selves, and teach Marble to lye" (l. 8, *LW*, 1:409). Summing up his first half century, he observes of himself;

> Yet counting as far as to Fifty his Years,
>   His Virtues and Vices were as other Mens are,
> High Hopes he conceiv'd, and he smother'd great fears,
>   In a Life party-colour'd, half Pleasure half care.
>
> Nor to Business a Drudge, nor to Faction a Slave,
>   He strove to make Intrest and freedom agree.
> In public Employments industrious and grave,
>   And alone with his Friends, Lord, how merry was He.

Now in Equipage Stately, now humbly on foot,
Both Fortunes he Try'd but to neither wou'd Trust,
And whirl'd in the round, as the Wheel turn'd about
He found Riches had wings, and knew Man was but dust.
(ll. 9–20, *LW,* 1:409–10)

The poem recognizes its own tentative nature; in case of robbery, hanging, or drowning, there may not even be bones to put beneath the stone. It closes by asking the reader to give Prior, significantly "a Smile, or a Tear / He cares not—Yet prythee be kind to his Fame" (ll. 31–32, *LW,* 1:410). It is this mixture of smiles and tears that gives the epitaph its special attraction—this quality of mixed laughter and regret, as Prior surveys his life and its ending and raises questions about both.

Songs

Majl Ewing, who pointed out musical settings for fifty-three lyrics by Prior, conjectured that "more are probably hidden away in the rarer Songbooks and Magazines of the 18th century."[7] Six of the fifty-three poems had two different musical settings; one had four, and one had six. Only a single decade between 1690 and 1800 had no new setting or reprint of Prior's lyrics. In a record decade, 1740–50, thirty-nine original settings and two reprints were published.[8] Ewing reminds us that three of Prior's ballads were specified by Prior to be sung to traditional tunes, and that two other longer poems were also set to music: "Hymn to the Sun" was "Set by Dr. Purcel" and "Henry and Emma" by Dr. Thomas Augustine Arne.[9] The *London Post* for 3–5 January 1700, states that Prior's "Carmen Seculare" was to be "sung before His Majesty" at St. James's on the next day;[10] Sir Henry Bate Dudley produced a musical version of "Henry and Emma" in 1774;[11] and two of Prior's lyrics—"HAST my Nannette" and "My Birth Day"—were still occasionally heard as songs in the mid-twentieth century.[12] Thus Prior, like Dryden, was writing many brief songs to be set to music but was simultaneously producing much longer occasional poems which also were sung in public.

The poet writing poems to be set to music faces special difficulties and demands. His lines are generally shorter, simpler, clearer, and more repetitive than those in his other poetry, for his audience must be able to follow the sung lyrics without losing the thread of thought even if occasional phrases are unclear. Prior's success in this medium is perhaps best shown by examining his two lyrics that Ewing states were still occasionally performed in the mid-twentieth century.

"HAST my Nannete" and "My Birth Day" are pastoral love poems with appropriate mythological trimmings, neither of which says anything that the audience has not heard often before. Thus the poems should be clear despite an occasional missed word or phrase.

In "HAST my Nannete" the shepherd begs the shepherdess to join him in love-making in the bower he has made, thanks Venus that sheep are dumb and cannot tell, asks Cupid to guard Nannete's flock from the wolves, but concludes that, if Cupid will not, he is not to ask that the shepherd and Nannete do so either. Their concerns are amatory, not pastoral:

> But of the Wolf if thou art afraid
> Come not to Us to call for Aid
> For with her Swain my Love shal stay
> Tho the Wolf Strole, and tho the Sheep Stray.
> (ll. 11–14, *LW*, 1:676)

In many ways the poem is a polished, conventional pastoral, yet it has survived when most pastorals have not through its last four lines, which both domesticate and defy Cupid. Here is a Cupid afraid of wolves; here are lovers who defy him and ignore the sheep while making love. In his best pastorals, Prior seems to follow the conventions, yet he alters them with covert touches of psychological realism without openly disturbing the meter or the figures.

"My Birth Day" was a poem that Prior originally intended to submit to the *Tatler,* along with a mock-pedantic prose letter of introduction. He apparently never submitted it, and the poem was not published till almost twenty years after his death. It has nevertheless become one of his most popular songs. It is a two-stanza poem in couplets in which the rejected lover is regaled by his friends on his birthday with "Music, Wreaths, and Mirth," yet wishes that he had never been born, rather than having to live and be rejected by Clotilda. In the second stanza, he implores Clotilda to give meaning to all the gifts tendered by his unknowing friends—and to his life. The poem has nothing surprising, no metaphysical turns of wit, but it has ease and polish, and is notable for its incremental repetition and for its thrice-repeated refrain, "I, my Dear, was born to Day—."

The two songs, then, embody many of the qualities that made Prior a successful writer of lyrics—simplicity, balance, artful repetition, the dressing of familiar material in a familiar guise, without sacrificing polish and elegance, the proper, easy placement of every word, and the touches of unobtrusive originality. They are qualities that link Prior, as a song-writer, as closely to the Renaissance and Restoration as to his Augustan fellows.[13]

Prologues and Epilogues

Prior wrote five dramatic prologues and two epilogues. One of the prologues, written in 1700 in collaboration with other members of the Kit Cat Club, was for Betterton in the role of Falstaff, to introduce *1 Henry IV*. Quite in character, he praises the audience but deprecates the men as far less virile (and less portly) than Falstaff himself. Unfortunately, Prior's share in this witty composition is impossible to determine.

Prior wrote two of his prologues for Westminster School performances of plays by Dryden and Otway. The earlier was spoken by the young Lord Buckhurst, to introduce a 1695 performance of Dryden's *Cleomenes*, three years after its original production. The performance may, in fact, have been in honor of Dryden, who, like Prior, was an alumnus of the school.[14] Well adapted to the play's young performers, the prologue reminds the audience that the boys purchased the lights and costumes and learned their lines at the cost of their leisure sports and sleep. The prologue gracefully compliments Dryden, Westminster School, and the Dorset family which had sponsored Prior when he was himself a schoolboy at Westminster.[15]

The second Westminster prologue introduced a performance of Otway's *The Orphan* twenty-five years later and was spoken by Thomas Hay, Viscount Dupplin, who acted the role of Cordelio. Not having published the prologue to *Cleomenes*, Prior plagiarizes from it freely, then contrasts the students' performance with that of the effete Italian opera, and closes with a pun on the name of the play: "For the Distress'd Your Pity We implore / If once refus'd, We trouble

You no more, / But leave Our ORPHAN squawling at your Door" (ll. 21–23, *LW,* 1:526).

About the same time (1719) Prior worked out a first draft of "A Prologue intended to the Play of Chit Chat, but never finished." A revised form of the prologue was later printed with the play, but it is not certain that the revision was Prior's. *Chit-Chat,* the only play by Thomas Killigrew the younger, was a great financial success in 1719, running for eleven nights, starring Booth, Wilks, Cibber, and Mrs. Oldfield, and making profits of over £1000.[16] Prior, perhaps for want of anything more positive to say, pleads for mercy for this first attempt at drama of the young Killigrew: "With gentle Stripes Correct the young beginner . . ." (l. 13, *LW,* 1:520), and excuses the play's episodic nature and formlessness on the grounds that modern life itself is like that, rather than neat, orderly, and clear. The play is also like a Lucretian universe, with atoms ruled by chance.

A final Prior prologue, of unknown date, is the "Prologue" beginning "LADIES, to YOU with pleasure we submit. . . ." Apparently written, as Allardyce Nicoll has suggested,[17] for a private performance of a young woman's first play, it addresses the ladies in the audience, whom Prior admonishes to learn from the play the lesson of fidelity in love. Its most interesting lines are a defense of the playwright's violation of the rules:

> Let Critics follow RULES, she boldly writes
> What NATURE dictates, and what Love indites.
> By no dull forms her QUEEN and LADIES move,
> But court their HEROES, and agnize their love.
> (ll. 9–12, *LW,* 1:689)

Both of Prior's epilogues were written for new plays, for Edmund Smith's *Phaedra and Hippolitus* in 1707 and for Mrs. Mary Manley's *Lucius* in 1717. For Smith's tragedy Addison had written the prologue, and thus, as Dr. Johnson was later to point out, the chief wit on each political side had given the play his support.[18] Johnson might have said much the same thing of *Lucius,* to which the prologue was written by Steele. In this epilogue, Prior manipulates the double standard in art like a two-handed sword; at one moment, a woman playwright is too delicate and defenseless to be attacked; in another, she is too dangerous to be trifled with.

In all these prologues and epilogues, Prior shows himself again to be a master of the occasional, able to treat what might have been a deficiency—youth, amateurism, formlessness, femininity, violation of rules—as an asset, thus disarming the critics. In the best of these exercises, the epilogue to Smith's *Phaedra,* Prior uses the play as an occasion for revising the plot in modern terms, so that the murderously jealous and incestuous villainess becomes simply an injured victim of bad heredity and a husband with no sense of decorum.

Philosophic Poems

Besides the very long *Solomon,* Prior wrote a number of shorter philosophic poems, among which were odes such as the "Ode. Inscribed to the Memory of the Honble Col. George Villiers," discussed above as an epitaph, and some of his laureate verse.[19] They were written in a number of different styles and forms, and date from his college days (at twenty-four) to the year of his death (at fifty-seven). An examination of four of these shorter philosophic poems, including the first and the last, should serve to demonstrate the range of Prior's philosophic interests and approaches and the essential unity of his philosophic position.

"On Exodus iii. 14," an ode in irregularly rhymed stanzas, was written, as Prior explained, as an exercise at St. John's College, Cambridge. It has been called by Louis I. Bredvold an embodiment of the skeptical attitude toward science in seventeenth-century England, the theme of the poem being "the inadequacy of reason to understand the world and the necessity of exercising faith and reverence to reach the high abode of the mysterious God who revealed himself to Moses."[20] In the poem man's pride in searching out the mysteries of the natural world is shown to lead him into error. Better, Prior advises, "To look to Heav'n, be blind to all below" (l. 99), because "Then Faith, for Reason's glimmering Light shall give / Her Immortal Perspective; / And Grace's Presence Nature's Loss retrieve . . ." (ll. 100–2, *LW,* 1:69). Man is more likely to reach "the Heav'n of Heav'ns" by Jacob's ladder than by "all the Volumes of Philosophy," he concludes. The poem is thus an early expression both of Prior's skeptical attitude toward science and of his resulting fideism.

In his 1692 epistle, "To the Honourable Charles Montague, Esq;" Prior examines the human condition and finds it one in which mankind balances "Imagin'd Pleasures" against "Real Cares." Here Prior's philosophical position has shifted from that in the Exodus Ode, for faith and hope have become deceptive, while reason and experience, though more trustworthy, afford a view of life so painful that it is better avoided.

A similar "occasional" philosophic poem written sixteen years later by Prior confirms this melancholy viewpoint. It is "Written in the Beginning of Mezeray's History of France," which points out in four six-line stanzas how tenaciously miserable men cling to life rather than accept its cure in death. No lame, blind beggar in the Invalides would trade his wretched life for the completed distinguished ones of Mezeray or of the kings he has described. "All covet Life, yet call it Pain: / All feel the Ill, yet shun the Cure: / Can Sense this Paradox endure?" (ll. 15–17, *LW,* 1:265). Even the old are reluctant to leave the stage of life, long after their parts, whether serious or comic, have been played out:

> The Man in graver Tragic known
> (Tho' his best Part long since was done)
> Still on the Stage desires to tarry:
> And He who play'd the *Harlequin,*
> After the Jest still loads the Scene,
> Unwilling to retire, tho' Weary.
> (ll. 19–24, *LW,* 1:265)

Again, men deceive themselves about their own lives because the truth—in this case that their lives are over—is unbearably painful.

The fourth philosophic poem to be considered is "Predestination," which is more like the Exodus Ode than the other two. Like the Exodus Ode, it is longer, it is not a response to a specific stimulus, and it not only examines man's misery but also offers a fideistic solution to his suffering. In heroic couplets, Prior wrestles with the problem of free will or predestination. If all man's actions are predestined, then how can he be praised or punished for them? Conversely, if God permits and foresees the actions of men, is He not willing what he foresaw? "Of this no further Mortal man can know, / Than as from Scripture God has deign'd to show" (ll. 41–42, *LW,* 1:560). But the Scriptures are often obscure, metaphorical, corrupted by time and complicated by the problems of translation. Man apparently exercises a will of his own, yet Grace would make such a will unnecessary and inoperative. The solution must be a matter of faith, left in the hands of God. Thus Prior's last serious philosophic poem says very much what his first had said—that man's reason provides insufficient answers to the most significant and troublesome questions of life, for which he must turn instead to faith.

Satires

A number of the poems already discussed could also be classified as satires. One of Prior's laureate modes, for example, is a satiric attack on the French enemy, its leaders and its laureate, and on political enemies at home. Similarly, most of his epigrams and some of his epitaphs have a satiric thrust. There are satiric touches in his prologues and epilogues and in the tales and light verse to be discussed later in this chapter. *Alma,* one of Prior's three longest poems, is essentially satiric. Prior also wrote four personal satires on friends and acquaintances, and three formal satires on his literary colleagues. All were written before Prior was twenty-six.

The personal satires include "On Mr: F. S. Killing the French K . . . " (1688), "On Fleet: Shepheards takeing away a childs bread and butter" (1689), "To Dr. F......... in a Letter to Beverley disswading him from drinking Waters" (1689), and "Letter to J...." (1690). "Satires" is almost too formal a term for these early efforts; they are simply verse letters to friends containing private jokes whose butt is often Prior himself, and they deserve to be classified with his other humorous verse epistles of the period, including two to Fleetwood Shepherd.[21]

With the three formal satires on his literary colleagues, the case is far different. Like other satires of the day, they hold up an implicit standard by which literary figures of the late Restoration are measured and found wanting. The "Satyr on the modern Translators," written while Prior was a student at St. John's College and provoked by the miscellanies edited by Dryden,[22] is an attack chiefly on Dryden, but also upon Mulgrave, Aphra Behn, Thomas Rymer, and Thomas Creech. Against each of these five persons, Prior strikes some telling—if somewhat uncivil—blows, in a poem that becomes a *Dunciad* of translators. "A Satyr on the modern Translators" is most interesting to us now because of its revelation of Prior's wit, trenchant though still uneven, and because it foreshadows *The Hind and the Panther Transvers'd* in its close knowledge of *The Rehearsal* and of Dryden's own works and in its realization that some method like that of *The Rehearsal* would again prove effective in satirizing the poet laureate.

Shortly after his graduation in 1697, Prior wrote "Satyr on the Poets. In Imitation of the Seventh Satyr of Juvenal," adapting the first one hundred lines of Juvenal's poem to the literary figures of his own age.[23] Prior later was to show the same unwillingness to acknowledge this poem that he felt about the earlier "Satyr on the modern Translators," probably for the same reasons—it was imprudent to attack the Duke of Buckinghamshire and unsound to attack Dryden. Unlike the earlier poem, however, "Satyr on the Poets" is not so much a satire on individual poets as it is on England, which permits its poets—good or bad—to starve. The theme of the poem is that poetry is not a paying profession in late seventeenth-century England. In a revealing contrast to "A Satyr on the modern Translators," written just two years before, the later poem reflects a colloquial ease (parts of it become a dialogue) and an ability to see social ills underlying individual faults.

In July 1687, just two months after the composition of "Satyr on the Poets," Prior brought out, in collaboration with Charles Montagu, *The Hind and the Panther Transvers'd,* a mixed prose and poetry attack upon Dryden's "Hind and the Panther," which had appeared on 27 May 1687. The satire brought Prior to sudden literary notice by displaying his ability to travesty and deflate the elegant beast-epic by applying to it prosaic common sense and plodding logic. Thirty-five years later, Sir James Montagu, in whose rooms the satire was conceived, described its occasion thus:

The Hind and Panther being at that time in every bodys hands Mr Prior accidently came one morning to make Mr Montagu a visit at his Brothers Chambers in the middle Temple London where the said Mr Montagu lodged when he was in London and the poem lying upon the table Mr Montagu took it up and read the four first lines in the Poem of the Hind and Panther . . . where stopping he took notice how foolish it was to commend a four footed beast for not being guilty of sin and said the best way of answering that Poem wou'd be to ridicule it by telling Horace's fable of the City mouse and Country mouse in the same manner which being agreed to Mr Prior took the book out of Mr Montagu's hands and in a short time after repeated the 4 first lines which were after printed in the City mouse and Country mouse. . . . The repeating these lines set the Company in Laughter and Mr Montagu took up the pen by him and wrote on a loose piece of paper and both of them making several Essays to transverse in like manner other parts of the Poem gave beginning to that work which was afterwards published to the Satisfaction of many people, and tho' no name was set to the book yet it was quickly known who were the Authors of it. . . .[24]

Although in a third of a century James Montagu can be supposed to have forgotten or garbled some of the details—he asserts later that the poem reconciled Prior and the Earl of Dorset, when we know that the reconciliation had taken place two or three years before—it is probably essentially correct in maintaining that both Prior and Charles Montagu worked on both parts of the poem, its poetry and its prose. With fraternal pride, James Montagu probably exaggerated his brother's role in its inception, but he is probably closer to the truth than those who claim that Prior produced it all, or that he produced all the verse while Montagu wrote all the prose.

In a long account of the occasion of his writing this satire, Prior raises two main objections to Dryden's poem. The chief objection was that its elegant language masked an insulting and slanderous attack on Anglicans and Dissenters alike. The second was that Dryden's allegorical figures did not follow the traditional beast-epic patterns for abstract meanings, but were new creations, not automatically to be identified with the institutions they were intended to represent. Believing Dryden's poem thus flawed, Prior states that he has decided to ridicule it by superimposing Horace's fable of the country mouse and the city mouse upon Buckingham's *The Rehearsal*. The method was a natural one for Prior, who had already used devices and names from *The Rehearsal* to satirize Dryden in two poems, and who was discovered by the Earl of Dorset reading Horace in a tavern.

Many of the wittiest effects of the poem are gained not from the direct attack upon Dryden but from the device of substituting the ludicrous mice for the elegant hind and panther, in lines following closely those of Dryden's original. In the first four lines of *The Hind and the Panther Transvers'd,* lines by James Montagu's testimony written solely by Prior, Dryden's regal opening

> A MILK-WHITE Hind, immortal and unchang'd,
> Fed on the lawns, and in the forest rang'd;
> Without unspotted, innocent within,
> She fear'd no danger, for she knew no sin. . . .

becomes in Prior's burlesque

> A *milk-white* Mouse *immortal and unchang'd,*
> *Fed on soft Cheese, and o're the* Dairy *rang'd;*
> *Without, unspotted; innocent within,*
> *She fear'd no danger, for she knew no* Ginn.
> (ll. 90–93, *LW,* 1:40)

Only six words have been changed, but four are key nouns, a change sufficient to create a new setting in which Dryden's lofty diction becomes ludicrous.

From *The Rehearsal* Prior borrows the device of introducing Dryden as Bayes, who is reading and "defending (as his way is) the foolishest things in his Poem" to Smith and Johnson, "by whom we mean any two Gentlemen of Tolerable Sense and judgment." In addition to the objections that Prior raises in his "Occasion of writing," he is ridiculing two other aspects of the poem and its poet as well—its tedium (Smith and Johnson keep trying to escape from Bayes and his interminable reading aloud of his poem) and its author's vanity (Bayes repeatedly congratulates himself on his most telling lines or contemplates his own life and person with fatuous self-satisfaction). *The Hind and the Panther Transvers'd* remains a very funny travesty of Dryden's poem, chiefly by its application of plodding common sense and strict logic to the beast-epic, which can be taken literally only when it is kept very short. For the most part, as Prior himself admitted, he has quoted the worst lines of Dryden's poem with alterations that make them silly in themselves and preposterous when applied to mice.

Despite the success of *The Hind and the Panther Transvers'd,* Prior found satires to be dangerous for an appointee to political office. Moreover, his youthful opinion of Dryden mellowed. He was to write no more literary satires. These three early productions are nevertheless useful in revealing one direction that Prior's wit could take. He was to find others, less dangerous to the politician and broader in scope, but he was never again to be funnier than he was in *The Hind and the Panther Transvers'd.*

Tales

One popular form in eighteenth-century English literature was the metrical tale, which no one in the century wrote better than Prior. These tales—often bawdy, always psychologically realistic even when they involved the gods, always rapid—are lively and entertaining reading yet. J. W. Draper, studying "The Metrical Tale in XVIII-Century England," points to the significant naturalness of diction in the realistic tales:

> the realistic tales . . . have their appeal, a certain masculine homeliness of style, happily illustrated in Prior's "ballads." Such a style may have inspired Wordsworth with his theory of diction, but Prior is swifter and more pungent and racier of the soil than Wordsworth's own poetry. Springing as it did from contemporary tavern-talk, the tale falls easily into vivid dialogue with quick give and take, and allows for an occasional pointed epigram.[25]

Prior's childhood in his uncle's tavern had made his ear alert to the diction of tavern-talk, and he concurred with Draper as to the tempo and length needed in a realistic tale. In "The Ladle" he contrasts the epic's accumulation of details with the tale's rapidity:

> How strong the Beer, how good the Meat,
> How loud They laught, how much They eat,
> In Epic sumptuous would appear;
> Yet shall be pass'd in Silence here:
> For I should grieve to have it said,
> That by a fine Description led,
> I made my Episode too long,
> Or tir'd my Friend, to grace my Song.
> (ll. 107–14, *LW*, 1:205)

If we use the term "tale" in the sense in which Prior employed it—any fairly long (more than fifty-line) narrative in verse, with realistic language and psychology—then Prior wrote fourteen of these metrical tales, all his later poetical career.[26]

Two of the tales are heavily autobiographical and have thus already been discussed—"The Conversation. A Tale" and "Down-Hall; A Ballad"—but these show the same colloquial dialogue, psychological realism, and speed as do the other tales. The impact of "Down-

Hall" has been particularly strong. The Reverend John Jones tells in 1764 of Caleb Parnham, the rector of Ufford, Northampton: "All was attention and delight in Mr. Bonfoy's parlour when he sung this ["Down-Hall"], and the ballad of Chevy Chace. . . ."[27]

Whether Prior is adapting a classical tale or making up a tale of his own, one of his most effective techniques is the modernizing of classical figures, largely shown by the colloquializing of their diction and by the human fallibility of their actions. In "Cupid and Ganymede" Cupid plays at dice with Ganymede and loses everything, including left-over gold picked up from Danae's shower, "A Snush-Box, set with bleeding Hearts," "His Nine-pins, made of Myrtle Wood," and "Two Table-Books in Shagreen Covers; / Fill'd with good Verse from real Lovers . . ." (ll. 13, 15, 19–20, *LW*, 1:273).

Perhaps the best of these classic tales turned modern is "Daphne and Apollo," a favorite of both Pope and Horace Walpole. Talking to Spence of Prior's collection of manuscripts, Pope said, ". . . there are nine or ten copies of verses among them, which I thought much better than several things he himself published. In particular, I remember there was a dialogue of about two hundred verses, between Apollo and Daphne, which pleased me as much as anything of his I ever read."[28] Walpole called "Daphne and Apollo" one of Prior's "wittiest and genteelest poems."[29] Though Prior misleadingly calls the poem "Faithfully translated from Ovids Metamorp. Book 1st. . . ." (*LW*, 1:413), only Apollo may come from Ovid; Daphne comes directly from eighteenth-century England. It is the collision of their disparate worlds that gives the poem much of its humor, for Apollo can offer Daphne nothing that interests her in her modern world. If he boasts that he rules Claros Isle and Tenedos, she replies, with sound English pride, "Thank you, I would not leave my Native Land" (l. 14, *LW*, 1:414). If he can foretell the future, so, she retorts, can Partridge. His beautiful locks do not interest her—they might be a Spanish Wig; she worries more about his bare chin. His healing arts are of no use to her in her wholesome English air. When he boasts that he composes fine verses, she retorts that she has already had her fill of verses: "So do your Brother Quacks and Brother Beaux / Memorials only and Reviews write Prose" (ll. 31–32, *LW*, 1:415). She likewise has no use for his skill at archery—it would only be dangerous to her, and it has its place only in the thicket. When, in despair, Apollo surrenders and implores, "Oh let me woo thee as thou wou'd'st be woo'd" (l. 41), she has a list ready of Augustan rules of well-bred country courtship. He is to bring gifts home from all his diurnal travels—"A Lacquer'd Cabinet some China Ware / You have them mighty cheap at Pekin fair" (ll. 60–61, *LW,* 1:416). He is never to philander as did his Father Jove; finally, he is to marry her, legally and properly. These are her Augustan terms; the choice is his. The Augustan world has met the classical world and beat it at its own game.

In "The Dove" the classical world again runs up against Augustan society—city society this time—and the victor is not so clear. Venus has lost her dove; Cupid says he will lead her to the culprit; they seek out Cloe's house, where they arrive at one in the morning. Cloe is indignant; she has only the coolest nodding acquaintance with the intruders. Nevertheless, at her invitation Cupid searches her wardrobe, her closet, her chest and box, "Turns all her Furbeloes and Flounces" (l. 100, *LW,* 1:436) but discovers no sign of the missing dove. The final victory is Cupid's, for he thus is enabled to search Cloe's person. But in another sense the victory is hers, for she has shown the gods to be ridiculous and unreasonable in her Augustan world.

In "Mercury and Cupid" there are only gods, but even they behave and talk in fallible human terms. Jove, "in sullen Humour," sends Hermes to destroy Cupid's arrows and quiver, almost like a constable serving a warrant. Cupid invites Hermes to rest an hour and drink a cooling cup of nectar in a toast to Jove, "this Celestial Hector"; it is a long, hot flight from heaven, and Hermes flies fast. As they drink, Cupid reminds Hermes of the power of his arrows. Hermes recognizes that Jove has more than met his match, and he departs without his prize. Again, the mortals have won, for it is Cloe who provides Cupid with his shafts: Jove is just a celestial Hector.

A final classically based tale is of a different type, a reworking, preferred by Horace Walpole to the original,[30] of an account found in Pliny's *Historia Naturalis.* "Protogenes and Apelles" recounts a painting competition between two mortal artists. Again, the tone and diction are folksy and colloquial—"Does 'Squire PROTOGENES live here?" (l. 29, 1:463)—though there is not the same striking distance between the characters, who are not gods, and their diction. This time the distance is simply between Greece two thousand years ago and England in Prior's time. The servant tells Apelles to return at six for tea:

> Tea, says a Critic big with Laughter,
> Was found some twenty Ages after:
> Authors, before they write, shou'd read:
> 'Tis very true; but We'll proceed.
> (ll. 45-48, *LW*, 1:464)

Even in two tales that function almost purely allegorically or didactically—"An English Padlock" and "Truth and Falshood. A Tale"—Prior operates in much the same fashion: by speed of narration and deliberately inappropriate colloquial diction. "An English Padlock" begins with an account of how "MISS DANAE" could not be locked away from Jove's embrace. How then is a modern English husband to keep his wife safe and faithful? There is a flaw in every scheme to confine her, to cut her off from other human intercourse. The solution is daringly simple. She must be sent out to see the world, returning only of her own free will.

"Truth and Falshood. A Tale" is an allegorical account of how Falshood steals the garments of Truth and goes out into the world in disguise, behaving very much like an Augustan coquette:

> In visits, still appears most wise,
> And rolls at church Her saint-like-eyes. . . .
> Her tongue so voluble and kind,
> It always runs before Her mind. . . .
> (ll. 35-36, 45-46, *LW*, 1:544)

In "The Thief and the Cordelier, A Ballad," the distance is between the ideal of the priest ministering to the man to be hanged and his actual performance. At first, the priest gives properly edifying lectures on the vanity of the condemned man's clinging to life, but when the wretch asks the priest to take his place in the banquet in heaven that night, the priest declines, saying that it is a fast night; he then turns and urges the hangman to "Dispatch me, I pr'ythee, this troublesome Blade: / For Thy Cord, and My Cord both equally tie; / And We Live by the Gold, for which other Men Dye" (ll. 57-59, *LW*, 1:460).

In "The Turtle and the Sparrow," another of Horace Walpole's favorites among Prior's poems,[31] the contrast is between two attitudes toward love, courtship, and marriage. The turtledove mourns Columbo, its dead mate, in language elegiac ("this BION-style") and lofty; the sparrow recounts its multiple marriages with colloquial jollity and surveys the death of its various spouses with wry relief, though his expectations still triumph over his experience, and he is looking forward to the end of this year of mourning so that he may marry again. The moral of the poem urges emulation of the turtledove's fidelity, but the sparrow has had the livelier and more winning part of the dialogue.

Finally, we come to the three poems often referred to as Prior's "merry tales": "Hans Carvel," "The Ladle," and "Paulo Purganti and His Wife: An Honest, but a Simple Pair." All three are fabliaux based on stories or motifs familiar to Prior and his audience; all three concern unhappy and incompatible marriages—in two of the cases, sexually incompatible ones.

Oliver Goldsmith called "Hans Carvel" "This bagatelle, for which, by the bye, Mr. Prior has got his greatest reputation. . . . It had been translated once or twice before into English, yet was never regarded till it fell into the hands of Mr. Prior. A strong instance how much everything is improved in the hands of a man of genius."[32] "Hans Carvel" is lively, colloquial, and bawdy, filled with the minute details of Augustan life that give realism and conviction.

"Paulo Purganti" concerns the same problem—an impotent husband and a sex-starved wife: "The Doctor understood the Call; / But had not always wherewithall" (ll. 81–82, *LW,* 1:262). Like "The Ladle," it contains a warning that tales must be brief: "Reduce, my Muse, the wand'ring Song: / A Tale should never be too long" (ll. 150–51, *LW,* 1:264).

"The Ladle" in most respects is like "Hans Carvel" and "Paulo Purganti." It concerns domestic conflict in a long-familiar form, told in a lively and racy manner, with colloquial speed. It is unlike the other "Idle Tales" in making a final point that Prior will reiterate in "Serious Reflections" and in *Solomon*: that the wishes of men are frivolous and vain. In "The Ladle" he reworks Ovid's story of Baucis and Philemon, supplying an ending that was apparently suggested by Edmund Gayton's *Pleasant Notes upon Don Quixot* (1654). Ovid's tale belongs to a much wider and older group of folktales that center upon three wishes, granted by the gods and wasted by human beings. Often the pattern of wasting is the same. A couple is granted the three wishes; one of them (usually the wife) wastes the first one on a triviality. The husband, angry at the waste, uses the second wish to humiliate the wife physically, and must use the third one to undo the painful and frustrating humiliation. Prior follows the Ovidian pattern in "The Ladle," but the moral is distinctively his, as it often is in his serious meditations upon the vanity and frivolity of human wishes.

> Against our Peace We arm our Will:
> Amidst our Plenty, *Something* still
> For Horses, Houses, Pictures, Planting
> To Thee, to Me, to Him is wanting.
> That cruel *Something* unpossess'd
> Corrodes, and levens all the rest.
> That *Something*, if We could obtain,
> Would soon create a future Pain:
> And to the Coffin, from the Cradle
> 'Tis all a WISH, and all a LADLE.
> (ll. 161-70, *LW*, 1:206-7)

The subsequent reputation of those "Idle Tales" reflects a shift in taste between the eighteenth century and the nineteenth. Dr. Johnson and Oliver Goldsmith considered them moral and unshocking tales but faced opposition in doing so. Reminded by Boswell of Lord Hailes's attack on Prior's "impure tales," Johnson retorted, "There is nothing in Prior that will excite to lewdness. If Lord Hailes thinks there is, he must be more combustible than other people." Boswell specifically brought up "Paulo Purganti," to which Johnson replied, "Sir, there is nothing there, but that his wife wanted to be kissed, when poor Paulo was out of pocket. No, Sir, Prior is a lady's book. No lady is ashamed to have it standing in her library."[33]

When Goldsmith in 1767 edited *The Beauties of English Poesy,* he intended it especially as an anthology for young people. "To our youth, particularly, a publication of this sort may be useful . . . ; every poem here is well known, and possessed, or the public has been long mistaken, of peculiar merit. . . ."[34] In this anthology he included both "Hans Carvel" and "The Ladle." A reviewer in the *Monthly Review,* however, attacked his choice of pieces, particularly his inclusion of "Hans Carvel"; the buying public, which agreed, objected also to "The Ladle," and Goldsmith's anthology had only a limited sale.[35] A modern adolescent would probably be more amused than shocked by these poems, but there is little chance that he would see them. They virtually disappeared during the nineteenth century, which found them embarrassingly frank. The

Chaucerian flavor of Prior's tales had been noted by Thomas Tickell in Prior's own century in these three tales and in "The Turtle and the Sparrow." It condemned the tales to disrepute and obscurity by the end of the eighteenth century.

Vers de Société

Most of Prior's remaining significant short poems may be classified as *vers de société*: polished, easy, light verses, brief and clear, in a conventional form, serving some social function, from the tendering of a dinner invitation to the winning of a woman. Several of the types of poems already discussed in this chapter—epigrams, playful epitaphs, songs, hudibrastic epistles, autobiographical tales—besides belonging to these more specific genres are also types of *vers de société*. In an even larger and looser sense, most of the best eighteenth-century poetry, Prior's included, is intended to serve a social function, and to serve it in a polished, easy, lucid fashion. That goal, natural to the eighteenth century, seemed repugnant to the nineteenth. For the eighteenth century, poetry, however individualized and personalized, is one social function of the world of educated men, as unsecluded and public as any other function. In it, a man might court his mistress or praise his patron or ponder the fate of his soul, but he did it in full awareness of the world of men going on about him and the world of literature that had preceded him. To be isolated, as Imlac reminds Rasselas of the unbalanced astronomer, is the first step toward madness, toward "the dangerous prevalence of the imagination"; to become again a part of society is the first step toward its cure. A poet who secludes himself from society is likely to become both obscure and irrelevant, to find in turn that society has secluded itself from him.

Though nineteenth-century critics tended to find *vers de société* trivial, the twentieth century does not. No category of Prior's poetry has been so praised and examined in the last eighty years as his social verse. Modern critics agree that Prior is one of the finest practitioners of *vers de société*, that he can work entirely within a highly conventionalized form yet do distinctive things with it; and that he is aided in his art by having mastered the techniques of Horace, the French lyricists, and such English figures as Ben Jonson, Carew, Suckling, and Rochester—the cavalier poets. The analyst of Prior's light verse, however, finds at last that he must examine in some detail single examples of his art in order to explain how it works. Some of the most illuminating studies of Prior's achievement in *vers de société* are of this kind; Oswald Doughty on "Down-Hall,"[36] Mark Van Doren on "An Ode" ("The Merchant, to secure his Treasure"),[37] Maynard Mack on "To a Child of Quality of Five Years Old,"[38] James Sutherland on "A Letter to the Honorable Lady Mrs. Margaret Candish Harley."[39]

The different tones that Prior was capable of striking within the bounds of conventional *vers de société* are nowhere better shown than in a closely related series of three poems: "Cloe Jealous," "Answer to Cloe Jealous, in the same Stile. The Author sick," and "A Better Answer." In the first poem, Cloe, by protesting that she does not care, complains that Damon's songs seem often addressed to other women. Perhaps she weeps, she says, "for my Two poor stragling Sheep / . . . or for my Squirrel dead" (ll. 3-4, *LW*, 1:448). As the poem proceeds, it becomes clear that Cloe feels herself a faithful mistress, mistreated by Damon because ignored in his verse. The poem ends:

> The secret Wound with which I bleed
> Shall lie wrapt up, ev'n in my Herse:
> But on my Tomb-stone Thou shalt read
> My Answer to Thy dubious verse.
> (ll. 41-44, *LW*, 1:449)

The poem is a conventional love lament of a woman loved, then abandoned; the imagery of flowers, the feigned reluctance to tell what then is told in detail, the fidelity of love-sickness even unto death are all frequent in poems of this type. It is polished, elegant, and largely conventional. Prior then wrote two answers to his own poem, very different in style and tone. The first is "Answer to Cloe Jealous, in the same Stile. The Author sick," which takes up the death-threat in the last stanza of the preceding poem and answers it in kind:

> Yet when some better-fated Youth
> Shall with his am'rous Parly move Thee:
> Reflect One Moment on His Truth,
> Who dying Thus, persists to love Thee.
> (ll. 13-16, *LW*, 1:450-51)

This is an effective answer, within the bounds of the serious love-lament. There is, however, "A Better Answer" to all such accusations, by refusing to react hyperbolically to hyperbole, by talking tolerant, amused common sense to a hysterical woman, still flattering her but reminding her that weeping ruins one's appearance and that poets write one language but talk another:

> DEAR CLOE, how blubber'd is that pretty Face?
> Thy Cheek all on Fire, and Thy Hair all uncurl'd:
> Pr'ythee quit this Caprice; and (as OLD FALSTAF says)
> Let Us e'en talk a little like folks of This World.
>
> How can'st Thou presume, Thou hast leave to destroy
> The Beauties, which VENUS but lent to Thy keeping?
> Those Looks were design'd to inspire Love and Joy:
> More ord'nary Eyes may serve People for weeping.
>
> To be vext at a Trifle or two that I writ,
> Your Judgment at once, and my Passion You wrong:
> You take that for Fact, which will scarce be found Wit:
> Od's Life! must One swear to the Truth of a Song?
>
> What I speak, my fair CLOE, and what I write, shews
> The Diff'rence there is betwixt Nature and Art:
> I court others in Verse; but I love Thee in Prose:
> And They have my Whimsies; but Thou hast my Heart.
>   (ll. 1–16, *LW,* 1:450–51)

The polish and elegance of these opening lines is frequently deflated by colloquial, chatty, ordinary terms ("blubber'd," "Folks of This World," "Od's Life"), for the whole poem is making that point: that underneath the elegance of *vers de société* are the ordinary ways of ordinary men, going about their unpastoral business. The balance of terms and tones is continued to the end of the poem, with its classical allusion carefully explained and its pronoun cases deliberately colloquialized:

> The God of us Verse-men (You know Child) the SUN,
> How after his Journeys He sets up his Rest:
> If at Morning o'er Earth 'tis his Fancy to run;
> At Night he reclines on his THETIS's Breast.

> So when I am weary'd with wand'ring all Day;
> To Thee my Delight in the Evening I come:
> No Matter what Beauties I saw in my Way:
> They were but my Visits; but Thou art my Home.
>
> Then finish, Dear CLOE, this Pastoral War;
> And let us like HORACE and LYDIA agree:
> For Thou art a Girl as much brighter than Her,
> As He was a Poet sublimer than Me.
> (ll. 17–28, *LW*, 1:451)

The poetical indiscretions have shaded into personal ones, but all are dismissed as inconsequential, trivial, beside the point, which is that Damon is essentially (if not accidentally) faithful to Cloe. This is one of Prior's strongest short poems—winning, witty, and gentle—and it operates by precisely the same method as do the successful tales such as "Daphne and Apollo," deliberately deflating highflown pastoral rhetoric by interspersing it with the colloquial common sense of "Folks of This World." The technique would not work if the classical material had not first been absorbed and mastered and loved—but the poem never forgets that the classical material is in certain ways absurd and irrelevant in the Augustan world. The technique further recognizes that the absurdity is as much a part of the unheroic modern world as of the inappropriately heroic classical one.

Chapter Four
Prior's Three Long Poems: *Henry and Emma, Solomon, Alma*

Though virtually all of Prior's literary reputation in the nineteenth and twentieth centuries has depended upon his shorter poems, particularly his familiar lyrics, his reputation in the eighteenth century was based just as firmly upon his three long poems: *Henry and Emma, Solomon on the Vanity of the World,* and *Alma: or, The Progress of the Mind.* Though very different in content, versification, and tone, the three poems have in common their initial popularity in their own century and their subsequent eclipse. Moreover, they are all explorations of some situation or system, conducting their inquiry at—for the modern reader—striking length. *Henry and Emma* is 773 lines long; *Solomon* is 2652; *Alma* is 1683. It was in large measure the success of these longer poems that made Prior for his own time a major poet.

Henry and Emma

Prior took as his model for *Henry and Emma* the anonymous late Middle English *Nut-brown Maid* (first published in 1502 but recently reprinted in the *Muses Mercury,* June 1707).[1] He printed the medieval poem immediately preceding his in both the 1709 and 1718 editions. The original *Nut-brown Maid* was a "test" poem written under the influence of the Franciscan defense of women; Prior sought to revive it, dress it in eighteenth-century apparel, and retell it in eighteenth-century terms. Like the original, Prior's poem has its heroine tested by her disguised lover, who presents her with increasingly painful alternatives to abandoning him. She is unswervingly faithful throughout the ordeal, and her lover finally reveals to her that he is no exiled murderer, harsh and changeable, but a young lord of high repute. Prior tells the tale at double its original length, in heroic couplets, with an alexandrine refrain for each lover: Henry's consists of variants of "Condemn'd in lonely Woods a banish'd Man to rove"; Emma's, of variants of "That I, of all Mankind, will love but Thee alone." Both Henry and Emma speak the rhetoric of poetic Augustan courtship: elegant, balanced, epigrammatic. Prior adds to the original poem a specific setting, a personal prologue within a long explanatory frame, and a mythological close which serves also to praise Queen Anne and the Duke of Marlborough.

The poem was highly and immediately popular. It was translated into Latin in 1748[2]; into German by F. J. Bertuch in 1753[3]; and into French prose by Mme Thiroux d'Arconville in 1764.[4] Sections of it were set to music in 1749 by Thomas Augustine Arne and used as an interlude; parts again were set to music in 1774 by Sir Henry Bate Dudley.[5] Critics as crotchety as John Dennis openly praised it.[6] Lady Mary Wortley Montagu, a true women's liberationist, objected to the "monstrous folly of [the] story in plain prose," yet so much admired Prior's version that even at seventy-three she could still recite the whole 773 lines by heart.[7]

In the later eighteenth century when two key critics expressed dislike for *Henry and Emma,* the pronouncements brought forth rebuttals from other critics of almost equal prominence. When Dr. Johnson objected to *Henry and Emma* on grounds of its morality and its tedium,[8] both William Cowper and John Wesley took specific exception to his censure.[9] When Thomas Warton the younger asserted that Prior had marred the design of the poem by softening the sternness of the man,[10] Horace Walpole angrily rejected the charge.[11]

Henry and Emma was as notable in the eighteenth century for its influence as for its reputation. Lady Mary Wortley Montagu could not only quote the poem by heart; her own poem, the "Basset-Table," is filled with echoes of Prior's poem. In 1739, William Shenstone went through his copy of Prior's *Poems on Several Occasions,* which he had purchased when an Oxford student four years earlier, "marking the Pieces I most admired with a proportionate Number of Crosses."[12] Marjorie Williams reports that two Prior poems—"The Garland" and *Henry and Emma*—receive Shenstone's highest commendation, the sevenfold cross.[13]

More important, two contemporaries of Alexander Pope—James Ralph[14] and Richard Savage[15]—insisted that Pope wrote *Eloisa to Abelard* in a deliberate attempt to compete with Prior's *Henry and*

Emma while capitalizing on its popularity. Lines from *Henry and Emma* are echoed in Pope's *Rape of the Lock,* in *Windsor Forest,* in the *Dunciad,* and in *Of the Characters of Women: An Epistle to a Lady,* but the main impact of Prior's poem undoubtedly came upon *Eloisa to Abelard.*[16]

With the beginning of the nineteenth century, the tables turned completely. *Henry and Emma* became the most steadily attacked of all Prior's poems, and has received a kind word only rarely in the last 180 years. The only detailed sympathetic treatment of the poem in the twentieth century was written by James Sutherland in 1948 in his *Preface to Eighteenth Century Poetry,* in which he examines the poem at some length, in the light of what Prior was attempting to accomplish. "What Prior has done is not so much to translate the poem into modern English as to inject it with some sort of poetical serum which completely alters the blood-content. He has treated it as a modern choreographer might treat sophisticated ballet."[17]

Prior's modernization of *The Nut-brown Maid,* like Dryden's and Pope's of Chaucer, had a double motivation. First, the poets wished to make the poems available to unsophisticated readers who would otherwise have had difficulty with the language. Dryden wrote of his Chaucer modernization in his preface to *Fables Ancient and Modern* (1700): "Tis not for the Use of some old *Saxon* Friends, that I have taken these Pains with him: Let them neglect my Version, because they have no need of it. I made it for their sakes who understand Sense and Poetry, as well as they; when that Poetry and Sense is put into Words which they understand."[18] Moreover, they wished to give more sophisticated readers the pleasure of seeing a familiar story treated in contemporary style, terms, and rhetoric.

It is a rare modernization that outlasts its own century; *Henry and Emma* did not survive its own age, nor did Dryden's and Pope's Chaucer modernizations. But to call these attempts mistakes or failures because they did not also speak in resounding terms to the nineteenth and twentieth centuries is to miss the point of modernization. Language and manners shift; there must be new modernizations of the best of the old tales in every century, so that the neophyte may encounter them for the first time and the learned may have the pleasure of seeing the original transformed into its modern-dress version. *Henry and Emma* was a spectacular success in its own age; succeeding ages must find their own frame of reference and their own rhetoric for testing the limits of female fidelity.

Solomon on the Vanity of the World

At about the same time (1707-8) that he was working on *Henry and Emma,* Prior was also writing a second major poem, *Solomon on the Vanity of the World,* though the latter was not to be printed till a decade afterwards. The longest of Prior's poems (2652 lines), *Solomon* was the most serious of his major efforts. It is a soliloquy by Solomon about his unsuccessful attempts to find happiness and meaning in three successive sources: knowledge, pleasure, and power. In a very interesting preface,[19] Prior writes of his efforts to choose the proper verse form for his meditation, and of his decision to choose heroic couplets but in a modified form, because "He that writes in Rhimes, dances in Fetters: And as his Chain is more extended, he may certainly take larger Steps."[20]

In Book I, Solomon seeks physical and metaphysical learning, only to be balked and baffled at every turn. Finally he concludes, Pyrrhonistically, that human reason is not sufficient to give certain answers to questions either material or spiritual. Not only common sense observation (and Pyrrho) but Scriptures as well show the futility of seeking certain knowledge.

Baffled in his search for knowledge, Solomon turns instead to pleasure, seeking happiness in wealth, architectural achievements, music, dance, drink, and finally love. He is most conspicuously unsuccessful in love. His first choice, a nameless Egyptian beauty, spurns him for her plighted Egyptian love. His second choice—or rather chooser, for it is she who seeks him out—is Abra, a simple low-born girl, who changes into a tyrant when he returns her love, filling his court with her friends and flatterers, leading him into ostentatious excesses and regal injustices and sloth. Finally, his sense of duty reasserts itself, and he throws off her power over him, resigning himself to "sigh in Royalty, and grieve in State" (2:806, *LW,* 1:355). Rejected and despairing, Abra kills herself. Solomon, plunged into grief, turns to range "Thro' Tribes of Women" while "Bury'd in Sloth, and lost in Ease . . . ," adopting the gods of whatever person he happens to caress. Eventually, however, he rises again and throws off his subservience to these women, concluding, "Of Lust and Love, with their fantastic Train, / Their Wishes, Smiles, and Looks deceitful all, and vain."[21]

In Book III, without much hope ("For Hope is but the Dream of Those that wake"—3:102, *LW,* 1:364), Solomon turns to all that is left for him on earth—power. He already foresees the answer here. He has observed the stages of man and the vicissitudes of fortune, even for great conquerors; he knows that today's hero (his laurel even now "Wet with the Soldier's Blood, and Widow's Tears"—3:308, *LW*, 1:369) is tomorrow's dishonored corpse or taunted captive. It would be best, he concludes, never to have lived. He sees all mankind, himself included, as trapped between the past and the future:

> Amid Two Seas on One small Point of Land
> Weary'd, uncertain, and amaz'd We stand:
> On either Side our Thoughts incessant turn:
> Forward We dread; and looking back We mourn.
> Losing the Present in this dubious Hast:
> And lost Our selves betwixt the Future, and the Past.
> (3:613–18, *LW*, 1:377)

In answer to his devout questioning, an angel appears and tells him to cease looking for relief from trouble and sorrow. The angel foretells the subsequent history of Israel, from the time of Rehoboam and Jereboam to the time of Christ, and counsels Solomon:

> Stop Thy Enquiry then; and curb Thy Sense;
> Nor let Dust argue with Omnipotence.
> 'Tis GOD who must dispose, and Man sustain,
> Born to endure, forbidden to complain.
> (3:840–43, *LW*, 1:383)

With the final injunction "Be Humble, and be Just," the angel flies upward, and Solomon accepts its orders:

> Benign Creator, let Thy plastic Hand
> Dispose it's own Effect. Let Thy Command
> Restore, Great Father, Thy Instructed Son;
> And in My Act may THY great WILL BE DONE.
> (3:887–90, *LW*, 1:385)

Solomon is by far Prior's longest and most detailed treatment of serious ethical and metaphysical questions. Hoxie Neale Fairchild in a study of Prior as a melancholy skeptic influenced by his early Calvinist background and later scientific determination, quips that

"Set amidst all the *vers de société* and bawdy tales, *Solomon* looks like a parson in a night club."[22] *Solomon* is nevertheless simply the longest manifestation of Prior's continuing interest in religious questions, from his "On Exodus iii. 14," written when he was still a student at St. John's College, Cambridge, to "Predestination," written in the last months of his life and left unfinished at his death. Throughout most of these works there is a consistent Pyrrhonism (an extreme skepticism about the efficacy of human reason) and a frequent fideism (accepting on faith matters that cannot be determined by this fallible reason). The chief point on which Prior vacillates is whether, in a world of vanities in which reason is but an erring guide, it is wise for a man to take his fill of the pleasures, however vain and transitory, that he can find at hand. Most of his poems, like "Jinny the Just," suggest that man should take his pleasures where he can find them, thus making life at least temporarily richer and fuller; *Solomon* warns that such pleasures are deceptive, dangerous, and ultimately unsatisfying.

Though never as widely popular as *Henry and Emma*, *Solomon* achieved a favorable response in its own day. It was translated into Latin verse by William Dobson (1734–36)[23] and later (1743–Book II only) by George Bally;[24] and into German by Simon Grynaeus in 1757.[25] Though Pope turned aside Prior's question as to how he liked *Solomon*, his avoidance of the question indicating that he did not,[26] Pope's own *Essay on Man* is heavily indebted to it.[27]

Because Prior's *Solomon* refuses to accept any rational way out, insisting that all things in this world are vanity and dust, it is both more philosophically consistent and more poetically tedious than Pope's *Essay on Man*. Tedium was the main charge that Dr. Johnson made against the poem: "The event of every experiment is foreseen, and therefore the process is not much regarded."[28] In this sense, *Solomon* suffers from its own consistency of idea and purpose, in a way that the *Essay on Man* does not. The impertinent Damon in Prior's "The Conversation" gives his pretended insider's view of Prior's key pieces. Of *Solomon* he opines: "Indeed poor SOLOMON in Rhime / Was much too grave to be Sublime" (ll. 63–64, *LW*, 1:525). It is, at least, probably too unwaveringly grave to arouse our curiosity; we know that no experiment—in knowledge, pleasure, or power—will long satisfy Solomon.

If Johnson found *Solomon* tedious as a whole, he learned a good deal from its parts. Both *Rasselas* and *The Vanity of Human Wishes* show strong and direct influence from *Solomon*.[29] Johnson's borrowings from Prior's *Solomon* partly vitiate his strictures upon the poem, but others answered his objections more directly. John Wesley, who called *Solomon* "one of the noblest poems in the English tongue . . . ,"[30] took specific exception to Johnson's dictum that *Solomon* was tedious. "Did any one ever discern it before? . . . So far from it, that if I dip in any of the three books, I scarce know where to leave off."[31] Wesley quotes forty-nine lines from *Solomon,* then asks "Now what has Mr. *Pope* in all his eleven volumes, which will bear any comparison with this?"[32]

Likewise, William Cowper called *Solomon* "the best poem, whether we consider the subject of it or the execution, that Prior ever wrote"[33]—and Cowper thought highly of much of Prior's work. Hannah More found *Solomon* exquisite; Edward Gibbon called it a verbose but eloquent poem; Crabbe and Scott praised it. But Voltaire apparently found it tedious, as Johnson had.[34]

Though the Victorians paid little attention to *Solomon,* the notice occasionally paid to it was not entirely unfriendly. *Solomon* did, after all, have a quality of high seriousness suited to the taste of many Victorians. Typical is Edmund Gosse's reaction to the poem. He seems to be praising *Solomon* highly; then, by the end of his sentence, he has dismissed it. "The poem has distinct merits; it is perhaps more 'correct,' in Walsh's sense, than any other in the language; but it cannot be read. . . ."[35] In the twentieth century, critics continued to mix praise and blame of *Solomon* in single pronouncements. Surely as a poem it may not arouse our curiosity—it is plain from the start that Solomon will find everything vain—but it has many strong lines, a number of memorable figures, and a versification worthy of notice. Moreover, it strongly influenced similar philosophical writing by both Pope and Johnson. Finally, it is a repository of Augustan attitudes—theological, ethical, scientific—both those that it accepts and those that it rejects. Professors Wright and Spears with good reason call *Solomon* "an important document in literary and intellectual history."[36]

Alma: or, The Progress of the Mind

About a decade after the writing of *Solomon,* Prior wrote the last of his major long poems, *Alma: or, The Progress of the Mind.* According to later accounts, he composed it in three weeks while he was being

held under house arrest and did not initially think highly of it—
"a loose and hasty scribble, to relieve the tedious hours of my
imprisonment, while in the messenger's hand"[37]—till it was praised
by Pope, Bathurst, and Harley. It is certain that Prior later revised
the poem extensively, and, as Professor Spears has observed, "poets
do not carefully revise trifles that they do not value."[38] Perhaps the
praise of his friends encouraged Prior in a higher opinion of the
poem and thus stimulated his revisions.

Alma, written in three cantos in hudibrastic couplets, is a mocking
attack upon all systems and system-building. In this one way, it
resembles *Solomon,* which had also pointed out the folly of system-
building.[39] In *Alma* Prior pretends to resolve a conflict between
Oxonian and Cantabrigian natural philosophers as to the seat of the
mind by proposing a compromise system. Those at Oxford, still
Aristotelian, insist that the mind or soul is everywhere throughout
the body: those at Cambridge, following Descartes, that it is in the
brain. As a compromise system, Prior (in a dialogue with his surly
but "fidus Achates," Richard Shelton) mockingly proposes a system
in which the mind progresses from the feet to the head as the man
ages—and thereby also provides a comic treatment of the stages of
man, which are tragically considered in *Solomon.* The question involved is larger, of course, than the foolish pretensions of the system-
builders. To question the site of the mind is also to question the
existence of soul (the usual translation of *alma*) and its relationship,
if it does indeed exist, to the body.

Canto I presents the Oxford and Cambridge systems and then
Prior's own. By the end of Canto I, Prior has traced the progress
of the mind as high as the waist in young adults. Dick Shelton
interrupts, reminding Prior that his admired classical poets place
the seat of romantic love in the heart or the liver. Prior dismisses
this position as mere poetical imagery, for the sake of pleasing and
meter, and insists on the waist as the seat of love, as of its fruits.

In Canto II, Prior pays tribute to Samuel Butler, whose hudibrastic verse he is employing, then turns to some corollaries of his
system—for example, the doctrine that wherever Alma has most
strongly resided in youth (in the leg, in the tongue) it will return
to reside in age, and the observation that the action of the mind is
partly determined by its environment: "In ALMA's Manners You
may read / The Place, where She was born and bred" (ll. 387–88,

LW, 1:495). Both corollaries give Prior rich opportunity to provide instances of human folly, individual and social.

Richard (now half-asleep) rouses himself in Canto III, to object that Prior has created a whimsical system in which he now insists that he and others believe. Prior replies by tracing the final progress of the mind, into the brain of the aging person. Richard proposes a counter-system built upon the hypothesis that the seat of mind is the belly, for foods determine temperament (individually and nationally) and lack of food kills Alma by killing the body. Prior replies that Shelton's system is too mechanistic and that he could "By dint of *Logic* strike Thee mute. . . ." (l. 381, *LW,* 1:510); ignoring Shelton's pleas to end the discussion, he points out the follies, disappointments, and frustrations of the aging man, with Alma now in his brain, and his strongest desire to forget her presence for a few minutes. Faced with his own mortality, all man can ask is amusements in the interim. Richard raises a final objection—all these follies he knows already, as well as his own mortality; he needs no new scientific-philosophic system to teach him these. He advises Prior to look instead for what he has said aging men seek: pastimes to make Alma temporarily forget herself.

The impact of *Alma* upon Prior's contemporaries and successors is revealing. *Alma* probably influenced similar passages in chapter 12 of the *Memoirs of . . . Martinus Scriblerus,* as revised by Pope, certainly influenced Diderot's *Les Bijoux Indiscrets* (1748), and was translated into Latin verse by Thomas Martin in 1763.[40] Pope called *Alma* a "masterpiece" and said that it was the only poem of Prior's that he would like to have written, "abating its excessive scepticism."[41] E. A. Richards, studying *Hudibras in the Burlesque Tradition,* establishes that *Alma* supplanted *Hudibras* itself in the esteem of the eighteenth century for polished hudibrastic verse.[42] Dr. Johnson, however, differed from the general opinion and rated *Alma* as inferior to *Hudibras,* writing that *Alma* "never . . . had a plan [or] any drift or design." He conceded that *"Alma* has many admirers."[43] Horace Walpole praised *Alma* as "far superior" to *Solomon* and much more learned.[44] Goldsmith thought "some parts of it very fine," others bad, but was puzzled as to its total intent: "What Prior meant by this poem I cannot understand. . . ."[45] William Cowper wrote that *Alma* owed "all its neatness and smartness" to its use of "the agreeable effect of rhyme or euphony."[46] Joseph Warton, toward the end of the eighteenth century, described *Alma* as "elegant and witty"[47] and later wrote of it: "Enquiries into the Seat of the Soul are finely ridiculed in the first canto of Prior's Alma; an original work, and perhaps the very best of all his compositions, which abounds equally in wit, pleasantry, humour, and good sense, and is a perfect pattern of facility of versification."[48]

The best explication of *Alma* for the first two centuries of its existence was provided by John Wesley, in rebuttal to Dr. Johnson's claim that *Alma* "never had a plan [or] any drift or design." Wesley replied, "The drift and design of it is tolerably plain. It is a strong satire on that self-conceited tribe of men, who pretend to philosophize upon every thing, natural or spiritual. It keenly exposes those who continually obtrude their own systems upon the world, and pretend to *account* for everything. His design is, if possible to make these men less wise in their own conceit, by showing them how plausibly a man may defend, the oddest system that can be conceived: and he intermixes many admirable reflexions, and closes with a very striking conclusion; which points out, where one would least expect it, that *all is vanity.*"[49]

Bredvold speaks for most twentieth-century critics of Prior's long poems in calling *Alma* his "only readable long poem."[50] Its wit, and its refusal to take itself seriously for long, appeal to the modern temperament in a way that the unrelieved seriousness of *Henry and Emma* and *Solomon* does not.

If the art of the heroic couplet, as practiced by Pope, was to conceal art by making the rhyme seem effortless and easy, Prior's octosyllabic couplets in *Alma* are seeking the opposite effect: to make the rhyme seem impossibly hard by continually rhyming with tortuous difficulty and frantic pain. Yet this too is a way in which art conceals art. Both of the most important scholars of the hudibrastic and the burlesque—E. A. Richards and Richmond P. Bond—agree that Prior took the hudibrastic as far as it could be taken in polite verse and thereby virtually exhausted its possibilities.[51] Prior adapted in *Alma* an ideal burlesque verse form, a modified hudibrastic, suited to his subject—both the verse and the content hide profundity and elegance behind a harlequin's mask.

The other aspect of *Alma* that particularly interests moderns is its revelation of the attitudes toward science and natural philosophy in the early eighteenth century. Prior's mock-system may indeed have its source in Montaigne,[52] but to Montaigne Prior added an epitome of eighteenth-century schools of natural philosophy, so that almost every study of eighteenth-century science has found *Alma* a valuable repository of ideas.[53] As Linacre Lecturer on medicine at St. John's College, Cambridge, and as an omnivorous reader, Prior knew a great deal about the new science. He did not like what he saw, but he was well aware of what he was seeing. For one who would understand eighteenth-century scientific philosophy, there is no livelier introduction than its unfriendly treatment in *Alma*.

Chapter Five
Prior's Prose and Dramas

Though Prior's literary reputation in his time and in ours rests on his poetry, he also wrote a number of pieces in prose and two unfinished plays. The prose is interesting because it supplements in many ways points of view and approaches taken in his poetry; the plays are interesting because they show a side of Prior not to be predicted from his nondramatic writing. The prose falls into five chief categories: 1) prefaces, dedications, postscripts; 2) two periodical essays; 3) two collections of observations (on Homer and Ovid); 4) two epistemological essays; and 5) four *Dialogues of the Dead*.[1]

Prefaces, Dedications, Postscripts

Several of Prior's prefaces, dedications, and postscripts show him simply as a graceful and winning eulogist, recounting the literary and personal virtues of the Earl of Dorset and, in less detail, of the Duke of Dorset, his son. These pieces are of interest now only in showing Prior's gift for presenting himself modestly while praising others aptly, for blaming others faintly while eulogizing strongly, for lauding them without fawning. They are characterized by warmth and critical acumen, and by a balance of sentence and phrase. Among such eulogistic pieces would be included the preface to the 1708 *Poems on Several Occasions*, the dedication to the same collection, and the postscript to the 1718 *Poems on Several Occasions*.

Two of Prior's prefaces, written to introduce individual poems, are more revealing, for they give us portions of his literary theory. In the first of these, the preface to "An Ode, Humbly Inscrib'd to the Queen. On the Glorious Success of Her Majesty's Arms, 1706," Prior explains that he felt a Horatian ode to be most appropriate for the august occasion; that the ode stanza suggested to him a similar long stanza in English; and that he chose for this similar stanza a modification of the Spenserian stanza, inserting between the eighth and ninth lines an iambic pentameter line rhyming with the closing alexandrine.² He writes further that he avoided many of Spenser's obsolete terms, while retaining a few expressions and proper names. He closes the preface with a comparison of the talents of Horace and Spenser, an unusual parallel for an Augustan to make: "My Two Great Examples, HORACE and SPENSER, in many Things resemble each other: Both have a Height of Imagination, and a Majesty of Expression in describing the *Sublime*; and Both know to temper those Talents, and sweeten the Description, so as to make it Lovely as well as Pompous: Both have equally That agreeable Manner of mixing Morality with their Story, and That *Curiosa Felicitas* in the Choice of their Diction, which every Writer aims at, and so very few have reach'd: Both are particularly Fine in their Images, and Knowing in their Numbers."³ The praise of Horace was usual in the Augustan period, but the praise of Spenser was not. It is possible that Prior's poem and its preface mark the beginning of the eighteenth-century revival of Spenser and imitations of his form; surely they represent an early manifestation of this tendency.

Of special interest for its criticism was the preface to *Solomon*, written in 1717 or 1718. Prior calls *Solomon* a poem that is either "*Didascalic,* or *Heroic,*" or a blending, being both narrative and moral, and seeking like Homer, Virgil, and others to teach a specific point as well as to tell a story. He sees Spenser as the English equivalent of the writers of classical epics; the *Faerie Queene,* had it been finished, "would have been an Heroic Poem, but in another Cast and Figure, than any that had ever been written before." Despite the diverse threads of plot in the *Faerie Queene,* all would have come together at last; "He lanches out into very flowery Paths, which still seem to conduct him into one great Road." Finally, he moves to a discussion of the proper versification for such a poem. Continually run-on couplets, like those of Donne and his contemporaries, are "too dissolute and wild, and came very often too near Prose." On the other hand, the closed heroic couplet, corrected by Davenant and Waller and perfected by Dryden, is too confined; it "produces too frequent an Identity in the Sound, and brings every Couplet to the Point of an Epigram. It is indeed too broken and weak, to convey the Sentiments and represent the Images proper for *Epic.*" The blank verse of Milton and the complexly rhymed stanza of Spenser are two attempts to find an adequate English verse and stanza form for the epic; Prior does not presume to pass judgment on them. He has however decided to write his own Didactic-Heroic poem in couplets arranged in stanzas and treated with more variations than Davenant, Waller, and Dryden would have allowed. (In *Solomon* he varied the couplets by occasional run-on first lines, by triplets, alexandrines, and hemistiches.) He praises Pope's use of the closed couplet in his Homeric translations, but reiterates that "He that writes in Rhimes, dances in Fetters: And as his Chain is more extended, he may certainly take larger Steps" (*LW*, 1:307–9).

Periodical Essays

At least twice in his lifetime Prior wrote periodical essays for the newspapers of his time, though his 1709 letter "To Isaac Bickerstaff commonly called the Tatler" was never printed in the *Tatler* and never acknowledged in it, and may not have been submitted.[4] It is a Scriblerian spoof, proposing marriage to Jinny Distaff, to whom he has never spoken in his life. He signs the letter "Walter Wou'd have Wit" and attaches to it his poem "My Birth Day," one of Prior's most effective lyrics despite its mocking introduction.[5]

A much more serious essay was published in the Tory political newspaper, the *Examiner*, no. 6, dated 7 September 1710. In a letter attacking the Whigs for imposing tyrannical power on the world of art as on the political world, all things in both being "weigh'd here by the unerring Balance of Party. . . ." (*LW*, 1:389), "Philodingle" devotes much of his attention to Samuel Garth's poem eulogizing the Earl of Godolphin, who had been forced to resign as lord treasurer on 8 August of that year. "Philodingle" reports that he has read Garth's eulogy carefully, "But so dull am I, that there does not appear to my Apprehension, either Poetry, Grammar, or Design in the Composition." Then he proceeds to analyze the poem, line by line and figure by figure, devastating it as he goes. Garth's image of the Nile, for example, is hopelessly trite: "I remember I us'd it, when I was about Twelve, in a *New-Years-Gift* to my Uncle, and was heartely asham'd of it a Year after" (*LW*, 1:391–92). He turns other figures against Garth and the Whigs. Garth has said that Godolphin as lord treasurer taught "the *Unpractis'd Crew to Steer*," but it is not the crew's business to steer: "This is a true Image of the Whig Scheme, where every Man is his own *Pilot*" (*LW*, 1:392). He cites an improper use of case, which

Dr. Busby would never have permitted at Westminster School, an instance of ingratitude to Queen Anne, and a line plagiarized from Dryden and altered for the worse: "This is being a meer *Banditti* in Poetry, to *Rob* and *Murder* too" (*LW*, 1:393). The piece closes with a sphinx-riddle in verse, the answer to which is "a Prime Minister," namely Godolphin. Line-by-line parody had made Prior's first literary reputation, with *The Hind and the Panther Transvers'd*; here he was using it to assist Swift and the Tories in attacking another controversial poem, the controversy this time being political rather than theological. That Prior's parody rankled is shown by the fact that Addison twice endeavored to reply to it: in the first issue of the *Whig-Examiner* (14 September 1710) and again in the *Tatler*, no. 239, 19 October 1710.[6]

The Collection of Observations on Homer and Ovid

Twice in his lifetime Prior put together sets of notes on major classical poets, but in neither case were the notes put into final form, presented to anyone, or published. The "Observations on Homer" is in paragraph form and reads fairly coherently; though Prior apparently did not consider it finished, it is at least a penultimate draft and a useful revelation of Prior's attitude toward Homer and the *Iliad*. The "Observation on Ovid's Metamorphoses" is much sketchier and more fragmentary, notes upon which Prior later intended to base a first draft of an essay.

The "Observations on Homer. A Letter" gives no indication of its intended recipient, except that he is "ever partial to Father Homer"; the letter was apparently never readied and sent. Prior calls the piece his "Diary" upon Homer; it focuses on the *Iliad* alone, and consists mainly of observations upon specific passages, similes, and images in the poem. The comments are undated but were probably completed no later than 1715.[7] Prior begins, ingratiatingly, by saying that he has recently "run over" the *Iliad* again "not in Greek don't mistake me but in French and Latin; recurring to the Original as well as my long Disuse of the Classic Writers gave me leave . . ." (*LW*, 1:417). Although Prior is being in part factual—he did own French and Latin translations of the *Iliad* and probably used them freely—he is also using the disarmingly over-modest device, which he often employs at the beginning of a prose letter or essay, disclaiming all expertise while covertly establishing his right to speak. To put his disclaimer in quite other terms, a man who has reread the *Iliad* in French, Latin, and Greek has every right to speak: he is a polylingual collator. But Prior has made what might have been a boast sound like an apology; he is rusty in his Greek. J. W. Johnson, studying *The Formation of English Neo-Classical Thought,* has shown that Prior "was pervasively affected by his study of Greek. A highly proficient Latin scholar and writer, Prior nevertheless found the Greek idiom and attitude a constant stimulation." Professor Johnson gives examples of Prior's particular interest in Greek and proves Prior's grasp of Greek metrics and prosody, concluding that Prior shared with Dryden and Pope "a preoccupation with Greek philology."[8]

In his "Observations on Homer," after his modest polylingual disclaimer, Prior begins with some general comments on the *Iliad.* He finds the books too closely connected to have been only distinct songs collected together after Homer's death. Horace had admitted that Homer sometimes nodded; Pope had denied it in 1711 in the *Essay on Criticism:* "Nor is it *Homer Nods,* but *We* that *Dream."* Prior's comment is "if Homer as our Friend Horace confesses Does sometimes Sleep, he makes a very glorious Noise whereever he is thorowly awake" (ll. 9–10, *LW,* 1:417). High praise, even if not the unqualified praise of Pope. Prior denies that the *Iliad* is the perfect epic poem, however, because it leaves too many persons and events unaccounted for, including the fall of Troy and the disposition of Helen. If the subject of the poem is not the destruction of Troy but simply "to Show how destructive the Disentions of the Great are to the Public," then the poem is "more Perfect, but his Design not so great" (ll. 17–18, 21–22, *LW,* 1:417–18). In any case, Prior observes, the whole quarrel is really brought on by three harlots—Helena, Chryseis, and Briseis—and he feels that all of these heroes carried on too much over women such as these, and in language low and inappropriate for "the Sons and Grandsons of Gods and Goddesses." He disapproves mythologically of Apollo's giving the Trojans a wind (that is AEolus's proper sphere) and theologically of Jupiter's sending a lying dream to Agamemnon (as he does of God's sending a lying spirit to seduce Ahab). "In these cases how can Heroic Virtue know how it is deceiv'd" (ll. 47–48, *LW,* 1:418). He seconds Scaliger's criticism that Homeric heroes should not properly "make long Speeches in the heat of their Battles . . . ," and he disapproves of the intervention of the deus ex machina, in human form, to save favorites: "This takes all merit and blame from human Action and is in a less degree the fault of all Epic Writers . . ." (ll. 55–56, *LW,* 1:419).

Most of the rest of Prior's "Observations on Homer" is taken up with his reactions to specific speeches, figures, episodes, and images in the *Iliad.* Some he finds "very fine," some not "very just," some "silly," some "horrible," some "rediculous." He is particularly displeased with the name-calling and cuffing among the gods and goddesses, which he finds "extreamly rediculous. Homer ought very often to remember what he makes Apollo say very finely to Neptune that the Gods should not be concerned about Men, who are short liv'd as flowers" (ll. 161–64, *LW,* 1:422). The cloud that hangs over all of Prior's serious religious poems, from the "Exodus Ode" to *Solomon* to "Predestination," is in part this—that the supernatural may indeed not care about insignificant men. It marks even his love poems such as "Parting with Flavia."

In closing, Prior again finds the *Iliad* structurally imperfect—either it stops too soon (before Troy falls and Helen is restored) or too late (continuing after the death of Hector). He is particularly afraid that the Trojan lamentation for Hector detracts from Achilles' achievement in killing him and makes the reader care too much about the victim—almost giving Homer an epic with two heroes on opposing sides.

As for Homer's praised achievement in keeping the time of the *Iliad* within a year, Prior retorts that its only real action—the quarrel and reconciliation of Achilles and Agamemnon and the death of Hector—could as well have taken place within a week.

Though not a polished critical essay, the "Observations on Homer" is useful because it is Prior's most extended piece of purely literary criticism, the Garth examination in the *Examiner* having been almost as long but politically motivated and dealing with a very minor poet and poem. Prior shows himself here a careful scholar of the *Iliad* and of its critics,[9] admiring Homer but never worshipping him, and differing with him wittily and winningly.

The "Observations on Ovid's Metamorphoses," though about five times as long as the "Observations upon Homer," is in much less finished form. It is nonetheless close, scholarly criticism concerning Ovid's episodes, characters, figures of speech, assumptions about his readers, strengths and weaknesses, with comments of broader impact scattered throughout: "It is greatly the fault of the Ancients to give insignificant Epithetes and dwell too long upon the description of Trifles" (ll. 30–32, *LW*, 1:664). ". . . the great fault of Epic bringing people for whom You have no Concern in to be killed, you are glad when you are rid of them at the Expence of their lives . . ." (ll. 51–53, *LW*, 1:664). He is particularly interested in parallels between the *Metamorphoses* and the Bible, in accounts of the creation, flood, paradise, promised land, giants endeavoring to scale heaven, general conflagration, father sacrificing his child at the behest of the gods, gods (or angels) being entertained by man, and the immortality of the soul. He inclines to humanize myth as superstition, the dragons slain by various heroes signifying "their having subdued famous robbers or Pyrats." He confesses himself moved by the *Metamorphoses* sometimes when he rationally ought not to be: "The force of Poetry is very strange, thô Dryope being turned into a Tree is as silly as imagination can well form a Story, her dying Speech to her family affects Me when I read it" (ll. 158–60, *LW*, 1:668). He points out obscurities and redundancies in Ovid's Latin, and similes unworthy of their subject: "Pyramus's blood spouted out like water from a crack't pipe: Ovid might as well have said 'He bled like a Stuck Pigg' " (ll. 190–92, *LW*, 1:669). Prior collects instances of a particular poetic device of Ovid's—a repetitive punning on words and their roots—and writes that "Ovid uses this way of Speech a hundred times over" (l. 210, *LW*, 1:670).[10] He finds the same fault of redundancy sometimes in Dryden: "The same thing is here according to Ovids usual redundance said three Times and the thought does not rise, Dryden Sometimes commits the Same fault, the four first verses of his Absolom" (ll. 247–49, *LW*, 1:671). Examining the story of Ceyx, Prior concludes that it is typical of Ovid: "We find that tenderness was his Masterpiece but he had no Strength" (ll. 233–34, *LW*, 1:671).

As in his own poetry Prior is best at domesticating the myth, so he is wittiest in the "Observations on Ovid's Metamorphoses" when he discovers characters behaving in ways that belie his human experience: "Proserpine was indeed very young or very silly that when She was in the hands of Pluto, had her cloaths torn and Squalled out to her Mother was griev'd that She dropt the flowers out of her lap. This was a great while since, Wenches that are bigg enough to be ravish't are not so infinitely concerned for their Nosegays" (ll. 253–57, *LW,* 1:671).

Prior praises Ovid for making "his People better bred then his fellow poets usually do" and concludes that "This proceeded from his knowing a Court" (ll. 260, 263, *LW,* 1:672). Almost surely Prior considered that his having had the same benefit in his own diplomatic career worked equally to his advantage as a poet.

The "Observations on Ovid's Metamorphoses" concludes with a general statement, suggested by Ovid and his heroes but going far beyond them, on the mutual interdependence of different classes and occupations of men that extends even to their fame after death. ". . . So is it in this imaginary life which We Seek after Death, Heroes and Conquerors perform great Actions which written and recorded may give them this kind of Immortality, Historians and Poets procure to themselves the Same advantage from the very writing of these Actions: princes build cities and palaces, Engineers and Architects come in for their share of the fame, and he that would be remembered by a Monument divides the honour with the Sculptor that Erects it" (ll. 288–95, *LW,* 1:672–73).

Both of these uncompleted essays show in Prior some of the same qualities that make his poems on classical topics so appealing. In them there is a combination of a man at ease with his classical learning and comfortable in his own modern world—and yet detached and unsentimental in viewing both. Behind both worlds are glimpses of a melancholy vision of something more—a world in which the gods may ignore man as too insignificant for their interest, or a world in which heroes and poets conspire together to save their names, for a while, from the ravages of time and death.

Two Epistemological Essays

Prior also worked during his lifetime on two essays that may be called, loosely, epistemological—that is, they deal with the method and grounds of knowledge, its limits and validity: the same question that Prior had raised repeatedly in his poetry, particularly in Book I of *Solomon* and in *Alma.* These essays are entitled "Heads for a Treatise upon Learning" and "Opinion." Neither is in final form (as the title of the first indicates), and neither was published in Prior's lifetime, both appearing for the first time in 1907 in the Waller edition of *Dialogues of the Dead and Other Works in Prose and*

Verse. Yet each essay helps to illuminate a topic of much interest to Prior.

Prior begins the "Heads for a Treatise upon Learning" by acknowledging the importance of school learning: "he who has it not in some degree can hardly be accounted a Man. . . ." Men cannot judge rightly, report accurately, or construct or enclose without arithmetic and geometry; they cannot understand their own or other modern languages without first knowing Latin and Greek. Having made these concessions, however, Prior states that his essay is going to examine the other side of the same coin: "The Good and Excellence of Learning has been the Theme of the greatest Writers for above three thousand years, the Inconveniences and Ills it may produce if not well regulated, is the Subject of my Present Letter" (ll. 11–14, *LW*, 1:578–79).

The rest of the essay is concerned with the limits of classical learning—the men it cannot help, the necessary subjects it does not touch upon. A multilingual coxcomb, for example, simply makes a fool of himself in many languages instead of one: "Languages in the Mouth of a Fool are like Weapons in the hand of a Madman, the more he has of them, the more harm he may do to himself as well as to every Body within his reach" (ll. 26–28, *LW*, 1:579).

Specialization in learning Prior holds to be a necessary evil, dangerous to a man's conversation and public use, but required in the professions, "for Life is so Short and the Avocations of it so various that without a peculiar application to one kind of Learning he cannot attain to a very Eminent Perfection in it" (ll. 37–39, *LW*, 1:579). He cites particularly theologians, lawyers, and doctors as such professional specialists.

"History in general is pleasurable" to study, Prior continues, and should be mastered when young, when the memory is most retentive. However, he deplores the tendency to teach only classical history, saying that it is equally necessary for modern Englishmen to know their own history from the time of the Norman Conquest and that of other countries of Europe from the time of the Renaissance. He finds chronology to be "the very life and Quintiscence" of history in general, and fears that antiquarians may be pleasing their eyes more than their minds, and hence may stop with contemplating the object itself rather than its historical authenticity and significance.

Prior prefers the classical poets to the classical historians, for their mythology, their morality, and the beauty of their ideas, but he warns against the indiscriminate employing of "a hundred Scraps of Verses which for above twice as many Years People have successively quoted; and by often hearing them, every Body are tired of . . ." (ll. 117–20, *LW*, 1:581). He advocates quoting from Italian, Spanish, French, and English writers, and points out the likeliest sources and uses of each of these literatures.

In a revealing aside, Prior praises the type of education that he received at Westminster School, with its insistence upon extemporaneous verses and declamations, which improved and dilated thought. This half-autobiographical observation, coupled with a later openly autobiographical tracing of his own education and literary career, makes this essay of special value in showing Prior's attitude toward his own writing. In this later aside, Prior tells of his early strong interest in poetry, an interest half-stifled by St. John's College ("where Prose was more in fashion than Verse") and by his diplomatic duties, which required a different style of prose and made satire a dangerous pastime.

In speaking of his own writing, Prior is giving an example of his more general observations upon style. He describes the ideal relationship between a man's reading and his writing style: "What ever you read you must so observe and digest, as to form from it in speaking especially your own Language a Stile close, distinct and Familiar; and in your Writing easy and Civil . . ." (ll. 154–56, *LW*, 1:582), avoiding all cant terms and professional jargon. In prose the ideal is "A plain free Polite Gentile Style," because all men must speak and write prose. As to poetry, "I would advise no Man to attempt it except he cannot help it, and if he cannot it is in vain to disswade him from it . . . he who has it will never be brought from it, do what you will . . ." (ll. 169–73, *LW*, 1:583). Boys with this urge must be educated very carefully; "they must begin soon and continue long in the Course of some severer Studies" (ll. 176–77, *LW*, 1:583).

As to wit in conversation, Prior continues, it "depends upon the Support of great Stock and plentiful variety of reading" (ll. 200–201, *LW*, 1:584); otherwise, even a witty man will become witty in one predictable manner. Except in theological or parliamentary debates, however, wit should be used only defensively, never offensively: "it should be used as a shield rather than a Sword to defend yourself but not to wound another" (ll. 218–19, *LW,* 1:584).

Besides his area of specialization, every man should develop, according to Prior, "some Secundary Science," such as architecture, sculpture, painting, or gardening, to fill his idle hours and entertain his companions without permitting or forcing them to enter into his specialized knowledge. He hesitatingly adds music to this list of usual secondary sciences, with the cautions "that it takes up too much of our Time and does not furnish us with the best Company" (ll. 269–70, *LW,* 1:585–86). Musicians spend so much time practicing that they have no time even to study music theory and history, much less any other more distant field.

The essay on "Opinion" is a more abstract essay than the "Heads for a Treatise upon Learning," seeking to determine "what this Opinion is, How it is commonly formed, upon what it subsists, and in what manner it is Altered" (ll. 4–5, *LW,* 1:586). Prior defines Opinion as "the Estimate, which every Man makes of every Thing he sees, the Product of what he calls common Sence . . ." (ll. 6–7, *LW,* 1:586) and General Opinion as "a majority of Voices."

Having observed that opinions change and that different people of the same age are moved by different passions, depending upon their temperaments, Prior then asserts that, for all men, "THE Two great Passions which Triumph over our Judgement and Consequently Subjugate our Opinion are Ambition and Love . . ." (ll. 73–74, *LW,* 1:588).

The opinions of specialists are suspect, Prior declares, both because they tend to be ignorant of all fields but their own ("hence it comes to pass that the Man who has Spent all his time in One Science and Consequently neglected the rest may talk finely upon some few Subjects and like a Child upon all others"—ll. 123–26, *LW,* 1:589) and because even in his own field he is likely to become a fanatic creator of some perverse system. Among such specialists are the collectors (of which Prior was certainly one) looking for the coin, book, picture, or medal that another man would throw away as old and useless.

Then Prior offers examples of the different ways in which different men, according to their private bents and interests, are affected by the same object. Further, he adds, "the common Herd of Mankind (and I am afraid the Majority is on their Side) have really no Opinion . . ." (ll. 173–74, *LW,* 590–91); they are always changing, simply picking up the first opinion they run across and adopting it as theirs, then changing it for a later one. All men resemble this "common Herd," for all change their opinions because of circumstances and external stimuli trivial in themselves yet decisive to those experiencing them.

A comic aspect of Opinion that Prior notes is that men's opinions are also subject to what other men conceive of their opinion, that even great men cannot be happy or successful unless their inferiors think them so: "the Opinion of One Man is altered by the Sentiment of an other in relation to the same Object. So plain is it that we do not See with our own Eyes, nor Judge by our own understanding" (ll. 305-8, *LW*, 1:594).

Furthermore, Prior writes, in forming our opinion we always pursue what we perceive as our own interest or our own pride: "under the Denomination of profit or pleasure we always pursue our Interest, or gratify our Vanity . . ." (ll. 322-24, *LW*, 1:595). Atop "the natural frailties of our minds falls yet another Incumbrance very hard to be removed . . . the prejudice of Education and Custom" (ll. 326-28, *LW*, 1:595), especially the prejudices of our impressionable youth.

The forming of opinions is an active principle; it does not wait for evidence in order to act. We react immediately to the stranger who enters the room, liking or disliking him; as we come to know him better, we either dismiss his faults or exaggerate them. The opinions of others intensify this jaundiced view, particularly the forced opinions of political parties. "A Party-Man indeed, and such most of us are, or must be, is an Animal that no Commentator upon human nature can sufficiently explain. He has not his own Opinion, how sorry a world so ever it may be, in his own keeping" (ll. 413-16, *LW*, 1:597). These prejudices of opinion have at least one advantage: "every Man is a Wit or a Hero somewhere" (ll. 427-28, *LW*, 1:597).

Finally, Prior observes how much our opinion depends on the results of an enterprise rather than upon its intrinsic merits. The example that he draws to support this generalization shows that he has come a long way from his poems denouncing the Duke of Monmouth as a traitor and praising William as a warrior king. He looks detachedly at both men and sees little difference except in results: "The DUKE OF MONMOUTH came to England with Liberty and Property, and the Protestant Religion on his Standard:

He was beaten and Beheaded, his Honors were taken from his Family. The Prince of Orange does the same thing, he is Successfull, is Crowned King of England, transmits an Imortal Memory to Posterity; Gives us a new Epoche of Time, and a different Sett of Principles from the Revolution" (ll. 472–78, *LW*, 1:599).

"Opinion" is thus a very useful prose supplement to *Alma*. Both works deal Pyrrhonistically with man's futile attempts to discover truth and with the factors which determine the opinions he substitutes for the certain knowledge that he cannot gain.

Dialogues of the Dead

Like his two epistemological essays, Prior's four *Dialogues of the Dead* were left incomplete at his death (he had projected at least six additional dialogues) and were not published until the 1907 A. R. Waller edition. However, unlike the epistemological essays, these four *Dialogues of the Dead* were generally known to exist because Alexander Pope had examined them in manuscript form (1723) and had later praised them to Spence:

> There are, also, four dialogues in prose, between persons of characters very strongly opposed to one another, which I thought very good. One of them was between Charles the Fifth and his tutor, Adrian the Sixth; to show the different turns of a person who had studied human nature only in his closet, and of one who had rambled all over Europe. Another between Montaigne and Locke, on a most regular and a very loose way of thinking. A third between Oliver Cromwell and his mad Porter: and the fourth, between Sir Thomas More and the Vicar of Bray.[11]

In 1785 the Duchess of Portland showed the *Dialogues* to Dr. James Beattie, who wrote of them to Mrs. Montagu, Aberdeen, 15 November 1785:

> Her Grace was so good as to permit me to read them, and I read them with great pleasure. One of them, a dialogue between Locke and Montaigne, is an admirable piece of ridicule on the subject of Locke's philosophy and seemed to me, when I read it, to be, in wit and humour, not inferior even to the "Alma" itself. I took the liberty to say to the Dutchess, that it was pity they were not given to the world; but I found her rather averse to the publication. She said, she could not bear to see her old friend criticised and censured by such people as the Critical Reviewers, &c. I hope the work will no longer be suppressed.[12]

Because the *Dialogues of the Dead,* unlike Prior's other prose pieces, belong to a clearly established literary tradition dating from Lucian, they have attracted a store of critical attention despite their late date of publication. Eugene R. Purpus, writing in 1950, counted Prior as among the "most prolific and best known" dialogue writers of this period.[13] Four other studies have treated Prior in some detail as a part of the specific tradition of the dialogue of the dead.[14]

The tradition of the dialogues of the dead dates back to Lucian, in the second century A.D., and it is to Lucian and to the later French practitioners of this form (Fontenelle in 1683, Fénelon in 1712) that Prior's *Dialogues* are most closely related, rather than to their English predecessors. What Prior does with his sources, nevertheless, in tone and approach, is essentially original, finding its closest analogues in his own *Alma* and his "Opinion" rather than in any of his predecessors. Although Prior can be seen somewhat to favor one disputant above his opponent in each dialogue, each is permitted to make sharp and valid points, and there is nowhere any victor in the debates. In each case, the ultimate quality of the life being debated lies in its values, its "opinion," and because the values of the opponents are so different, the issue cannot ultimately be resolved.

The first of these four debates, "A Dialogue between Charles the Emperor and Clenard the Grammarian," pits Charles V, Holy Roman Emperor and King of Spain, against Nicolas Kleynaerts, a sixteenth-century priest-philologist. Each man was monarch of his own world, and the dialogue begins in earnest when Clenard proposes "That each of Us should give a fair and just Account of himself as a Man . . ." (ll. 20–21, *LW,* 1:599). Charles remembers his victories; Clenard reminds him of his defeats. Charles remembers his applause and attention; Clenard reminds him that people heartily wished him a thousand miles away. Charles quotes Prior's own "First Hymn of Callimachus" to justify his glory; Clenard replies contemptuously that "Prior may say what he will in Verse, that Hymn was all Enthusiasm. All Heros, Stars, and Gods. In Prose I am sure he is of another Opinion" (ll. 150–52, *LW,* 1:603). In a poem Clenard reminds Charles that the hero is likely to draw, tied to his chariot wheels, both "His En'mies Ensigns, and his Peoples Laws" (l. 199, *LW,* 1:604). When Charles retorts that Clenard is "a dangerous Person, and ought to be laid in a gentle Confinement for the good of the Public" (ll. 206–7, *LW,* 1:604), Clenard laughs and replies, "dont You imagin that we think such as You dangerous Persons, only that for our private Safety we dare not say so. . . . I tell You, that for the good of the Public You should all have your Swords taken from You as if You were actual Lunaticks, and not be suffered to go a Madding with this rattle of a Globe to play with" (ll. 208–10, 211–14, *LW,* 1:605). Charles' reputation is now merely that of a vexatious, aggressive, troublesome fellow.

Having thus deposed Charles from his throne of greatness, Clenard attempts to put himself there. Clenard, for example, could travel quietly and safely in these countries that Charles could not conquer. Happiness and glory are within the reach of every wise man; fame depends upon the opinions of others.

Though Clenard can out-argue him, Charles still suspects that the truth is somehow on his side, "Facts, Clenard, real visible Facts are on my side. Thy Glory is only Speculative, Meer imagination" (ll. 295–96, *LW,* 1:607). But Clenard argues (as Prior had at the end of his "Observations on Ovid's Metamorphoses") that the scholar is necessary to keep the fame of the hero alive. Charles answers with the other half of Prior's observation at the end of the comments on Ovid, that the hero is equally necessary to preserve the fame of the grammarian. When Charles plays his trump card—his abdication and retirement to a monastery—Clenard replies, "A Physitian, who cures himself of a Dropsey has great Skill, but a Man who never had the Distemper has Sounder health" (ll. 474–75, *LW,* 1:612). He asks Charles by the way of conclusion, "Now, which of Us Two was the Happyest Man?" and Charles is hard put for an answer. But then Clenard makes, in a sense, a surprising concession: "You are a Silly Combatant, to Fight me at my own Weapon." That is, Charles has been out-argued, but the truth has not been found; the debate has merely been won by the more experienced debater. Or perhaps not even that. Charles is not convinced and refuses to refer the dispute to Dionysius, who having been both prince and schoolmaster, might be able to tell which state had been better. He refuses any arbiter because "I was always Subject only to my own Will, and can be tryed by nothing else." Clenard observes, justly, "So that we end just where We begun. . . . But however, Charles, if Princes are Governed only by their own Will, You must Confess at least it was a Mad World that We Lived in" (ll. 557, 560–62, *LW,* 1:614). It is this theme of the madness of the world that informs *Alma* and runs through the four *Dialogues of the Dead.*

Clenard has apparently won the debate (Charles makes him promise not to repeat it to his fellow princes), but he has not convinced Charles, and he has won it partly because, as he himself admits, the weapons were those he used best and he had only to prove that "You would not find so much difference between us Two as You imagine"; Charles had to prove a clear superiority. Charles still feels superior but cannot prove it. It is all, as Prior's "Opinion" had said, a matter of opinion; every man is a hero somewhere.

The second of these pieces is "A Dialogue between Mr: John Lock and Seigneur de Montaigne." Prior's poetry up till this time had already shown his dislike of Locke and his admiration of Montaigne. Thus, following the pattern of the first dialogue, Locke is the proud first speaker, Montaigne the antisystematic antagonist. Locke believes that human understanding can be systematically analyzed; Montaigne does not: "There is some Crany, some winding Meandre in every Mans brain, which he himself is the last that finds out" (ll. 40–41, *LW,* 1:616). Montaigne has read Locke, "Just as I read other Books, with care where they instruct me, with pleasure where they amuse me and half asleep where they tire me" (ll. 78–80, *LW,* 1:617). Montaigne parodies items discussed by Locke, saying that he has made a hundred plain things ambiguous, that his readers are grateful if he gives them six or eight words that make common sense every six or eight chapters, and that this obscurity may be deliberate, for men "are most prone to admire what they do not perfectly understand . . ." (ll. 143–44, *LW,* 1:619). Locke perceives the difficulty of the debate for him: "You, the loosest of Writers, have no great respect for my close way of Reasoning" (ll. 193–94, *LW,* 1:620). Montaigne replies: "One may read your Book over as the Irish Man eat Whipt Cream, and when they asked him what he had been doing, he said he had been tasting a great Nothing" (ll. 195–98, *LW,* 1:620). The irreconcilable difference between the debators is shown by Locke's asking "Should not a Man know himself?" and Montaigne's reply, "he that does not talk with a Wiser Man than himself may happen to Dye Ignorant" (ll. 299–300, 302–3, *LW,* 1:623). That is, Locke believes that self-knowledge is possible; Montaigne believes that self-deception is inevitable. Locke goes to sleep while Montaigne is giving him "half a Dozen" (closer to three dozen) of his axioms, but, awakened, complains of Montaigne's chaotic method. Montaigne replies that he glories in his lack of method. The best method is to imitate Nature, irregular and copious. In answer to Locke's charge that he plagiarizes, Montaigne replies, "Truth and reason lye in common to all the World like Air and Water (ll. 569-70, *LW,* 1:631). But Locke, precipitating a debate upon the Ancients and the Moderns, in the very terms of Swift's *Battle of the Books,* responds with his most palpable hit, that if all the ancients took back their own from Montaigne's books, "Montaigne hath writ no Book." Locke pursues his advantage by boasting that he spins his work out of his own thoughts; so, replies Montaigne, does the "Spider out of her own Bowels; and yet a Cobweb is good for Nothing else that I know of but to catch flies, and Stanch cut Thumbs" (ll. 605-7, *LW,* 1:632). Montaigne, likening his method to that of the bee, calls what he does composing, not creating; Locke calls it mere compilation. Montaigne replies that no man is an original creator, though he may deceive himself into thinking all ideas originally his: "probably neither [Locke's servants] Robin, John, Margrate You or I, or any other five Persons alive have either the same Idea's of the same thing, or the same way of Expressing them" (ll. 852-54, *LW,* 1:639). Locke perceives that they have at last come to the heart of the question—and indeed they have. No one has been convinced; no one has really won, though Montaigne (like Clenard) has been allowed the choice of weapons and the greater latitude for brandishing them. The only point upon which they may agree—at least Locke does not argue it—is that the world outside them is chaotic and irregular. Locke believes it vital to impose order upon this chaos; Montaigne believes it impossible to do so. Prior has not played fair with Locke, of course: for example, he has permitted Locke to espouse order and to be unconvinced by Montaigne's engaging disorder.

The most serious of the four *Dialogues of the Dead* is "A Dialogue between the Vicar of Bray, and Sir Thomas More," between a man beheaded for his faith and his conscience when he was fifty-three and his appointee to a country parish, who held his post by three times changing his faith and died in his bed at eighty. It is the only one of the four dialogues in which even the reader is uncertain which debater might be said to have won. Once again, the two debaters seem in agreement on the kind of world they live in: it is as mad as Charles and Clenard's, as chaotic as Locke and Montaigne's. But whereas the other pairs of debaters have carried on at least a semblance of an organized debate, because they have positions in common—Charles and Clenard are both proud emperors of their own realm, Locke and Montaigne are both philosophical authors—the vicar of Bray and Sir Thomas More are so diametrically opposed that they cannot properly be said to carry on a debate at all. Rather, each man simply states parts of his philosophical position, to be interrupted from time to time by the other man.

More's position is that "A Man must do his Duty what soever may be the Event of it . . ." (ll. 80–81, *LW*, 1:642). The chief duty of all men is clear, "every Man is obliged to suffer for what is right as to oppose what is unjust" (ll. 419–20, *LW*, 1:652). Even if his conscience misleads him, he must follow it, and be blessed even in seeking right, though he may not find it. By his own death, More did more good than he would have by living a long, cowardly, and time-serving life; many better heads "have been Confirmed by my Example, and I . . . Answered the end for which life was given me" (ll. 526–28, *LW*, 1:655).

The vicar's philosophy is as clear to him as More's is to him: "never Strive against the Stream, always drive the Nail that will go, eat Your pudding and hold Your Tongue, dont pretend to be Wiser than your Master, or his Eldest Son" (ll. 117–19, *LW*, 1:643). It was his business "to teach my Parish and Receive my Tythes" (l. 139, *LW*, 1:644), and he taught them whatever Parliament told him he should be teaching them. He did what he holds to be enough: "I never mist my Church, was civil to my Parishioners, and gave Something to the poor" (ll. 174–75, *LW*, 1:645). When he preached, he always lauded those in power and drew Biblical analogies to support his praise, so that Mary was "Deborah or Judith, who Restored the Ancient Laws and Customs of the People of Israel" (ll. 191–92, *LW*, 1:645) in her own reign, and "Jesabell or Athalia" during the reign of Elizabeth. His greatest fear was losing his vicarage.

Of course, each speaker finds the other's choice of life incomprehensible, a dangerous precedent. The vicar can never see beyond "that ugly Seam, Sir; that remains stil about your Neck"; it is the first thing he notices when he meets Sir Thomas and the last thing when they part. He thinks that "that Grave is an ugly hole indeed, when once a Man Slips his foot into it—" (ll. 263–64, *LW*, 1:247), and that Sir Thomas, like Cicero before him, "had his Head cutt off because he would be running it too far into Affairs, From which he had better to have Receeded" (ll. 96–98, *LW*, 1:643). Sir Thomas has called himself keeper of the King's conscience; the vicar reminds him that one can hardly keep the conscience of a man "who never knew his own Mind half an Hour." The vicar honors the martyrs on their holy days "and set out their Relicts to be kist by the People," but their way is not his. "Lord, Sir, They had their way to Heaven, which in all probability was the nearest; You were pleased to take That; very well, I had mine, it was a little about indeed. . . . We were not all Born to be Martyrs any more than Lord Mayors" (ll. 371–74, *LW*, 1:650–51). In short, the vicar finds Sir Thomas to have been a brave but foolish man, the object of pity rather than emulation.

Sir Thomas's judgment on the vicar is harsher. He finds that all the vicar's maxims reduce to a single principle: "take care of your Self, or keep out of harms way." (The vicar agrees.) By his own account, the vicar had preached not sermons but panegyrics. In sum, says Sir Thomas, the vicar "trifled fourscore Years without doing any good or intending it" (ll. 218–19, *LW*, 1:646). Again the vicar is unmoved, agreeing with Sir Thomas's summation. Sir Thomas concludes: "This Man now would not commit any famous Wickedness, yet how far is he from being honest; Well; as bad as they say the World is, there are fifty Idle Knaves in it for one determined Villain" (ll. 516–19, *LW*, 1:655).

Prior has not given us a victor in this debate; we simply select the man whom we would have selected before the debate began. As the two part, Sir Thomas says, "Adieu, thou poor Spirited Parson with thy Vicarage of Bray," to which the Vicar replies, "Thou Great Chancellor of England, without a head, Adieu." Each man knows that the other speaks the truth of him, but each feels that the other's evaluation is essentially trivial, making too much of something too small. Sir Thomas as a man of conscience has quietly given up this world with a jest about his beard; the vicar as a man of the world has quietly laid down his conscience. Each one finds the sacrifice regrettable but necessary. If men were to vote their sentiments, Sir Thomas would probably be the victor, but as he himself twice acknowledges, if men were to vote their actions, they would follow the vicar of Bray—a paradox that makes this the most interesting of Prior's four dialogues. It is notable too that the ambivalence of the debate resembles that of Prior the politician, who at one point votes to impeach his childhood friend in order to protect his king and himself, yet at a later one saves his old friends from the Tower at the risk of his own neck.

The fourth and last of Prior's *Dialogues of the Dead*, "A Dialogue between Oliver Cromwell, and his Porter," returns to the usual pattern for Prior, in which a proud man is defeated in debate (though not convinced) by a man whom he at first condemns, but who proves himself to be his equal, at least in debate. Of the four dialogues, this is the one with the most underworld flavor: there are references to the "chattering Ghosts" and to the rules under which the underworld operates. The conquerors and heroes whom Cromwell seeks are on the other side of the river, "making of Dirt pies or playing at Cudgells. . . . Every Man acts in Jeast here what He did in t'other World in Earnest" (ll. 250–51, 254–55, *LW*, 1:662). Cromwell is much like Charles V, a proud tyrant who finds his power suddenly dissipated in his death. Death has been the true leveler; now Cromwell cannot even command his old porter.

But the porter argues with Cromwell, as Clenard did with Charles, that they were also equal in the other world, for each ruled an area that pleased him most, though the mad porter had more joy of his imaginary kingdom in Bedlam than Cromwell did of his real one in Britain. The porter went mad on the day that Charles I was executed: "I confess when You Cut off the Kings head you turned mine into the bargain." His only defense in this mad, chaotic world was to turn mad himself, into a world of his own making and more to his liking. Cromwell, like Charles, feels that he was the true emperor: "My Power was real, Your Authority was only imaginary. . . ." But when Cromwell insists that "Thousands of People can Witness that they Submitted to Me," the mad porter reminds him that no outsider can testify as to a man's happiness. When Cromwell objects that the porter is arguing that "to Act or not to Act is just the same thing," he corrects his old master: "To Act or to think one Acts is just the same." The porter quotes Epictetus: "It is not the thing it Self . . . that Pleases or disquiets a Man but the Opinion he conceives of the thing" (ll. 152–54, *LW*, 1:659–60). The porter later makes the same point that Clenard has made; heroes and conquerors are undisciplined children, troubling the world with their own madness. He finds that Cromwell was ten times madder than himself, "So Mad that no Man durst either Advise, or tye You. . . ."

As in each of the four dialogues, the madness or chaos of the world has been asserted and not denied; as in each, no one is converted or convinced. Cromwell has made the mistake of Charles and of Locke: he has permitted the mad porter to choose his weapons and to hold the floor at much greater length. The porter has therefore been able to divert the original discussion of the exercise of real power into a discussion of whether respect was merited and happiness experienced. On these grounds, as the porter knows at once but Cromwell does not see until too late, it is all a matter of opinion.

Prior's *Dialogues of the Dead* have been virtually without influence, because of the accident of their not having been published till almost two centuries after their composition. Pope and Beattie knew them in manuscript, but most of their contemporaries did not—and when they were finally printed in the twentieth century, the taste for such dialogues had died out. Nevertheless, they are witty and moving, showing Prior's ability to build memorable characters as well as to write vivid prose. He had written in "Heads for a Treatise upon Learning" that "History in general is pleasurable," and it is indeed so if those come alive who made it and if the issues with which they dealt are seen to be the basic, universal conflicts, dreams, and desires of mankind. These are the things that happen in Prior's *Dialogues of the Dead*. Prior's various prose works—prefaces, dedications, postscripts, periodical essays, observations upon classical writers, epistemological essays, and the four *Dialogues of the Dead*—show him to have been a writer of great skill and charm, learned without being pedantic, lively and charming without being sentimental, witty and detached yet always somehow involved in the mad, chaotic world which he describes.

Prior's Two Plays: *Ladislaus* and *Britanicus and Junia*

Besides his wide rangings in the field of poetry and his little-known but effective occasional sallies into prose, Prior twice attempted to write plays, but he left both unfinished. *Ladislaus* and *Britanicus and Junia* bear certain resemblances, though they are essentially very different in type. Both were serious plays, based on French models. Both were to have been wholly or in part in blank verse. *Ladislaus* was based upon the most famous play of Jean de Rotrou, *Venceslas* (1647), which Horace Walpole called "the best of the French tragedies, anterior to Corneille."[15] *Britanicus and Junia* was based upon Racine's *Britannicus* (1669). The great difference in the two plays, however much Prior modified them, is largely a difference in these sources. Rotrou as a dramatist was not really a classicist, but was more like the heroic dramatist in England—creating a crammed plot, with many characters, much violence (even if off-stage), sudden shifts of character, with weakness of motivation disguised under a great deal of lively movement. Racine, at the height of French classicism, had a much smaller cast, with motivations and destinies so interwoven that no character could make a decision or take an action without altering the positions and dilemmas of all the others.

All that Prior left to us of his *Ladislaus* is a completely worked out, lengthy "argument" and four fragmentary scenes unconnected to one another but placeable in terms of the argument. The argument reads like *The Conquest of Granada,* with a large cast and frequent half-explained shifts of position: a heroine who agrees to marry the attempted rapist whom she has avoided throughout the play, a power-loving king who suddenly "retires to his Religion and Rural pleasures," a young fratricide who turns out to be beloved by his subjects, who refuse to execute him and instead crown him king. Prior had often commented that the world is mad, but *Ladislaus* demonstrates the point almost too strongly. The speeches that Prior prepared for the play are frequently hyperbolical fustian, though there is one, apparently intended for the king, on the mixture of justice and mercy for his condemned fratricidal son, interesting for its balancing of parts and use of antitheses and for its echo of Horatio on the dead Hamlet:

> Stern Justice
> Demands no further than the Murtherers life
> Then blood for blood, She leaves to gentle Mercy
> The Man's immortal part, and while the Judge
> Forct by strict law transmitts the Malefactor
> An Exil from this world, and human race
> Whom he by Crimes has injured, Kind clergy
> With fervent tongues and hands lift up are suffered
> To send their wishes up that Heaven would pardon
> The dying Penitent, and guarding Angells
> Convey his parting Spirit to endless Joy.
> (*LW,* 2:1002)

It is difficult to judge a play that exists only as argument and four scattered and unfinished scenes. Admittedly, the argument of *Antony and Cleopatra* would sound crowded and frenzied. The extant dialogue nevertheless is not particularly striking or effective; there are no "Ah, soldier" passages here.

Prior's *Britanicus and Junia* lacks the finished argument of *Ladislaus* but contains several more nearly finished scenes. Professors Spears and Wright report that Prior's manuscripts "consist of a mixture of rough notes, synopses, and dramatized scenes, written on sheets, half-sheets, and small scraps of paper that have been put together in accidental order." They have printed in Prior's *Literary Works* "those passages of dialogue that are most finished"; on the basis of this evidence, they conclude that Prior intended "to enliven the French play [Racine's *Britannicus*] by adding the necessary pageantry and movement demanded by the English stage."[16] In this play, Racine had taken a topic superficially very unclassical—the youth of Nero—and had given it a classical treatment, stopping it as soon as Nero takes the decisive step toward depravity—as if Shakespeare had stopped *Macbeth* immediately after the murder of Duncan. That act done, the rest inevitably follows, and does not need to be shown.

In the scenes from *Britanicus and Junia,* there is sufficient development for some characters to be plainly shown: Nero, Burrhus, Agrippina, and especially Narcissus are all clearly delineated. Nero is in the grip of passion and wavering toward vice, but still hesitant; Burrhus is the blunt, uncourtly Roman soldier; Agrippina is the mother scorned, still ambitious for power, still plotting; Narcissus, the most interesting of them all, a secondary Iago, goads Nero toward murdering Britanicus while scoffing at virtue as simply a useful propagandistic weapon in the hands of the powerful. Two of the three most memorable speeches in the fragmentary play belong to Narcissus. In one, a soliloquy, he sets forth the doctrine of the ruling passion, saying that the one who discovers the ruling passion of another may easily manipulate his reason, and that he has discovered that love is the passion of Britanicus: "Who wou'd prevail o'er Men must first observe / Their Darling Passion of their hearts and thence / Govern their ductile Reason, in Britanicus / The power of Love prevails the dazled Lover" (ll. 103–6, *LW,* 1:574). In the other, in answer to Nero's troubled question "But what is vertue?" Narcissus replies, "Tis a dream, all alow tis nothing in itself, yet all: tis that whose Influence governs the world, it is the Tyrant of the mind. It is a weapon, whose point you should always offer against your Enemies breast, but never turn it to your own, tis What priests should teach the people that Kings may reign in safety" (ll. 171–75, *LW,* 1:577). The other memorable lines in Prior's play come in Nero's retort to Agrippina, who has just reminded him that hers are the breasts that gave him suck. Nero finds an apt if unfilial parallel: "Romulus, founder of the Roman Empire / Was nurst by a Shee wolf—" (ll. 152–53, *LW,* 1:576)—a bit of repartee that might have come out of *Dialogues of the Dead.*[17]

As a dramatist, Prior may have found that his own philosophy stood in his way. If a man sees the world as a mad and chaotic place, in which changeable men follow first one opinion, then another, as age, custom, and passion dictate, more often the victims than the masters of forces outside themsleves—then it is difficult for him to write either heroic or classical drama. It would be easier to write theater of the absurd, but Prior was two centuries too early for that. As it was, he was destined, like Browning after him, to display his dramatic talents best in his nondramatic work.

Chapter Six
The Major Impact of a Minor Poet

This study began by asking the question raised by Prior's impressive monument in the Poets' Corner of Westminster Abbey: in what sense may a so-called minor poet have made a major contribution to literature? Matthew Prior's contribution to British literature was a major one in at least four senses.

First, Prior produced a respectable body of literary work, in prose and verse, including effective and influential works in a number of genres: serious and mocking full-length philosophical poems, imitations of classical sources, a long amorous dialogue, tales, *vers de société,* epigrams, epitaphs, lyrics, songs. A number of his shorter lyrics, mixing laughter and tears, are still often quoted and frequently anthologized.

Second, through the impressive financial success of the 1718 subscription edition of his *Poems on Several Occasions,* Prior established a direct connection between practicing writer and reading public without dependence upon an intervening patron. Earlier similar successful financial ventures had been made by Dryden with a translation of Virgil and by Pope with translations of Homer, but in both cases the subscribers themselves would have been hard put to say whether they were pledging their guineas to Virgil or to Dryden, to Homer or to Pope. Prior's 1718 edition was not a translation but a collection of his own work; subscribers were buying Prior. The edition was thus, in its conspicuous financial success, a milestone in literary history.

Third, in an age often treated as if it were monolithically dedicated in poetry to the heroic couplet, Prior wrote competently and well in at least six different line or two-line patterns: iambic pentameter in both heroic couplet and blank verse, octosyllabics both lyric and comic, and anapaests in trimeter and tetrameter, the last two of which he brought to a height they had never reached before. He arranged these lines, moreover, into a variety of stanzaic patterns besides couplets and blank verse—a modified Spenserian stanza, Horatian and Pindaric odes, quatrains, triplets, sestets—using the last three groupings as effectively as they had ever been employed in English, and in an astonishing variety of tones and approaches. He led the way for a Spenserian revival in the eighteenth century, and his other forms reminded the poets who followed him in the eighteenth century that there always existed workable alternatives to the heroic couplet form. Dr. Johnson, a reluctant witness for the defense, stated that it was Prior's variety that had given him his great reputation.

Last, Prior's writing exercised a marked influence upon the writings of the three most important literary figures of the eighteenth century—Swift, Pope, and Johnson—and upon a number of lesser figures in Great Britain and America throughout the eighteenth and nineteenth centuries.

Prior's Influence upon Jonathan Swift

Prior and Swift had become friends as early as 1704,[1] for a letter from Dr. Francis Atterbury to Robert Harley, first Earl of Oxford, in that year indicates that Prior was in possession of either the proofs or an advanced copy of one of Swift's books.[2] Prior appears repeatedly in Swift's *Journal to Stella,* the first mention being in the entry for 15 October 1710.[3] Swift and Prior were both members of the Brothers Club, which met in London every Thursday.[4] Swift refers frequently to their dining, drinking, jesting, walking, quarreling, punning, reading their poetry, or planning political maneuvers together while Prior was in London. Later, when Prior began to be sent on secret missions to France, he and Swift corresponded.[5] Prior arrived in Paris on 17 August 1712, and did not live in London for any lengthy period again until March 1715. Meanwhile, Swift returned to Ireland on 16 August 1714, and did not come back to England until March 1726, over four years after Prior's death. Thus, the last portion of their friendship was conducted exclusively by letter, yet the warmth of affection seems never to have cooled. Swift subscribed for four copies of Prior's 1718 *Poems on Several Occasions* and expended great amounts of time and effort in raising and collecting subscriptions to this edition, an activity that he continued even after Prior's death.[6]

From Gaulstown, Swift wrote to Archbishop King on 28 September 1721: "I am just now told from some newspapers, that one of the King's enemies, and my excellent friend, Mr. Prior, is dead; I pray God deliver me from many such trials. I am neither old nor philosopher enough to be indifferent at so great a loss; and therefore I abruptly conclude. . . ."[7] On 25 January 1722, Adrian Drift, Prior's amanuensis and close friend, wrote to Swift from Prior's home in Duke Street, Westminster, of a ring "which you will be pleased to accept and wear in memory of Mr. Prior, whom you so dearly loved. . . ."[8] On 3 February 1722, Swift replied to Drift that he would be "very thankful of a memorial of Mr. Prior, though I need nothing to make me remember him with all regard due to his merits, and whose friendship I so highly esteemed."[9] When on 19 February 1729, Swift drew up his list of twenty-two acquaintances, "Men famous for their learning, wit, or great employments or quality, who are dead," Prior's name was included.[10]

Swift's friendship for Prior and his high opinion of him as diplomat and as poet exercised a profound influence on Swift's own poetry. F. Elrington Ball, the foremost twentieth-century critic of Swift's poetry, sees Prior as a chief influence on Swift's verse from 1710 on, teaching him "art and ease." Ball adds: "Of the power of Prior, to whom Cowper, Thackeray, and Dobson unite in giving pre-eminence in familiar verse, to impart such qualities, there cannot be question. Of the situation and disposition of Swift to receive them there can be as little doubt."[11] Sir Harold Williams in his more recent edition of Swift's poems states that "the unhappiness of Swift's life" was partially caused by the fact that his poetry fell short of that of his friends, Pope, Prior, and Gay, that Pope was his superior in verse while "Gay and Prior had a more lyrical gift."[12]

Occasional anonymous poems, such as "The Fable of the Widow and Her Cat," were attributed by some critics to Prior, some to Swift, and some to the two men jointly.[13] Swift loved Prior as a man, deferred to him as a diplomat, and learned from him as a poet. Swift was writing tetrameter lines and *vers de société* before the two men became friends, but Prior taught him to write them more gracefully and elegantly. Though the influence persisted throughout the last thirty years of Swift's lifetime, it was particularly marked in the period 1710–12, when the two politician-poets were frequently and intimately associated. Ball cites evidence of Prior's influence upon three of Swift's best poems of this period: two Horatian imitations (of the Epistle *Quinque dies* and the Satire *Hoc erat*) and the famous 900-line *Cadenus and Vanessa*. Even years later, when Prior's only contact with Swift was through letters, Swift, in the last four stanzas of "The Bubble," takes a statement that Prior had written him in prose about the South Sea speculation and expands it in verses influenced by Prior's own poetry.[14] Prior's greatest gift to Swift as a poet, however, was not so much of specific lines, concepts, and echoes as it was of tone and style. Prior taught Swift a courtliness and ease of familiar verse that he had not hitherto mastered; it was a gift that Swift never forgot, either to practice or to repay.

Prior's Influence upon Alexander Pope

With Alexander Pope, a generation younger than Prior and Swift, indebtedness to Prior was much deeper and more specific.[15] Few poets have had a better opportunity to analyze another man's poetry from many sides than Pope did to study Prior's. Pope was young and avidly reading during Prior's period of greatest fame and survived Prior by twenty-three years, long enough to consider all his works. Pope and Prior had many mutual friends; they were also personally acquainted and for five years moved in some of the same circles. In preparing the 1718 subscription edition of Prior's *Poems on Several Occasions* and, in 1723, the projected posthumous edition of Prior's works, Pope read, in print or in manuscript, almost everything extant of Prior's—an unusually full grouping, for Prior had, as Pope later told Spence, "kept every thing by him, even to all his school exercises."[16]

The result of this close literary association between Prior and Pope was that the young Pope decided, more or less consciously, to make use of Prior in the same sense that, on a larger scale, he made use of Dryden. With each, he was focusing attention on a figure whose unusual merit both he and the public conceded without question. He formulated for himself a detailed analysis of the poetical virtues and limitations of each: his forte, his contributions, the relative merits of his individual pieces. Then, at certain key points, he set out first to emulate and then to surpass him. Later, he merely borrowed from him phrases or ideas that were particularly apt for his own purposes.[17]

Pope's earliest open competition with Prior on a literary theme came in versions of the "Adriani Morientis," the valedictory to his soul attributed to the dying Roman Emperor Hadrian in the second century A.D. Fontenelle, Prior's dinner companion in France, had published a French version of the poem in 1683; Prior's English version of the poem—"POOR little, pretty, flutt'ring Thing"— was included in the 1703/4 Dryden edition of *Miscellany Poems* and later, revised, in the 1718 *Poems on Several Occasions,* which Pope assisted in bringing out. On 12 June 1713, Pope wrote to John Caryll, senior, from London, enclosing Prior's poem and two by himself—"The Same by Another Hand" ("Ah, fleeting spirit! wandering fire") and "Christiani Morientis Ad Animam."[18] The first Pope poem is heavily influenced by Prior's; the second, an expanded and Christianized version, is most influenced by Thomas Flatman's "A Thought of Death." Caryll preferred the Christianized version, but for most modern readers Prior has won this particular competition. His version seems both closest to the spirit of Hadrian and most satisfactory as a poem in itself. Pope's versions seem elevated in diction but not improved.[19]

Four years later (in 1717) Pope again put himself into deliberate competition with a successful Prior poem, at least if we are to believe James Ralph and Richard Savage. In *Sawney. An Heroic Poem. Occasion'd by the Dunciad,* Ralph had written that Prior's *Henry and Emma* had "charm[ed] the finest Tastes" and that Pope had, in an effort to compete with its success, created *Eloisa to Abelard,* with its "enamour'd, raging, longing Nun. . . ."[20] Pope retorted that Prior had himself praised *Eloisa to Abelard* in his *Alma,*[21] but he never replied to the specific charge that he was attempting to outdo Prior with his *Eloisa.* The Pennsylvania-born Ralph had come to London with Benjamin Franklin in 1724 and was little better than a Grub Street hack; more significant testimony comes from Richard Savage, who had worked closely with Pope on the *Dunciad* itself and on its prefatory prose material as well. Sutherland has called Savage Pope's chief link with Grub Street during this period and his chief informant.[22] Savage later told Dr. Johnson that Pope's poem had been motivated by Prior's, for Johnson wrote in his "Life of Pope" that "Of the *Epistle from Eloisa to Abelard,* I do not know the date. His first inclination to attempt a composition of that tender kind arose, as Mr. Savage told me, from his perusal of Prior's *Nut-brown Maid.* How much he has surpassed Prior's work it is not necessary to mention, when perhaps it may be said with justice, that he has excelled every composition of the same kind."[23] Though modern critics of Pope have not been inclined to take Savage's testimony seriously,[24] there is considerable external and internal evidence of Pope's indebtedness to Prior in this poem. *Henry and Emma* had first appeared in 1708, when Pope was twenty, and had gained instant popularity; moreover, it was to reappear in the 1718 *Poems on Several Occasions,* which Pope was helping to bring out. It was also a great favorite of Lady Mary Wortley Montagu, who exercised such a strong personal influence in Pope's maturing years that he liked to imagine himself in love with her, as he hints strongly at the close of *Eloisa to Abelard.* Lady Mary, as we have seen, was such an enthusiastically untiring admirer of *Henry and Emma* that she could recite the entire 773 lines by heart, even when she was old.[25] At least four times, lines from *Henry and Emma* are echoed in other poems by Pope—in *The Rape of the Lock, Windsor Forest, The Dunciad,* and *Of the Characters of Women;* there are also a number of less plainly marked parallels between *Henry and Emma* and other Pope poems.[26] *Henry and Emma* was thus a highly successful poem by a renowned poet, and Pope may well have hoped to outdo Prior at his own game while profiting from the popularity that Prior had helped to build for the high-flown rhetoric of bitterly tested love.

Both *Henry and Emma* and *Eloisa to Abelard* are extended pieces of elegant amorous verse, concerning a pair of lovers already familiar to the English reading public. Thus the task of each poet was not to inform his readers of an amorous dilemma, but rather to present that dilemma with a pointedness and a polish that it had never before received—to tell what had oft been told before, but never so intricately, to exploit what Professor Tillotson has called an Ovidian geometry of amorous situation.[27] In both pairs of lovers the total attention is ultimately focused on the woman, the man playing not only a subsidiary part but an essentially unsympathetic one. In each instance the woman is subjected to a peculiarly sharp torment, in which a choice that at one point seems to be between love and reputation becomes no choice at all—at least, one in which sexual love is not an alternative. Emma finally is told by Henry that she must either part from him or follow him into the woods only to act as servant to his new love. Eloisa is repeatedly forced to remember that she is no longer free to choose whether she may love Abelard illicitly or not; the attack upon him has made it impossible for him to love her sexually at all. The only choice that the future can offer her, as Professor Tillotson has remarked, is complete acquiescence to her vows as a nun or death.[28] Thus in both poems the amorous dilemma is so painful that the woman contemplates with melancholy pleasure the prospect of her own death, somewhat comforted by the consciousness that she is to become a heroine of stories in future ages.

There are other resemblances in the structure of the two poems. Both poets use their fiction in order to plead a personal amorous cause of their own: Prior to Cloe (probably Anne Durham, as Professor Wright has shown[29]); Pope, more obliquely, to Lady Mary Wortley Montagu.[30] Both poems are also essentially speeches, the main body of Prior's piece being a dialogue between Henry and Emma, and of Pope's a reply to Abelard's letter in a manner that seems to be spoken rather than written.

Eloisa to Abelard incorporates at least two modified passages from Prior's "Celia to Damon,"[31] but its greatest verbal debt to Prior comes from *Henry and Emma*. Of the eleven distinct parallels between the two poems, over half occur in the first third of *Eloisa to Abelard* (the first 122 lines), although there was no reason in the structure or subject matter of *Eloisa to Abelard* for Pope to resemble Prior less as his poem progressed. As Pope's poem grew under his hand, he seems to have become more confident of his own rhetoric and less dependent upon the Prior poem. Some of the more striking parallels are merely fitted into convenient places in Pope's poem, but others are altered by Pope in a manner that illuminates his poetical intention as contrasted with Prior's.[32]

Pope's *Eloisa to Abelard* owes much to sources other than Prior's *Henry and Emma*, particularly to English versions of amorous epistles. Professors Root and Tillotson have established clearly that Pope was writing *Eloisa to Abelard* in the tradition of the heroic epistle, with his greatest single debt being to John Hughes's 1713 translation of the letters of Abélard and Héloïse.[33] Pope's debt to Prior, however, is also significant. Pope probably owed to him the original incentive for writing a female amorous declamation that would outdo the popularity of *Henry and Emma*. He owed to him some of the variations in general structure of the poem that differentiate it from Hughes's version of the letters, particularly the personal coda, considered by Tillotson "original, for an epistle,"[34] though corresponding in purpose exactly to Prior's personal prologue. Finally, he owed to Prior the verbal patterns of certain phrases, lines, and passages, which in *Eloisa to Abelard* frequently serve a new purpose but retain something of their Prior form.

As an effort to excel Prior at his own poetical game, *Eloisa to Abelard* is much more successful than Pope's *Adriani Morientis* had been four years earlier. Most modern readers would prefer *Eloisa to Abelard* to *Henry and Emma,* and even in Pope's own age Eloisa began to overshadow Emma. *Eloisa to Abelard* is more concise (half the length of *Henry and Emma*). Its ordeal has greater dramatic melancholy: Eloisa's dilemma is real; Emma's test is merely a trick known in advance by the audience. The rhetoric is more appropriate to the situation of Eloisa, who has had years in which to contemplate the various nuances of her amorous dilemma, whereas Emma is suddenly surprised by hers and should be active rather than verbal.

Another of Prior's long poems, *Solomon on the Vanity of the World,* heavily influenced another of Pope's major poems, the *Essay on Man,* written over a decade after *Eloisa to Abelard. Solomon* achieved a highly favorable response in its own century, being twice translated into Latin verse (by William Dobson and by George Bally) and once into German (by Simon Grynaeus).[35] Sixty years after the death of Prior, John Wesley praised *Solomon,* concluding "Now what has Mr. *Pope* in all his eleven Volumes, which will bear any comparison with this?"[36] On another occasion, Wesley described *Solomon* as "one of the noblest poems in the English tongue. . . ."[37] Earlier in 1782, the year that Wesley's essay appeared, William Cowper had called *Solomon* "the best poem, whether we consider the subject of it or the execution, that [Prior] ever wrote."[38] Pope himself apparently did not like the poem; he turned aside Prior's direct question about his opinion of *Solomon* by praising *Alma* instead.[39] Nevertheless, Pope's own *Essay on Man* is heavily indebted to *Solomon,* as it also owes lines to Prior's "On Exodus iii. 14" and his "Essay on Opinion."[40]

There are some forty verbal parallels between Prior's *Solomon* and Pope's *Essay on Man.* These generally occur in passages concerned with brief and painful human existence, with the search for happiness, with man's reason and his passions, or with the animal kingdom. Prior and Pope also resemble each other in their treatment of two of the poetical-philosophical figures popular throughout the eighteenth century: the Great Chain of Being and the Ages of Man.

A comparison of Prior's *Solomon* and Pope's *Essay on Man* clarifies the nature, limitations, and merits of each piece as a philosophical poem. Prior's ideas in *Solomon* appear only in certain sections of the *Essay on Man,* but in these sections the resemblances are strong. That is, parts of the *Essay on Man* are very much like the Pyrrhonistic, pessimistic, sceptical philosophy of *Solomon,* but other parts are much more optimistic and sound much more like Shaftesbury than like Prior.[41] Pope, in order to vindicate the ways of God to Man, looked closely at the worst aspects of human existence, then endeavored to explain reasonably how and why they were ultimately right. So long as Pope is examining the moral and physical evils of this world, he and Prior run closely parallel; but as soon as he begins to explain why these partial evils produce universal good, he and Prior diverge sharply. The only solution that Prior's *Solomon* can offer to human suffering is fideism—an acceptance by faith of a difficult universe and an inscrutable God. Pope, on the contrary, attempts to establish reasonably that those things that appear to be evil and unjust to man are not so when viewed in the whole scheme of things.

Because Prior's *Solomon* refuses to accept any rational way out, insisting that all things in this world are vanity and dust, it is both philosophically more consistent and poetically more tedious than Pope's *Essay on Man*. Dr. Johnson wrote in criticism of *Solomon* that "The event of every experiment is foreseen, and therefore the process is not much regarded."[42] Because we know in advance that knowledge or pleasure or power will not long satisfy Solomon, we are held to the reading not by the interest of the framework of plot that Prior has provided but by the phrasing and individual ideas. Though these deserve more attention than the nineteenth or twentieth centuries have paid them, perhaps verbal purity and ideological precision are not enough to sustain over 2600 lines of verse. Prior's single theme of Pyrrhonistic philosophical belief, which he refused to relinquish in favor of any optimistic rational solution, has nevertheless continued to impress those who do manage to read through *Solomon*. George Saintsbury maintained that "If he had not Pope's intense craftsmanship, Prior . . . has something of the 'behind the veil' touch that Pope never even hints at."[43] This "something . . . behind the veil" in Prior's *Solomon* is the philosophical consistency that forced him to eschew any Shaftesburian hope of human benevolence and the rational rightness of the present universe and to retain instead the position of unresolved doubt which led Professor Spears to call him "a harbinger of future dissatisfactions."[44]

Pope in the *Essay on Man* views the suffering and injustice of this world quite as clearly as does Prior and often in much the same terms. Yet, having taken this full look at the worst, Pope endeavors to establish by reason what Christian mystics sometimes perceive extrarationally: that all suffering and evil are part of a divine plan that will bring a unity of good from this apparent multiplicity of evil. Pope's difficulty is that he is trying to vindicate the ways of God to man by the very reason that he has elsewhere in the same poem asserted to be weak, fallible, presumptuous, and misleading. Thus the *Essay on Man* seems to shift back and forth between two incompatible positions—the Pyrrhonistic doctrine that man's reason is unable to cope with either the problem of God or that of the natural universe and the Deistic concept that man can do a fairly efficient job of dealing rationally with both.

The distance between Prior's and Pope's ultimate position is shown by their differing use of a similar figure to embody the human predicament. Prior in *Solomon*, 3:697, speaks of human existence as "Lab'rynths," as Pope calls it in the *Essay on Man*, 1:6, "A mighty maze!" Either figure suggests a complex puzzle, but one with a builder and a plan. Pope sets out to find this plan, asserting some ten lines later (1:16) that he intends to "vindicate the ways of God to Man." But Prior, painfully aware that he is neither Daedalus nor Theseus, never feels that he can see the plan of the labyrinth and instead finds himself (3:696–97) "unable to explain / The secret Lab'rynths of Thy Ways to Man. . . ."[45]

Twice Pope imitated a Horatian ode already Anglicized by Prior. Both men imitated Horace's Satires, II, vi, which contained the account of the country mouse and the city mouse, Prior in *The Hind and the Panther Transvers'd,* Pope in the octosyllabic *An Imitation of the Sixth Satire of the Second Book of Horace.* In each case, the poet had a collaborator (Prior had Charles Montagu, Pope had Jonathan Swift), but the lines telling the story of the city mouse and the country mouse are believed by most critics to have been written by Prior and by Pope. The relevant lines in Pope's poem begin

>   Our Friend Dan *Prior* told, (you know)
>   A Tale extreamly *a propos:*

Name a Town Life, and in a trice,
He had a Story of *two Mice*.[46]

Despite this friendly reference to Prior, Pope's version of the same story owes to Prior's *Hind and the Panther Transvers'd* at most only three small details.[47] What the *Imitation of the Sixth Satire of the Second Book of Horace* may actually demonstrate is that both Swift and Pope learned from Prior's colloquial use of octosyllabics but that each man adapted his learning to his own gifts. Swift's colloquialism is straightforward and flexible; Pope's is brilliant, balanced, and perhaps a little rigid.

Both Prior and Pope translated Horace's Ode I, iv, which Ben Jonson had also translated. Jonson's version was called "Ode the First. The Fourth Booke. To Venus"; Prior's is "Cantata. Set by Monsieur Galliard" (1716); Pope's is "The First Ode of the Fourth Book of Horace" (1737). In general Pope's version is more like Jonson's than like Prior's, for Prior is not simply translating but is writing words to be set to music, divided into five parts for recitative and arias.[48]

The methods of Jonson, Prior, and Pope with this same Horatian ode offer an illuminating contrast. Jonson is cautious, fairly literal, somewhat rough, and powerful. Prior takes his material where it pleases him and suits it to his own purposes, creating a Restoration love-lyric that resembles Horace's farewell to love only in general outline. Pope follows Horace rather closely, though not so closely as Jonson, substituting for Roman geographical and amorous details equivalents more familiar to English thought or acceptable to English taste. Pope's version is as polished, easy, and elegant as Prior's but much closer to his Horatian original. In general, Jonson modifies Horace to make a more powerful metaphor; Prior, to simplify and generalize; and Pope, to polish and "modernize."

The influence of one poet on the next is slight; each seems to have worked primarily with the Horatian original. Prior shows no indebtedness to Jonson; Pope possibly owes to Jonson his verse form, but little else, and he owes to Prior only a single line ("Ah sound no more thy soft alarms"), the addition of Chloe, and the change of the beloved "wanton boy," Ligurinus, to a more acceptable girl (a shift explicit in Prior and implicit in Pope).[48]

The problem of Pope's more general indebtedness to Prior is an intriguing one. When Edward Harley in 1723 asked Pope to read through all of Prior's manuscripts with a view toward editing and bringing out a comprehensive edition, Pope replied, "I now not only desire, but want, & long, to read the Remains of Mr Prior. My Respect for him living extends to his memory; & give me leave to say, In this I resemble your Lordship, that it dies not with his person."[49] Twice in the *Dunciad* Pope coupled Prior's name with those of major contemporary literary figures (Congreve, Addison, Swift) as the models of good writing against which the dunces were weighed in the balance and found wanting. In his last two years of life, when he was projecting a dictionary "that might be authoritative for our English writers," Pope listed Prior as one of the nine "that might serve as authorities for poetical language. . . ."[50] Three of these—Dryden, Swift, and Prior—were drawn from the Restoration-Augustan period, but Swift was restricted to being an authority for burlesque language only. Prior and Dryden had no such restrictions.

The question then becomes what Pope—who set out to become England's first "correct" poet—learned in general from Prior, one of his projected dictionary "authorities for poetical language." As an assistant in planning the 1718 *Poems on Several Occasions* and as the chief editor of the projected posthumous edition of Prior's works, Pope had dealt either casually or closely with almost everything that Prior had written. Moreover, Pope had an extraordinary literary memory for lines of poetry read years before[51] and a sharply sensitive personal recollection of the friends of his youth.[52] In general, then, it is likely that Pope learned from Prior—or intensified because of Prior's tutelage—what Charles Kenneth Eves has called "that rococo style which pointed directly to the *Rape of the Lock.*"[53] Prior's deft placing of the floridly ornamental mantle of style upon subjects deliberately too small for it may have foreshadowed that same mixture of high style and low subject in Pope. The matter of a delicate and easy tone, which also has been suggested as a skill perfected by Prior and passed along to Pope, is another facet of the same question of style. To a young man aiming, like Pope, to become England's first correct poet, Prior had much to teach of tone and style.

In addition to teaching Pope a delicacy and ease of perfect light verse tone, Prior improved the heroic couplet which was to become Pope's masterpiece. Robert Southey commented that "For improving [the heroic couplet], too much has been ascribed to Waller, and not enough to Prior. From Prior, Pope adopted some of the most conspicuous artifices of his verse."[54] Nevertheless, though Prior improved the heroic couplet which Pope was to perfect, it was probably in matters of lightness, delicacy, and ease of tone that Prior had the most profound influence upon Pope.

Prior's Influence upon Samuel Johnson

Though the third great literary figure of the eighteenth century, Samuel Johnson, disapproved of Prior and damaged his poetical reputation by a very unfriendly and unsympathetic "Life of Prior," he also learned from Prior in his own writings, particularly in *Rasselas,* which is heavily indebted to Prior's *Solomon.* Both works are elegant, serious narratives in which a young prince is attempting to make a choice of life, only to find one pathway after another leading to a dead end—or a minotaur. In both works the prince acts a little and talks and listens a great deal. Ian Jack has pointed out that both works employ a "remote, vague, and Oriental" setting, are heavily indebted to the Bible, and are basically "Christian satires on the lot of Man."[55] Though Johnson found *Solomon* tedious— "Tediousness is the most fatal of all faults. . . ."[56]—he also found it a mine of useful observations, a number of which he incorporated into *Rasselas* and into *The Vanity of Human Wishes.* All three works stand squarely, as Jack has pointed out, in the tradition of Christian pessimism, but Prior's specific three-fold division in *Solomon* of areas to be examined—knowledge, pleasure, and power—finds specific parallels in those questions that Rasselas and Imlac and Nekayah and Pekuah raise in *Rasselas* and in those goods that the poet finds it vain and dangerous to wish for in *The Vanity of Human Wishes.*

Prior taught the English poets of the eighteenth century more than matters of style and subject. Along with Dryden and Pope, he also taught them that it was possible for a practicing poet to support himself handsomely from his writings without dependency upon patrons if he would deal directly, in a businesslike fashion, with his reading public. All three poets used the subscription method to secure advances while they worked upon projects and hence to support themselves rather well with funds drawn directly from their potential readers. Prior died a wealthy man not because of his diplomatic career, which often proved a financial disaster, but because of the 1718 *Poems on Several Occasions.*

Prior's Influence upon Other Writers

Prior's poetry also exerted a discernible influence upon lesser poets of the eighteenth and nineteenth centuries, in England and in five other countries. Anne Finch, the preromantic Countess of Winchilsea, frequently mentioned Prior in her poems, in the most notable instance, a thirteen-line section of "The Nymph whose Virgin-heart thy charms have taught," calling Prior her Teacher and Master.[57]

William Cowper reacted against Johnson's censure of Prior, and J. W. H. Atkins has praised Cowper as a corrective "with exquisite taste" to Johnson, who had condemned Prior's use of classical fable as insincere and missed Prior's "most subtle quality."[58] Oswald Doughty has shown the influence of Prior upon Cowper's light verse: "in it he continued Prior's vein of humour, though with less subtlety than Prior showed at his best, while he possessed also Prior's facility in rhyme and rhythm, when writing in the 'familiar style.'"[59]

In this same period Prior's poetry was prized by three of the Wesleys: Samuel the younger, John, and Charles. John Wesley in his journal, letters, and sermons quoted from Prior some sixty times, more than from any other poet of that century and more than from any other poet of any age except Milton. In 1779 he printed *Henry and Emma* whole in the *Arminian Magazine*. Sixteen times the Wesleys' hymns incorporate phrases borrowed from Prior,[60] the most familiar being the third line of "Jesus, Lover of My Soul"—"While the nearer waters roll"—a direct borrowing from Prior's *Solomon*. Samuel J. Rogal explains the Wesleys' continued interest in Prior thus: "Either firsthand or by way of the printed page, the brothers discovered in this Augustan poet a model of perfection for eighteenth-century man: the scholar, the poet, the statesman whose Tory principles anchored him firmly to the trinity of God, king, and nation, and whose sense of loyalty allowed him to endure harassment and even persecution from an overzealous Whig ministry."[61] Henry Bett argues that Prior also taught the Wesleys "Something of the freedom of their versification. . . ."[62]

Prior likewise exerted a strong influence on a number of German poets of the eighteenth and nineteenth centuries. Wieland's *Musarion* was inspired by Prior's *Alma*[63]; Friedrich von Hagedorn was praised as the "deutsch Prior"[64]; Spiridion Wukadinovic has shown that in

Germany Prior also influenced Uz, J. N. Götz, Herder, J. G. Struckmann, Fr. Justin Bertuch, and Gleim.[65]

The Scottish pastoral poet Allan Ramsay (1686–1758) wrote his best pastoral occasional poem[66] in "Robert, Richy, and Sandy: A Pastoral on the Death of Matthew Prior"; in the poem Prior is praised as a satirist, wit, teller of poetic tales, and love poet, in whose work, "Nae word stood wrang."[67] Ramsay's most scholarly biographer, Burns Martin, has, in fact, called Prior one of the two strongest contemporary influences upon Ramsay's work, a model for his attempts at *vers de société*.[68]

In Ireland the nineteenth-century lyricist Thomas More owed a considerable debt to the earlier light verse of Prior, a debt pointed out by William Thackeray, and in nineteenth-century England, Prior's influence fell almost exclusively upon the Victorian writers of familiar verse, Thackeray among them. Thackeray defended Prior against the strictures of Dr. Johnson, calling his lyrics "amongst the easiest, the richest, the most charmingly humorous of English lyrical poems."[69] Brander Matthews named Prior the master of Praed and of Locker-Lampson, classifying all three poets as among the ten great writers of English *vers de société*.[70] Still another Victorian writer of polished, elegant verse, heavily influenced by classical models, William Johnson Cory, paid tribute to Prior in 1877 in a revision of his collection *Ionica* by titling his translation of a Greek mirror-epigram "In Honour of Matthew Prior."[71] Cory's lyrics plainly show the influence of Prior.

In nineteenth-century America, Prior's influence is most apparent in the familiar verse of Oliver Wendell Holmes, who wrote to Locker-Lampson from Boston, 14 January 1873, that "My mother was brought up on the literature of Queen Anne's men & used to quote Pope & I am afraid sometimes Prior without knowing the length to which his vivacities sometimes went, I am quite certain."[72] Holmes shows in his own verse a marked influence from Prior, though not from his bawdier poems.

Thus, throughout the eighteenth century Prior exerted a broad and significant influence upon British and German poets writing in many different forms: long philosophical poems either serious or half-mocking, Horatian imitations, tales, lyrics. Though his influence was still plainly discernible in Britain, Germany, and the United States throughout the nineteenth century, it was felt almost exclusively, especially in the English-speaking countries, in the one genre of *vers de société*. Because the twentieth century does not prize any of the forms in which Prior excelled, he has had little to teach it thus far, though he and similar writers may yet offer a particularly attractive alternative to irregular and obscure verse or to the laceratingly personal confessional poem.

Prior willed to those poets who followed him his immediate inheritance from the Restoration: gifts of lyricism and levity, of octosyllabics and anapaests. Like Swift, though not a rebel against Augustan poetic practices, by his use of other verse forms and other tones, he retained for poets the precedent of a nonpentameter, noniambic verse in various moods. It is in this role that he had his major impact as a minor poet.

Even more than most poets, Prior lived in an age of transition. Just as he managed quietly to pass from the Whig to the Tory party when it became apparent that the country that he wished to serve had changed its allegiance, so he passed smoothly from the Restoration to the Augustan mode of verse when the muse whom he wished to serve shifted her taste. Horace Walpole commented that Prior as a politician "left his party, but not his friends"; so too in poetry Prior managed to retain (without any show of nostalgia) some of the Restoration language, lyricism, and levity, along with certain verse-forms popular during that earlier period. When Pope commented to Spence that Sir John Suckling, Sir John Mennes, and Matthew Prior all belonged to the same school of poetry, he was grouping three men whose style was often burlesque, anti-Petrarchan, familiar, and colloquial, expressing its easy informality in varied metrical patterns. It is to a considerable degree because of Prior that this school of poetry continued as a current within the mainstream of Augustan elegantly formal poetry, written in heroic couplets and highly serious in its estimate of itself. It is likely, moreover, that Prior's major significance in the late twentieth century is that he offers certain alternatives—in genre, tone, polish, style, approach—to the chief types of poetry that we currently practice. He may justly continue to claim that elaborate tomb in Westminster Abbey, at the feet of Spenser, on the grounds that what he meant to English poets in the eighteenth and nineteenth centuries he may once again come to mean to us.

Notes and References

Chapter One

1. "The Birth of Prior," [London] *Times Literary Supplement*, 14 March 1918, 130.

2. The best detailed biography of Prior remains Charles Kenneth Eves, *Matthew Prior: Poet and Diplomatist* (New York, 1939). It has been supplemented and modified by various later studies, especially those made by H. Bunker Wright and by Professors Wright and Monroe K. Spears in their 260-page commentary to *The Literary Works of Matthew Prior* (Oxford, 1959), 815–1077. Hereafter cited as *LW*.

3. Harold Bunker Wright, "Matthew Prior: a Supplement to His Biography" (Ph.D. diss., Northwestern University, 1937), 128.

4. *LW*, 1:583. All subsequent references to Prior's poetry and prose are taken from this standard edition, unless otherwise noted, and will be cited parenthetically in the text.

5. Lawrence E. Tanner, *Westminster School, a History* (London: Country Life, 1934), 14–20.

6. "Heads for a Treatise upon Learning," *LW*, 1:580.

7. For a full account of Prior's relationship to his best-loved relative, see H. Bunker Wright, "Matthew Prior's 'Welbeloved and Dear Cossen,'" *Review of English Studies* 15 (July 1939):318–23.

8. See Brice Harris, *Charles Sackville, Sixth Earl of Dorset, Patron and Poet of the Restoration*, Illinois Studies in Language and Literature, vol. 26, nos. 3–4 (Urbana: University of Illinois Press, 1940).

9. As reported by William Kellaway, assistant librarian, University of London Institute of Historical Research, to Richard B. Kline, "Matthew Prior and 'Dear Will Nuttley': An Addition to the Canon," *Philological Quarterly* 47 (April 1968):161.

10. Joseph Spence, *Anecdotes, Observations, and Characters, of Books and Men. Collected from the Conversation of Mr. Pope, and Other Eminent Persons of His Time*, ed. Samuel Weller Singer (London: W. H. Carpenter, 1820), 111.

11. Samuel Johnson, "Prior," in *Lives of the English Poets*, ed. George Birkbeck Hill (Oxford: Clarendon Press, 1905), 2:182.

12. *LW*, 841.

13. See Monroe K. Spears, "Matthew Prior's Attitude toward Natural Science," *PMLA* 63 (June 1948):485–507.

14. See Marjorie Nicolson, "The Microscope and English Imagination," *Smith College Studies in Modern Languages* 16, no. 4 (1934–35):32–33.

15. *LW,* 1049.

16. For the most detailed and convincing discussion of Prior's affection for William, see Jon Sherman Lawry, "A Critical Study of the English Poetry of Matthew Prior" (Ph.D. diss., Northwestern University, 1955), 31–41.

17. "To My Lady Exeter, on New Years day. Her Birth-Day," "To the Countess of Exeter, Playing on the Lute," and "The Crest of the Arms of the Earl of Exeter a Wheatsheaf supported by Two Lyons" (in Latin).

18. "To the Right Honourable the Countess Dowager of Devonshire, On a Piece of Wissin's; Whereon were all her Grandsons Painted"; "Picture of Seneca dying in a Bath. By Jordain. At the Right Honourable the Earl of Exeter's at Burleigh-House"; "A Flower, Painted by Simon Varelst."

19. "There be Those that leave Their Names behind them"; "Many Daughters have done well, but Thou Excellest them all"; "Ad illustrissimam Dm: Margaritam Coll: C. Jo: Fundatricem" (a close Latin rendering of "Many Daughters have done well. . . .").

20. Public Record Office, *Stepney Papers,* 105/82.

21. Peter Motteux, *Gentleman's Journal* (February 1692), 3. (The poem is on pp. 3–4.)

22. For a clear, brief account of Prior's "extraordinary expenses" at The Hague, see Coleman O. Parsons, "Matthew Prior's Extraordinaries," *Notes and Queries* 166 (3 March 1934):148–50.

23. Historical Manuscripts Commission, *Report on the Manuscripts of the Duke of Buccleugh and Queensberry, K. G., K. T., Preserved at Montagu House, Whitehall* (London: Mackie & Co., 1903), 2:397.

24. Narcissus Luttrell, *A Brief Historical Relation of State Affairs from September 1678 to April 1714* (Oxford: University Press, 1857) 4:278.

25. Spears, "Matthew Prior's Attitude toward Natural Science," 488 n.

26. Robert Joseph Allen, *The Clubs of Augustan London,* Harvard Studies in English, vol. 7 (Cambridge, Mass: Harvard University Press, 1933), 47.

27. Letter to William Cole, 10 June 1778, in *Horace Walpole's Correspondence,* ed. by W. S. Lewis et al. (New Haven: Yale University Press, 1937–), 2:90.

28. Wright, "Matthew Prior: A Supplement to His Biography," 45.

29. Ibid., 24.

30. See Richard G. Brown, "The Role of the Duchess of Marlborough in Augustan Literature" (Ph.D. diss. University of Rochester, 1971), 124–84.

31. For the fullest treatment of Prior's courtship, see H. Bunker Wright, "Matthew Prior and Elizabeth Singer," *Philogical Quarterly* 24 (January 1945):81–82.

32. H. Bunker Wright, "Matthew Prior's Cloe and Lisetta," *Modern Philology* 36 (August 1938):9–23.

33. John Macky, *Memoirs of the Secret Service of John Macky, Esq: During the Reigns of King William, Queen Anne, and King George I. . . .*, ed. A. R. (London: n.p., 1733), 135.

34. *Poems on Several Occasions* (London: R. Burrough, and J. Baker, and E. Curll, 1707).

35. *The Present State of Wit in a Letter to A Friend in the Country.* (Reprinted Augustan Reprint Society, ser. 1: Essays on Wit, no. 3, 1946), 2.

36. Herbert Davis and Irvin Ehrenpreis, eds., "Memoirs, Relating to That Change which happened in the Queen's Ministry in the Year 1710. Written in October, MDCCXIV," in *Prose Works of Jonathan Swift, Political Tracts, 1713–1719* (Oxford 1953), 8:123–24.

37. Jonathan Swift, *Journal to Stella,* ed. Harold Williams, 2 vols. (Oxford, 1948), 1:98, 115, 167, 198, 248, 417, 249, 228; 2:510; 1:65, 428, 422–23.

38. Davis and Ehrenpreis, eds., *Prose Works,* 7:44.

39. George Macaulay Trevelyan, *England Under Queen Anne: The Peace and the Protestant Succession* (London: Longmans, Green & Co., 1934), 183.

40. Jonathan Swift, *A New Journey to Paris* (London: John Morphew, 1711). This piece is reprinted in Davis and Ehrenpreis, eds., *Prose Works,* 3:207–18.

41. Harold Williams ed., *The Poems of Jonathan Swift* (Oxford: Clarendon Press, 1937), 1:143.

42. Historical Manuscripts Commission, *Calendar of the Manuscripts of the Marquis of Bath Preserved at Longleat, Wiltshire,* vol. 3, *Prior Papers.* (Hereford, 1908), 217.

43. Swift, *Journal to Stella,* 417.

44. 13 March 1712, Swift, *Journal to Stella,* 2:513.

45. For this interpretation of the poems, see *LW,* 2:929.

46. 28 October 1712, Swift, *Journal to Stella,* 566.

47. Historical Manuscripts Commission, *Manuscripts of the Marquis of Bath . . . Longleat,* 230.

48. William Makepeace Thackeray, *The History of Henry Esmond, Esq. A Colonel in the Service of Her Majesty Queen Anne Written by Himself* (New York: Charles Scribner's Sons, 1904), 2:206–7.

49. Herbert Davis and Irvin Ehrenpreis, eds., "An Enquiry into the Behaviour of the Queen's last Ministry, with Relation to their Quarrels among themselves, and the Design charged upon them of altering the

Sucession of the Crown. June—1715," in *Political Tracts, 1713–1719* (Oxford: Basil Blackwell, 1953), 158.

50. "What passed at Mr. Prior's Examination, before a Committee of the Privy-Council. Drawn up by Himself," in *The History of His Own Time. Compiled from the Original Manuscripts of His late Excellency Matthew Prior Esq; . . .*, 2d ed. (London: n.p., 1740), 417–35.

51. Ibid., 427.

52. *LW*, 2:941.

53. Williams, ed., *Poems of Jonathan Swift*, 312, ll.29–34.

54. Owen Ruffhead, *The Life of Alexander Pope, Esq. Compiled from Original Manuscripts; with a Critical Essay on His Writings and Genius* (London: C. Bathurst et al., 1769), 482.

55. John Hill Burton, *Life and Correspondence of David Hume* (Edinburgh: W. Tait, 1846), 2:501.

56. 23 January 1717, F. Elrington Ball, ed., *The Correspondence of Jonathan Swift* (London: G. Bell & Sons, 1910–14), 2:360.

57. Harry Ransom, "The Rewards of Authorship in the Eighteenth Century," *University of Texas Studies in English* 18 (1938):52.

58. A point argued convincingly by Wright, "Matthew Prior, A Supplement to His Biography," 55.

59. John Dennis, "Matthew Prior," in *Studies in English Literature* (London, 1876), 129.

60. Letter from Arbuthnot to Henry Watkins, 30 September 1721. *European Magazine and London Review* 13 (January 1788):8.

61. For a detailed treatment of Prior's relationship to these two women, see Wright, "Matthew Prior's Cloe and Lisetta," 9–23.

62. Historical Manuscripts Commission, *Report on the Manuscripts of His Grace the Duke of Portland, K.G., Preserved at Welbeck Abbey* (London: Mackie & Co. 1901), 7:306.

63. H. Bunker Wright and Henry C. Montgomery, "The Art Collection of a Virtuoso in Eighteenth-Century England," *Art Bulletin* 27 (September 1945):195–204.

64. W. Roberts, "Prior as a Book Collector," *Athenaeum*, 19 June 1897, 810. Wright, "Matthew Prior: A Supplement to His Biography," lists every book now known to have been in Prior's library, 1898 items, apparently about half the total library, 144–384.

65. Welbeck MS., f. 121v.

66. For a fuller treatment of Prior's relationship with Drift, see Wright, "Matthew Prior: A Supplement to His Biography," 64–69.

67. "Verses Spoke to the Lady Henrietta-Cavendish Holles Harley, in the Library of St. John's College, Cambridge, November the 9th. An. 1719" (*LW*, 1:521); the brief Latin-and-English "Engraved on Three Sides

of an Antique Lamp given by me to the Right Honorable the Lord Harley" (*LW*, 1:522–23); and the lengthy "Colin's Mistakes" (*LW*, 1:545–49).

68. "A Letter to the Honorable Lady Mrs: Margaret Candish Harley," *LW*, 1:527.

69. As reported by Lady Louise Stuart, "Introductory Anecdotes," in *The Letters and Works of Lady Mary Wortley Montagu* (London: George Bell & Sons, 1898), 1:cxii.

70. Historical Manuscripts Commission, *Manuscripts of the Marquis of Bath . . . Longleat*, 3:483.

71. Gibbs's plans are shown in *A Book of Architecture, containing Designs of Buildings and Ornaments* (New York: B. Blom, 1968), plate 55.

72. Historical Manuscripts Commission, *Manuscripts of the Marquis of Bath . . . Longleat*, 3:488–90.

73. Wright, "Matthew Prior: A Supplement to His Biography," 39.

74. Letter from Pope to Edward Harley, 22 January 1726, in. George Sherburn, ed., *The Correspondence of Alexander Pope* (Oxford: Clarendon Press, 1956), 2:364.

75. Eves, *Matthew Prior: Poet and Diplomatist*, 398.

76. The history of Down Hall and of John Morley of Halstead, Harley's agent and the landjobber from whom Prior purchased the estate, is traced by Alfred Hills, "Matthew Prior in Essex," *Essex Review* 44 (October 1935):236–42.

77. Nikolaus Pevsner, *The Buildings of England: Essex* (London: Penguin Books, 1954), 211.

78. "The Thief and the Cordelier, a Ballad," written in 1718, was to be sung to the same ballad tune. *LW*, 1:459.

79. H. Bunker Wright, writes: "On October 13, 1717, Prior gave Harley £2000, receiving Harley's bond for that amount, and his agreement to pay £200 per annum during Prior's natural life, beginning with Michaelmas 1717. Almost two years later, on July 27, 1719, Prior gave Harley £1000 more, for an additional annuity of £100, and had Harley's note to that effect." "Matthew Prior: A Supplement to His Biography," 43–44.

80. Welbeck MS., f. 51.

81. Richard Savage, *An Author To be Lett* (London: A. Moore, 1729), 3.

82. See Pope's letter to Prior of February 1720, returning the poem to him and suggesting that Prior's first speech might be shortened. Sherburn, ed., *The Correspondence of Alexander Pope*, 2:30.

83. *LW*, 2:997–98.

84. H. Bunker Wright, "Matthew Prior's Funeral," *Modern Language Notes* 57 (May 1942):344.

85. Ibid., 345.

86. J. Bridges, in Thomas Hearne, *Remarks and Collections* (Oxford: Oxford Historical Society, 1885–1921), 7:283.

87. Wright establishes that Prior had "invested upwards of 3000 pounds" in the South Sea Company, 1719–1720, and lost a little more than £1200, while earning cash dividends of £95. 10s. 4d." Matthew Prior: A Supplement to His Biography," 42-43.

88. Ibid., 51.

89. Ibid., 52.

Chapter Two

1. Harris, *Charles Sackville*, 175.

2. Two very useful analyses of the panegyric poems are Ronald Eugene Rower, "Matthew Prior: A Critical Study" (Ph.D. diss., Columbia University, 1968) and Lee Anderson Orr, "The Zeal of the Patriot: Matthew Prior as Panegyrist" (Ph.D. diss., University of Virginia, 1971).

3. Ll. 62–63, *LW*, 1:3.

4. Trevelyan, *England Under Queen Anne*, 183, was to write of Prior as "Devoted to the memory of the Stadtholder-King. . . ." See also Jon Sherman Lawry, "A Critical Study of the English Poetry of Matthew Prior" (Ph.D. diss., Northwestern University, 1955), 31–41. William Stebbing writes of Prior's "genuine admiration of the obstinate heroism of William's character. . . ." "Two Poet-Politicians: Abraham Cowley, Matthew Prior," in *Some Verdicts of History Reviewed* (London, 1887), 101. The latter half of the essay is a reworking of Stebbing's "Article III," *North British Review* 27 (November 1857):366–401.

5. Peter Motteux, "August the 22d, 1692," *Gentlemen's Journal*, August 1692, 1.

6. Historical Manuscripts Commission, *Manuscripts of the Marquis of Bath . . . Longleat*, 3:25.

7. H. Manners Sutton, ed., *The Lexington Papers; or, Some Account of the Courts of London and Vienna; at the Conclusion of the Seventeenth Century. Extracted from the Official and Private Correspondence of Robert Sutton, Lord Lexington* (London: J. Murray, 1851), 63.

8. Historical Manuscripts Commission, *Manuscripts of the Marquis of Bath . . . Longleat*, 3:49.

9. 29 April 1695, ibid., 3:50.

10. Letter reproduced in full in H. T. Swedenberg, Jr., "George Stepney, My Lord Dorset's Boy," *Huntington Library Quarterly* 10 (November 1946):25–26.

11. Ibid.

12. Herbert J. C. Grierson describes it as "One of his cleverest hits," in Grierson and J. C. Smith, *A Critical History of English Poetry* (London: Chatto & Windus, 1962), 197. Gilbert Highet calls it a "brilliant parody,"

better than Boileau's original. *The Classical Tradition: Greek and Roman Influences on Western Literature* (Oxford: Clarendon Press, 1949), 633. Oswald Doughty, a quarter of a century before Highet, had used precisely the same terms to describe the poem—"brilliant parody"—and wrote that Prior in his burlesque had turned "the pompous and sycophantic ode" against Boileau "with great effect." "Matthew Prior (1664-1721)," in *The English Lyric in the Age of Reason* (London, 1922), 48. William Stebbing wrote of it, "The poem is full of open daylight and plain sound English." "Two Poet-Politicians: Abraham Cowley, Matthew Prior," 103.

13. "Letter from Prior to Tonson," *Gentleman's Magazine*, n.s.2 (November 1834):464.

14. *LW*, 2:895–96.

15. He would employ the same altered Spenserian meter once more, in "Colin's Mistakes," written in 1721.

16. Sigurd Hustvedt singles out "The Viceroy" for special attention, as an example of Prior's "large faith in the possibility of the ballad as poetic material," though he also finds it "a good example of his more imitative manner." Sigurd Bernhard Hustvedt, *Ballad Criticism in Scandinavia and Great Britain during the Eighteenth Century*, Scandinavian Monographs, vol. 2 (New York: American-Scandinavian Foundation, 1916), 86.

17. Maynard Mack, "Matthew Prior: et multa prior arte," *Sewanee Review* 68 (Winter 1960):167,170.

Chapter Three

1. Henry Philip Dodd, *The Epigrammatists*, 2d ed. (London: George Bell & Sons, 1876), 283.

2 *LW*, 1:527.

3. See chapter two.

4. See chapter two.

5. The second epitaph, ostensibly concerned with an earlier Bishop of Rochester, was translated at this time because of its applicability to the present Bishop of Rochester as well.

6. Sherburn, ed., *The Correspondence of Alexander Pope*, 2:465–66.

7. Majl Ewing, "Musical Settings of Prior's Lyrics in the 18th Century," *ELH* 10 (June 1943):161.

8. Ibid., 170. Ewing's figures are only slightly affected by the fact that he is counting among these settings one poem, "The Female Phaeton," which we now doubt to be Prior's. See *LW*, 2:1073–75, where Simon Harcourt is considered a likelier author of the piece.

9. Ibid., 171n.

10. *LW*, 2:876.

11. Ibid., 909.

12. Ewing, "Musical Settings of Prior's Lyrics," 160–61.

13. For a consideration of the Renaissance qualities in the poetry of Matthew Prior, see Frances Mayhew Rippy, "Matthew Prior as the Last Renaissance Man," in *Studies in Medieval, Renaissance, American Literature: A Festschrift* (Fort Worth, 1971), 120–31, 203.

14. Harris, *Charles Sackville*, 129.

15. In 1704, four years after Dryden's death, Prior wrote a second prologue which accompanied a Dryden play, this time Dryden's best, *All for Love*. But Prior's "Prologue, Spoken at Court before the Queen, on Her Majesty's Birth-Day, 1704" is not really a prologue to Dryden's play, which it never mentions, but to the whole performance, and was preceded by an overture and followed by a symphony before Dryden's play was finally performed. *LW*, 2:891.

16. *LW*, 2:977. See also Allardyce Nicoll, *A History of Early Eighteenth Century Drama 1700–1750* (Cambridge: University Press, 1929), 132, 187–88.

17. *LW*, 2:1031.

18. Johnson, "Edmund Smith," in *Lives of the English Poets*, 2:15.

19. Among poems not yet discussed this category would include "On Exodus iii. 14. I am that I am. An Ode" (1688), "To Dr. Sherlock, on his Practical Discourse Concerning Death" (1690), "Charity never faileth" (1690), "God is Love" (1690), "To the Honourable Charles Montague, Esq:" (1692), "Considerations on part of the Eighty Eighth Psalme" (1693), " 'Who would, says Dryden, Drink this draught of Life' " (1697), "Adriani Morientis ad Animam Suam. Imitated" (1703), "Charity" (1703), "Written in the Beginning of Mezeray's History of France" (1708), "The First Hymn of Callimachus" (1708), "Seneca, Troas, Act 2d. the Chorus Translated" (1708), "Gualterus Danistonus Ad Amicos. Imitated" (1710), "The Second Hymn of Callimachus" (1718), and "Predestination, A Poem" (1721).

20. Louis I. Bredvold, *The Intellectual Milieu of John Dryden: Studies in Some Aspects of Seventeenth-Century Thought* (Ann Arbor: University of Michigan Press, 1934), 64n.

21. "An Epistle to Fleetwood Shephard, Esq;" and "To Mr. Fleetwood Shepherd," both written in 1689.

22. *Ovid's Epistles* (1680–83), *Miscellany Poems* (1684), and *Sylvae* (1685). For details of the contents of these three miscellanies which Prior is attacking, see *LW*, 2:823.

23. For the best study of Prior's place in the English literary tradition of the imitation, see Harold F. Brooks, "The 'Imitation' in English Poetry, Especially in Formal Satire, Before the Age of Pope," *Review of English Studies* 25 (April 1949):124–40. Brooks asserts that Prior, like Cowley

and Oldham and unlike Swift, Pope, and Johnson, imitates by closely paralleling his original, sentence by sentence.

24. *Memorandums Concerning the late Celebrated Poet & Statesman Mr Matthew Prior Copy'd from a MSS of Sir James Montagu Ld Chief Baron of the Exchequer,* fols. 15–19, a manuscript volume preserved at Longleat, Wiltshire. A fuller quotation from this volume is given in *LW*, 2:831–32.

25. J. W. Draper, "The Metrical Tale in XVIII-Century England," *PMLA*, 52 (June 1937):396.

26. "Hans Carvel" (1700), "The Ladle" (1703), "An English Padlock" (1704), "Paolo Purganti and His Wife: An Honest, but a Simple Pair" (1708), "Cupid and Ganymede" (1708), "Daphne and Apollo" (1715), "The Dove" (1717), "Mercury and Cupid" (1718), "The Thief and the Cordelier" (1718), "Protogenes and Apelles" (1718), "The Conversation. A Tale" (1720), "The Turtle and the Sparrow" (1720), "Truth and Falshood. A Tale" (1720), and "Down-Hall; A Ballad" (1721). I have eliminated from the list three of Prior's longer narrative poems that show little realism of diction or motive: "Love Disarm'd" (1708), "Colin's Mistakes. Written in Imitation of Spenser's Style" (1721), and the undated "Amaryllis. A Pastoral."

27. John Nichols, *Literary Anecdotes of the Eighteenth Century* (London: Nichols, Son & Bentley, 1814), 8:378.

28. *Anecdotes, Observations,* 48.

29. Letter to Miss Mary Berry, 16–18 October 1790, in Lewis, ed., *Horace Walpole's Correspondence,* 11:121.

30. "Introduction," in *AEdes Walpolianae: or, A Description of the Collection of Pictures at Houghton-Hall in Norfolk,* 2d ed. (London: [Dodsley], 1752), xvii–xix.

31. Letter to Miss Mary Berry, 16–18 October 1790, in Lewis, ed., *Horace Walpole's Correspondence,* 11:121.

32. "Introductory Criticism to Vol. II of *The Beauties of English Poesy,*" in *The Works of Oliver Goldsmith,* Turk's Head Edition, ed. Peter Cunningham (New York and London: G. P. Putnam's Sons, 1908), 9:236.

33. George Birkbeck Hill and L. F. Powell, eds., *Boswell's Life of Johnson* (Oxford: Clarendon Press, 1934), 3:192.

34. Cunningham, ed., "Introductory Criticisms to Volume II," 227–28.

35. Ralph M. Wardle, *Oliver Goldsmith* (London: Constable & Co., 1957), 176.

36. Oswald Doughty, "The Poet of the 'Familiar Style,' " *English Studies* 7 (February 1925):9–10.

37. Mark Van Doren, *Introduction to Poetry* (New York: Dryden Press, 1951), 17–21.

38. Mack, "Matthew Prior: et multa prior arte," 172–73.
39. James Sutherland, *A Preface to Eighteenth Century Poetry* (Oxford: Clarendon Press, 1948), 4.

Chapter Four

1. *LW,* 2:909.
2. London: Lintott, Tonson, and Draper, 1748.
3. F. J. Bertuch, trans., *Heinrich und Emma. Ein gedicht aus dem Englischen des Herrn Prior* (Stralsund and Leipzig, 1753).
4. Thiroux d'Arconville, trans., *Mélanges de poesie angloise contenant . . . Henry et Emma, imité de la belle brune de Chaucer, par Matthieu Prior* (Paris, 1764).
5. Thomas Augustine Arne, *Songs in Henry and Emma . . . a New Musical Drama (1749)* and Sir Henry Bate Dudley, *Henry and Emma, a New Poetical Interlude* (1774).
6. Eves, *Matthew Prior: Poet and Diplomatist,* 392.
7. Oliver Elton, *A Survey of English Literature 1730–1780* (New York: Macmillan, 1928), 1:63–64.
8. Johnson, "Prior," in *Lives of the English Poets,* 2:202–3.
9. Letter 88, in William Hayley, ed., *The Life and Letters of William Cowper, Esq.* (London: Baldwin, Cradock et al., 1824), 1:234–35; John Wesley, "Thoughts on the Character and Writings of Mr. Prior," *Arminian Magazine* 5 (December 1782):661.
10. *The History of English Poetry, from the Close of the Eleventh to the Commencement of the Eighteenth Century* (London: J. Dodsley et al., 1774–81), 3:140–41.
11. Lewis, ed., *Horace Walpole's Correspondence,* 29:118.
12. So Shenstone writes on the first blank page of his copy.
13. Marjorie Williams, *William Shenstone. A Chapter in Eighteenth Century Taste* (Birmingham: Cornish Brothers, 1935), 119–20.
14. Ll. 11–26, *Sawney, An Heroic Poem. Occasion'd by the Dunciad* (London: 1728), 11–12.
15. Johnson, "Pope," in *Lives of the English Poets,* 3:105.
16. The problem of Pope's indebtedness to Prior in this poem is discussed in more detail in chapter six, and in Rippy, "Matthew Prior and Alexander Pope: Their Personal and Literary Relationship."
17. Sutherland, *Preface to Eighteenth Century Poetry,* 92–93.
18. John Dryden, "Preface," in *Fables Ancient and Modern* (London: Jacob Tonson, 1700), n.p.
19. Discussed more fully in chapter five.
20. "The Preface," *LW,* 1:309. These modifications are pointed out in the discussion of the preface in chapter five.
21. *LW,* 2:994–95, 1:360.

22. Hoxie Neale Fairchilde, *Religious Trends in English Poetry,* vol. 1, *1700-1740. Protestantism and the Cult of Sentiment* (New York: Columbia University Press, 1939), 33.

23. Oxford, reprinted in 1740.

24. Cambridge and London.

25. Basel: J. J. Schorndorff.

26. Ruffhead, *The Life of Alexander Pope,* 482n.

27. For a fuller discussion of the impact of Prior's *Solomon* upon Pope's *Essay on Man,* see chapter six, and Rippy, "Matthew Prior and Alexander Pope," 466–92.

28. Johnson, "Prior," in *Lives of the English Poets,* 2:206.

29. See chapter six. Also see Ian Jack, "The 'Choice of Life' in Johnson and Prior," *Journal of English and Germanic Philology* 49 (October 1950):523–30.

30. *The Works of the Rev. John Wesley, A.M.,* 5th ed. (London: Wesleyan Conference Office, n.d.), 6:433.

31. Wesley, "Thoughts on the Character and Writings of Mr. Prior," 622.

32. Ibid., 663.

33. Letter to the Rev. William Unwin, 5 January 1782, in Hayley, ed., *The Life and Letters of William Cowper,* 1:232.

34. "Sur M. Pope et Quelques Autres Poètes Fameux," in *Lettres sur les Anglais,* lettre 22, in *OEuvres complètes de Voltaire,* vol. 24. *Mélanges Historiques,* vol. 1 (Paris: Antoine, Augustin Renouard, 1819), 126.

35. Edmund Gosse, *A History of Eighteenth Century Literature (1660–1780)* (London: Macmillan and Co., 1889), 134.

36. *LW,* 2:913.

37. Ruffhead, *Life of Alexander Pope,* 482n.

38. Monroe K. Spears, "The Meaning of Matthew Prior's *Alma,*" *ELH* 13 (December 1946):270.

39. See Louis I. Bredvold, "The Gloom of the Tory Satirists," in *Pope and His Contemporaries: Essays presented to George Sherburn,* ed. by James L. Clifford and Louis A. Landa (Oxford: Clarendon Press, 1949), 3.

40. Thomas Martin, trans., *Alma* (Sarum: Typis E. Easton, 1763).

41. Ruffhead, *Life of Alexander Pope,* 482n.

42. E. A. Richards, *Hudibras in the Burlesque Tradition,* Columbia University Studies in English and Comparative Literature, no. 127 (New York, 1937), 145–46.

43. Johnson, "Prior," in *Lives of the English Poets,* 2:205.

44. Letter to Mrs. Hannah More, Strawberry Hill, 13 November 1784, in Lewis, ed., *Horace Walpole's Correspondence,* 31:221.

45. "Introductory Criticisms," in *The Works of Oliver Goldsmith,* 9:238.

46. Letter to Lord Thurlow, August 1791, *Correspondence of William Cowper*, ed. Thomas Wright (London: Hodder & Stoughton, 1904), 4:113.

47. Joseph Warton, *Essay on the Genius and Writings of Pope* (London: J. Dodsley, 1782), 2:126.

48. Joseph Warton, *Works of Alexander Pope, Esq. With notes and illustrations by J. Warton, and others* (London: B. Law, 1797), 6:142n.

49. Wesley, "Thoughts on the Character and Writings of Mr. Prior," 661.

50. Louis I. Bredvold, "The Literature of the Restoration and the Eighteenth Century, 1660–1798," in *A History of English Literature*, ed. Hardin Craig (New York: Oxford University Press, 1950), 392.

51. Richards, *Hudibras in the Burlesque Tradition*, 148–51; Richmond P. Bond, *English Burlesque Poetry, 1700–1750*, Harvard Studies in English, no. 6 (Cambridge: Harvard University Press, 1932), 151, 154, 293.

52. See W. P. Barrett, "Matthew Prior's *Alma*," *Modern Language Review* 27 (October 1932):454–58, and H. B. Wright, "William Jackson on Prior's Use of Montaigne," *Modern Language Review* 31 (April 1936):203–5.

53. See, for example, Carson S. Duncan, *The New Science and English Literature in the Classical Period* (Menasha, Wis.: Collegiate Press, 1913), 123, 133, 181; and three studies by Marjorie Nicolson, "The Microscope and English Imagination," *Smith College Studies in Modern Languages* 16, no. 4 (July 1935):32–33; "A World in the Moon: A Study of Changing Attitudes toward the Moon in the Seventeenth and Eighteenth Centuries," *Smith College Studies in Modern Languages* 17, no. 2 (January 1936):31, 67; *Newton Demands the Muse: Newton's Opticks and the Eighteenth Century Poets*, History of Ideas Ser., no. 2 (Princeton: University Press, 1946), 92.

Chapter Five

1. I have not chosen to include *The Hind and the Panther Transvers'd* in this chapter, though its satire mixes poetry and prose, because it has already been discussed at some length in chapter three, and because it is impossible to determine which parts of its prose were written by Prior and which by Charles Montagu.

2. He was also utilizing a less heavily linked rhyme scheme for the earlier lines of each stanza.

3. *LW*, 1:231–32.

4. Prior, Swift, and Rowe did collaborate on another letter to the *Tatler*, published in no. 258 (30 November-2 December 1710), but it is impossible to determine Prior's part in this second letter. See Jonathan Swift, 2 December 1710, in Swift, *Journal to Stella*, 1:111.

5. See chapter three.

6. *LW*, 2:920.

7. Ibid., 940.

8. J. W. Johnson, *The Formation of English Neo-Classical Thought* (Princeton: Princeton University Press, 1967), 74–75, 87.

9. J. W. Johnson states that Prior's "Observations on Homer" shows the influence of Byzantine literary criticism, specifically that of Eustathius. Ibid., 131.

10. Professors Wright and Spears have counted eighty-two such instances collected by Prior in these "Observations on Ovid's Metamorphoses." *LW,* 2:1022.

11. Spence, *Anecdotes, Observations,* 48–49.

12. Sir William Forbes, *An Account of the Life and Writings of James Beattie, LL.D.* (Edinburgh: Arch. Constable & Co., 1807), 2:370.

13. Eugene R. Purpus, "The 'Plain, Easy, and Familiar Way': The Dialogue in English Literature, 1660–1725," *ELH* 17 (March 1950):54.

14. The earliest of these was Johan S. Egilsrud's *Le "Dialogue des Morts" dans les Litteratures Française, Allemande, et Anglaise (1644–1789)* in 1934, which found Prior's work the best in English in their genre, written with French lightness and delicacy, yet still somehow labored rather than spontaneous (Paris: L'Entente Linotypiste, 1934), 151–55. Almost a decade later, Benjamin Boyce, writing "News from Hell," classified Prior as working in the tradition of "the heathen and skeptic varieties" of dialogues of the dead, "Witty and intellectual," making "no pretence of describing the scenery or customs or inhabitants of the nether world." *PMLA* 58 (June 1943):424. Richard Morton wrote in 1967 that Prior is witty in his dialogue and willing to write at length, so that ideas can be "scrutinized closely and pointedly," although "To the extent that one character, representing an apparent ideal, debates with a less admirable interlocutor, Prior's dialogues are conventional." He concluded that "Prior goes beyond skillful conventionality in some passages . . . in his dialogues, regardless of obvious opinion, he takes care to manage his tube with consistency and, when the reader least expects it, he bowls counter to the bias and startles our complacency" ("Matthew Prior's *Dialogues of the Dead," Ball State University Forum* 8 (Summer 1967):76–78). The fullest treatment of Prior's *Dialogues of the Dead* came a year later (1968) in Ronald Eugene Rower's "Matthew Prior: A Critical Study," in which he takes issue with Morton's assumption that Prior's dialogues were essentially philosophical literature, not dramatic literature. Rower believes that Prior makes his ghosts deliberately poor philosophical debaters because he insists that they be very much themselves; condemned by death to a perpetually impotent spiritual playground, they give dramatic vigor to the *Dialogues* by behaving as complicated individual human beings, contradictory and troubled (Ph.D. diss., Columbia University, 1968). See also Maynard

John Higby, "Matthew Prior's 'Dialogues of the Dead' and the Dialogue Tradition" (Ph.D. diss., University of South Carolina, 1971).

15. Horace Walpole, *Walpoliana* (London: R. Phillips, 1804), 26.

16. *LW,* 2:1003–4.

17. Richard B. Kline, who has made the only detailed study to date of Prior's plays, justly concludes that Prior's dialogue in *Britanicus and Junia* "was a great improvement over the dialogue in 'Ladislaus.' " "Supplement to the Biography and Criticism of Matthew Prior" (Ph.D. diss., Duke University, 1965). Because we cannot date the two plays, the superiority of *Britanicus and Junia* may simply demonstrate that if one chooses a French model to adapt into English, it is wiser to choose Racine than Rotrou.

Chapter Six

1. The most detailed study of Prior's relationship to Swift has been made by James Alfred Koger, "The Personal and Literary Relationship of Matthew Prior and Jonathan Swift" (Ph.D. diss., Rice University, 1971).

2. Historical Manuscripts Commission, *Report on the Manuscripts of His Grace the Duke of Portland. Preserved at Welbeck Abbey* (London: Eyre & Spottiswoods, 1897), 4:155. L. G. Wickham Legg conjectures that this book shown by Prior was probably *A Tale of a Tub. Matthew Prior: A Study of His Public Career and Correspondence* (Cambridge: University Press, 1921), 127, n.2.

3. Swift, *Journal to Stella,* 59.

4. Allen, *Clubs of Augustan London,* 78.

5. The first extant letter from Prior to Swift was written from Paris, 8 April 1713. Ball, ed., *Correspondence of Jonathan Swift,* 2:18–19.

6. For a detailed account of Swift's share in this subscription edition, see Rippy, "Matthew Prior and Alexander Pope," 154–59.

7. Ball, ed., *Correspondence of Jonathan Swift,* 3:103.

8. Ibid., 6:235.

9. Ibid., 236.

10. The list was first printed in Sir Walter Scott's "Life of Swift," in *The Works of Jonathan Swift, D.D.* (Edinburgh: Archibald Constable & Co., 1814), 1:359, later reprinted in appendix 17 to Ball, ed., *Correspondence of Jonathan Swift,* 5:465–66. For documentation of Swift's high opinion of Prior as politician, see Rippy, "Matthew Prior and Alexander Pope," 6–7.

11. F. Elrington Ball, *Swift's Verse: An Essay* (London: John Murray, 1929), 102–3.

12. Williams, ed., "Introduction," in *The Poems of Jonathan Swift,* 1:xiv–xv.

13. Ball, *Swift's Verse,* 124.

14. Westminster, 28 February 1721. "I am tired with politics and lost in the South Sea: the roaring of the Waves and the madness of the people were justly putt together. . . ." Williams, ed., *Correspondence of Jonathan Swift*, 2:378. Ball (*Swift's Verse*, 160–61) argues that the Prior letter produced the four stanzas in the Swift poem; Williams believes that the Swift poem produced the Prior letter (*Poems of Jonathan Swift*, 1:250).

15. For a full treatment of this question of the literary influence of Prior upon Pope, see Rippy, "Matthew Prior and Alexander Pope."

16. 211, Joseph Spence, *Observations, Anecdotes, and Characters of Books and Men Collected from Conversation*, ed. James M. Osborn (Oxford: Clarendon Press, 1966), 1:91.

17. For a discussion of four Prior epigrams that linked him in some fashion with Pope, see Rippy, "Matthew Prior and Alexander Pope," 376–405.

18. Sherburn ed., *Correspondence of Alexander Pope*, 1:179. Pope's contributions to the *Adriani* imitations are complicated by his love of mystification, for he redated and readdressed letters, substituted one version of the poem for an earlier one, and even wrote footnotes conjecturing about his own editorial practices. Norman Ault has unraveled many of the details of Pope's devious readjustments of fact and chronology in "The 'Hadrian' Poems," in *New Light on Pope with Some Additions to His Poetry Hitherto Unknown* (London: Methuen & Co., 1949), 60–67.

19. For a full discussion of these versions of the *Adriani Morientis*, see Rippy, "Matthew Prior and Alexander Pope," 406–32.

20. Ralph, *Sawney*, 11–12.

21. James Sutherland, ed., *The Dunciad*, vol. 5 of *The Twickenham Edition of the Poems of Alexander Pope*, gen. ed. John Butt (London: Methuen & Co., 1943), 28.

22. Ibid., xxv–xxvi. See also Sir Leslie Stephen, *Alexander Pope*, English Men of Letters Series (London: Macmillan & Co., 1880), 126.

23. Johnson, "Pope," in *Lives of the English Poets*, 3:105.

24. See Robert Kilburn Root, *The Poetical Career of Alexander Pope* (Princeton: Princeton Unversity Press, 1938), 235, and Geoffrey Tillotson, ed., *The Rape of the Lock and Other Poems*, vol. 2 of *The Twickenham Edition of the Poems of Alexander Pope* (London: Methuen & Co., 1940), 397. Tillotson's appendix N (pp. 397–98) is devoted to a consideration of *Eloisa to Abelard* and *Henry and Emma*.

25. Elton, *A Survey of English Literature 1730–1780*, 1:63–64.

26. For a full enumeration of these parallels and a more detailed discussion of the relationship of *Henry and Emma* to *Eloisa to Abelard*, see Rippy, "Matthew Prior and Alexander Pope," 433–65.

27. Tillotson, ed., *The Rape of the Lock and Other Poems*, 281.

28. Ibid., 285.

29. Wright, "Matthew Prior's Cloe and Lisetta," 9–23.
30. See Tillotson, ed., *The Rape of the Locak and Other Poems,* 291–93.
31. Prior's ll. 9–10 become Pope's 11. 59–60; Prior's ll. 41–44 become Pope's ll. 45–48. See Rippy, "Matthew Prior and Alexander Pope," 454–55.
32. For a detailed itemization and discussion of these verbal parallels, see ibid., 456–63.
33. Root, *The Poetical Career of Alexander Pope,* 94–99; Tillotson, ed., *The Rape of the Lock and Other Poems,* 275–88.
34. Tillotson, ed., *The Rape of the Lock and Other Poems,* 288.
35. For a fuller discussion of the reputation of *Solomon,* see chapter four.
36. Wesley, "Thoughts on the Character and Writing of Mr. Prior," 600–3, 660–65.
37. *The Works of the Rev. John Wesley,* 6:433.
38. Letter to the Rev. William Unwin, 5 January 1782, in Hayley, ed., *Life and Letters of William Cowper,* 1:232.
39. Ruffhead, *Life of Alexander Pope,* 482n.
40. For a full discussion and itemization of the indebtedness of the *Essay on Man* to Prior's various works, see Rippy, "The Ways of God to Man': Prior's *Solomon* and Pope's *Essay on Man,*" in "Matthew Prior and Alexander Pope," 466–92.
41. See two articles by William E. Alderman, "Shaftesbury and the Doctrine of Benevolence in the Eighteenth Century," *Transactions of the Wisconsin Academy* 26 (1931):137–59; "Shaftesbury and the Doctrine of Optimism," *Transactions of the Wisconsin Academy* 28 (1933):297–305.
42. Johnson, "Prior," in *Lives of the English Poets,* 2:207.
43. George Saintsbury, *The Peace of the Augustans: A Survey of Eighteenth Century Literature as a place of Rest and Refreshment* (London: Oxford University Press, 1946), 57.
44. Spears, "Matthew Prior's Attitude Toward Natural Science," 506.
45. Comparing these two passages in the *Essay on Man* and *Solomon,* Professor Spears concludes: "Against the dominant rationalism and optimism of his age, Prior upholds an Anglican Fideism; he is, in a sense, a tragic figure, for without the calm certainty of faith he remains a Fideist manqué." "Matthew Prior's Religion," 180.
46. Ll. 153–56, John Butt ed., *Imitations of Horace with An Epistle to Dr. Arbuthnot and the Epilogue to the Satires,* vol. 4 of *The Twickenham Edition of the Poems of Alexander Pope,* gen. ed. John Butt (London: Methuen & Co., 1939), 259.
47. For an identification and discussion of these details and of the broader question of Prior and Pope as Horatian imitators, see Rippy, " 'I

Have Taken Horace's Design': Prior, Pope, and Four Horatian Imitations," in "Matthew Prior and Alexander Pope," 493–516.

48. In two instances, Pope's Horatian imitations draw lines directly from Prior pieces other than his reworkings of Horace. In his *Letter to Monsieur Boileau Despreaux: Occasion'd by the Victory at Blenheim, 1704*, Prior had written:

> amongst our selves, with too much Heat,
> We sometimes wrangle, when We should debate;
> (A consequential ILL which Freedom draws;
> A bad Effect, but from a Noble Cause:)
> (11.191–94, *LW*, 1:226)

Pope makes the same specific observations upon the same English political situation in "The First Epistle of the Second Book of Horace, Imitated":

> But Britain, changeful as a Child at play,
> Now calls in Princes, and now turns away.
> Now Whig, now Tory, what we lov'd we hate;
> Now all for Pleasure, now for Church and State:
> Now for Prerogative, and now for Laws:
> Effects unhappy! from a Noble Cause.
> (ll. 155–60, Butt ed., *Imitations of Horace*, 209)

In the second instance, Pope borrowed a contrast from Prior's manuscript prose and turned it into a line of poetry. Pope had praised Prior's four manuscript *Dialogues of the Dead* to Spence, recalling the precise content of each, including "another between Montaigne and Locke on a most regular and a very loose way of thinking. . . ." (Spence, *Observations, Anecdotes, and Characters of Books and Men*, 1:92). Into his "First Epistle of the First Book of Horace Imitated," a decade later (1737), Pope incorporated the lines:

> But ask not, to what Doctors I apply?
> Sworn to no Master, of no Sect am I:
> As drives the storm, at any door I knock.
> And house with Montagne now, or now with Lock.
> (ll. 23–26, in Butt, ed., *Imitations of Horace*, 281)

49. Letter of 24 August 1723, in Sherburn, ed., *Correspondence of Alexander Pope*, 2:193.

50. Item #390, Spence, *Observations, Anecdotes, and Characters of Books and Men*, 1:171.

51. Samuel Johnson wrote of Pope: ". . . he is said to have had great strength and exactness of memory. That which he had heard or read was not easily lost; and he had before him not only what his own meditation suggested, but what he had found in other writers that might be accommodated to his present purpose." Johnson, "Pope," in *Lives of the English Poets*, 3:217.

52. Pope wrote to Swift on 30 December 1736: ". . . I find my heart harden'd and blunt to new impressions, it will scarce receive or retain affections of yesterday; and those friends who have been dead these twenty years, are more present to me now, than these I see daily." Sherburn, ed., *Correspondence of Alexander Pope*, 4:51.

53. Eves, *Matthew Prior: Poet and Diplomatist*, 181–82.

54. Robert Southey, "Preface," in *Specimens of the Later English Poets* (London: Longman, Hurst, Rees & Orme, 1807), 1:xxix-xxx.

55. Jack, "The 'Choice of Life' in Johnson and Prior," *Journal of English and Germanic Philology* 49 (October 1950):523–30. J. W. Johnson, "Rasselas and His Ancestors," *Notes and Queries* 204 (May 1959):185–88, cautions that "Johnson certainly received hints for *Rasselas* from reading Prior's *Solomon* . . . but despite striking similarities . . . there are several important differences between the 'plots', tone, and implications of the two works."

56. Johnson, "Prior," *Lives of the English Poets*, 2:206.

57. Samuel Humphreys, "Some Account of the Author: Memoirs of the Life of Mr Prior," in *Poems on Several Occasions. By Matthew Prior, Esq;* 4th ed. (London: C. Hitch & J. Hodges, 1754), 2:lxxii.

58. J. W. H. Atkins, *English Literary Criticism: 17th and 18th Centuries* (London: Methuen, 1951), 323.

59. Doughty, "The Poet of the 'Familiar Style,' " 5.

60. Henry Bett, *The Hymns of Methodism*, 3d ed. (London: Epworth Press, 1945), 154–60.

61. Samuel J. Rogal, *John and Charles Wesley*, Twayne's English Authors Series, no. 368. (Boston: Twayne Publishers, 1983), 102. See also two works by T. B. Shepherd: "John Wesley and Matthew Prior," *London Quarterly and Holborn Review*, July 1937, 368–73, and *Methodism and the Literature of the Eighteenth Century* (London: Epworth Press, 1940).

62. Bett, *Hymns of Methodism*, 159.

63. Johan S. Egilsrud, *Le "Dialogue des morts" dans les littératures française, allemande et anglaise (1664–1789)* (Paris: L'Entente linotypiste, 1934), 140.

64. Spiridion Wukadinovic, *Prior in Deutschland* (Graz: K. K. Unicweaitäts-Buchdruckerei und Verlags-Buchhandlung 'Styria," 1895), in Anton E. Schoenbach and Bernhard Seuffert, *Grazer Studien zur deutschen Philologie*, 4:7.

65. Ibid., passim.
66. Burns Martin, *Allan Ramsay, A Study of His Life and Works* (Cambridge: Harvard University Press, 1931), 68.
67. L. 103, in Burns Martin, ed., *The Works of Allan Ramsay* (Edinburgh and London: A. Fullarton & Co., [1851]), 2:176.
68. Martin comments further, "we need hardly add that the Scot never achieved the polish and urbanity of his master." Ibid., 59.
69. "Prior, Gay, and Pope," in *The English Humourists of the Eighteenth Century,* ed. by Derek Stanford (London: Grey Walls Press, 1949), 164. For specific instances of Thackeray's indebtedness to Prior, see William P. Trent, "Thackeray's Verse," in *Longfellow and Other Essays* (New York: Thomas Y. Crowell & Co., 1910), 182.
70. Brander Matthews, "Familiar Verse," in *Gateways to Literature and Other Essays* (New York: Charles Scribner's Sons, 1912), 163–64.
71. William Johnson Cory, *Ionica,* introduction and notes by Arthur C. Benson, Sesame Library (London: George Allen & Unwin, n.d.), 218.
72. Letter quoted in full in Augustine Birrell, *Frederick Locker-Lampson: A Character Sketch* (New York: Charles Scribner's Sons, 1920), 96.

Selected Bibliography

PRIMARY SOURCES

1. Standard Edition

Wright, H. Bunker, and Monroe K. Spears, eds. *The Literary Works of Matthew Prior*. 2d ed. 2 vols. Oxford: Clarendon Press, 1971. The definitive edition, further enriched by detailed biographical and textual materials available only in commentary.

2. Letters

Historical Manuscripts Commission. *Calendar of the Manuscripts of the Marquis of Bath Preserved at Longleat, Wiltshire*. Vol. 3, *Prior Papers*. Hereford: Anthony Brothers, 1908. The most important single source of Prior materials.

Swift, Jonathan. *Journal to Stella*. Edited by Harold Williams. 2 vols. Oxford: Clarendon Press, 1948. Swift's first-hand accounts of his friendship with Prior and of Prior's personal and political comings and goings, London, 15 October 1710, to 18 November 1712.

Williams, Harold, ed. *The Correspondence of Jonathan Swift*. 5 vols. Oxford: Clarendon Press, 1963–65. Letters to, from, and about Prior from his most significant friendship.

SECONDARY SOURCES

1. Full-Length Biographies

Bickley, Francis. *The Life of Matthew Prior*. London: Sir Isaac Pitman & Sons, 1914.

Eves, Charles Kenneth. *Matthew Prior: Poet and Diplomatist*. Columbia University Studies in English and Comparative Literature, no. 144. New York: Columbia University Press, 1939. The best single biographical study of Prior.

Johnson, Samuel. "Prior." In *Lives of the English Poets*, edited by George Birkbeck Hill, 2:180–211. Oxford: Clarendon Press, 1905.

Kline, Richard B. "Supplements to the Biography and Criticism of Matthew Prior." Ph.D. diss., Duke University, 1965. Second part adds to the biographical data.

Legg, L. G. Wickman. *Matthew Prior: A Study of His Public Career and Correspondence.* Cambridge: University Press, 1921.

Wright, H. Bunker. "Matthew Prior: A Supplement to His Biography." Ph.D. diss., Northwestern University, 1937. Remains most important biographical dissertation.

2. Other Major Sources

Aitken, G. A. "Matthew Prior." *Contemporary Review* 57 (May 1890):715–29. Carefully and usefully biographical.

Barrett, Wilfred Phillips. "Matthew Prior and His Literary Relations with France." Ph.D. diss., Cambridge University, 1931.

———. "Matthew Prior's *Alma.*" *Modern Language Review* 27 (October 1932):454–58. Suggests source for main conceit of *Alma* (Montaigne) and influence of *Alma* on Diderot.

Bassil, Veronica. "The Faces of Griselda: Chaucer, Prior, and Richardson." *Texas Studies in Literature and Language* 26 (Summer, 1984):157–82. Sees Prior's *Henry and Emma* as facilitating the "movement from the piety and militarism of the Nut Brown Maid to sadomasochistic pornography, from joyful reunion to epic solitude, from the compactness of the dramatic ballad to the infinite details of melodrama."

Bastide, Charles. "Un Secrétaire d'Ambassade anglais à Paris sous Louis XIV." *Revue des Sciences Politiques* 48 (April-June 1923):231–48. An analysis of Prior's two diplomatic sojourns in France, French reactions to him, and his gradual mellowing toward France, seduced by the charms of its culture.

Bett, Henry. *The Hymns of Methodism.* 3d ed. London: Epworth Press, 1945. Cites sixteen borrowings from Prior in the Wesleys' hymns and argues that the Wesleys owed to Prior "Something of the freedom of their versification."

Bickley, Francis. "New Facts about Matthew Prior." *Quarterly Review* 218 (January 1913):91–117. New light shed on various facets of Prior's biography, chiefly from Longleat vol. 3, "a volume which, had it not appeared as an official publication, would probably have been hailed as a literary discovery."

Blackmur, R. P. "Homo Ludens." *Kenyon Review* 21 (Autumn 1959):662–68. Begins as high praise of Wright-Spears edition but ends as high praise of Prior himself for skill in octosyllabic and in anapaest and as "homo Ludens," a type of poet almost nonexistent in our own serious day.

Brown, T. J. "English Literary Autographs XXIII: Matthew Prior, 1664–1721." *Book Collector* 6 (Autumn 1957):279, plate. Comments on the two extremes of Prior's handwriting, illustrating both with photographic reproductions from the Portland Papers.

Carroll, Edward L. "A Memoir of Matthew Prior." *Union College Bulletin* 26 (1932):43–61. Chiefly a biographical summary, paralleling Prior's life and times to our own.

Cibber, Theophilus, [and Robert Shiels]. "Matthew Prior, Esq;" In *The Lives of the Poets of Great Britain and Ireland,* 4:43–57. London: R. Griffiths, 1753. An unreliable but interesting mid-18th-century account of Prior's life and valuation of his poems.

Conron, Alfred Brandon. "The Classical Influence in Matthew Prior's Poetry." Ph.D. diss., Harvard University, 1951. A bringing together of materials hitherto scattered in numerous books on the influence of single classical authors on English literature.

Cox, Mary Elizabeth. "Prior's Conversation Poems." *Bulletin of the West Virginia Association of College English Teachers* 1 (Spring 1974):20–27. A study of Prior's delight in mixing styles.

Crinò, Anna Maria. "L'Opera Letteraria di Matthew Prior." In *Atti e Memorie della Accademia di Agricoltura Scienze e Lettere di Verona,* 12:239–359. Ser. 6. Verona: Linotipia Veronese Ghidini e Fiorini, 1962. The first full-length study in Italian of Matthew Prior, considering him mainly by genres and particularly strong in treating the relationship between Dryden and Prior.

Dennis, John. "Matthew Prior." In *Studies in English Literature,* 109–47. London: Edward Stanford, 1876. A biographical and critical study of Prior, as diplomat and as poet, useful for its study of his influence on his contemporaries and on later poets.

Dobson, Austin. "Matthew Prior." *New Princeton Review* 6 (November 1888):281–311. Reprint. In Dobson, Austin. *Eighteenth-Century Vignettes.* Ser. 2. London: Dodd, Mead, & Co., 1894. A biographical and critical account of the poet, with lengthy quotations from him.

Doughty, Oswald. "Matthew Prior (1664–1721)." In *The English Lyric in the Age of Reason,* 46–56. London: Daniel O'Connor, 1922. Writes of Restoration qualities in Prior's lyrics and mixture of laughter and tears.

———. "The Poet of the 'Familiar Style.'" *English Studies* 7 (February 1925):5–10. Sides with Cowper against Johnson in defending Prior's "inimitable" social verse.

Ewing, Majl. "Musical Settings of Prior's Lyrics in the 18th Century." *ELH* 10 (June 1943):159–71. Prior's "long continued popularity as a lyric poet": fifty-three lyrics set to music, plus three ballads and two longer poems.

Frederickson, Kent Walter. "Matthew Prior: A Study of the Poetry of a Minor Augustan." Ph.D. diss., Harvard University, 1964.

Frey, Engelbert. *Der Einfluss der englischen, französischen, italienischen und lateinischen Literatur auf die Dichtungen Matthew Priors.* Strassburg: Karl

J. Trübner, 1915. An important study of European influences on the poetry of Prior.

Goad, Caroline. *Horace in the English Literature of the Eighteenth Century.* Yale Studies in English, no. 58. New Haven: Yale University Press, 1918. Devotes a chapter (pp. 90–116) to influence of Horace upon Prior's poetry and prose and resemblances and differences between the two poets.

Higby, John. "Ideas and Art in Prior's *Dialogues of the Dead.*" *Enlightenment Essays* 5 (Summer, 1974):62–69. Interprets the fourth dialogue as summing up the other three and the total work as deserving more attention.

———. "Matthew Prior's 'Dialogues of the Dead' and the Dialogue Tradition." Ph.D. diss., University of South Carolina, 1971.

Jack, Ian. "The 'Choice of Life' in Johnson and Prior." *Journal of English and Germanic Philology* 49 (October 1950):523–30. Influence of *Solomon* upon *Rasselas* and *Vanity of Human Wishes,* all in tradition of Christian pessimism.

Johnson, J. W. "Rasselas and His Ancestors." *Notes and Queries* 204 (May 1959):185–88. *Solomon* important to *Rasselas* chiefly for reminding Johnson of its source, *Ecclesiastes.*

Ketton-Cremer, R[obert] W[yndham]. *Matthew Prior.* Rede Lecture. Cambridge: University Press, 1957, 25 pp. A sympathetic and thoughtful tracing of Prior's public and poetic career.

Koger, James Alfred. "The Personal and Literary Relationship of Matthew Prior and Jonathan Swift." Ph.D. diss., Rice University, 1971.

Lawry, Jon S. "A Critical Study of the English Poetry of Matthew Prior." Ph.D. diss., Northwestern University, 1955. A close analysis of Prior's English poems, chiefly by genres.

Mack, Maynard. "Matthew Prior: et multa prior arte." *Sewanee Review* 68 (Winter 1960):165–76. Initially a review of the Wright-Spears edition of Prior, it becomes a tough modern estimate of Prior's strengths and weaknesses.

McGaw, Leslie Emerson. "Matthew Prior's Response to John Locke's 'Essay Concerning Human Understanding.' " Master's thesis, University of Western Ontario, 1966. A 132-page examination of *Alma* and of the Montaigne-Locke dialogue as reflections of Prior's response to Locke's "Essay."

Meier, T. K. "Prior's Adaptation of 'The Nutbrown Maid.' " *Moderna Sprak* (Stockholm) 68 (1974):331–36. Finds "gentle irony and amused worldliness" in Prior's treatment of the "Christian, mythological, classical, and heroic traditions" in *Henry and Emma.*

Morton, Richard. "Matthew Prior's *Dialogues of the Dead.*" *Ball State University Forum* 8 (Summer 1967):73–78. "From the traditional

forms of the *dialogue des morts* Prior absorbs what is meaningful, and he adds insights of his own."
Orr, Lee Anderson. "The Zeal of the Patriot: Matthew Prior as Panegyrist." Ph.D. diss., University of Virginia, 1971.
Ransom, Harry. "The Rewards of Authorship in the Eighteenth Century." *University of Texas Studies in English* 18 (1938):47–66. A discussion of the agreement under which Prior contracted *Poems on Several Occasions*, "One of the more interesting contracts for the publication of poetry in the early eighteenth century. . . ."
Richards, E. A. *Hudibras in the Burlesque Tradition*. Columbia University Studies in English and Comparative Literature, no. 127. New York: Columbia University Press, 1937. A detailed and thorough study of Prior as a writer of comic octosyllabics; also a contrast of *Alma* and *Hudibras*.
Rippy, Frances Mayhew. "Matthew Prior and Alexander Pope: Their Personal and Literary Relationship." Ph.D. diss., Vanderbilt University, 1957. 547 pp.
———. "Matthew Prior as the Last Renaissance Man." In *Studies in Medieval, Renaissance, American Literature: A Festschrift*, 120–31, 203. Fort Worth: Texas Christian University Press, 1971. An identification of markedly "Renaissance" traits in the writings of Prior.
Roberts, Gerald L. "A Commentary on Prior's 'Poems on Several Occasions.' " Master's thesis, University College of Swansea, Wales, 1956–57. A commentary on the 1718 edition of Prior's *Poems on Several Occasions*, it was the first full annotation attempted on Prior's work and included a short biographical account and a criticism of his poetry.
Rogal, Samuel J. *John and Charles Wesley*. Twayne's English Authors Series, no. 368. Boston: Twayne Publishers, 1983. Considers John Wesley's *Thoughts on the Character and Writings of Mr. Prior* to have been used more as an excuse to castigate Pope than to quarrel with Johnson (pp. 101–7).
Rower, Ronald Eugene. "Matthew Prior: A Critical Study." Ph.D. diss., Columbia University, 1968. 250 pp. Especially valuable for its full and informative analyses of the panegyric poems and of the *Dialogues of the Dead*.
———. "Pastoral Wars: Matthew Prior's Poems to Cloe." *Ball State University Forum* 19 (Spring 1978):39–49. "The Cloe poems are impressive examples of Prior's talent for depicting with warmth and understanding the intimate, somewhat childish, but central concerns of ordinary people. . . ."
Rubin, Emanuel Leo. "The English Glee from William Hayes to William Horsley." Ph.D. diss., University of Pittsburgh, 1968. 1635 pp. Has seven entries for "glee" settings in the second half of the eigh-

teenth century for five different Prior poems, including three for "A Song" ("If wine and music").

Saintsbury, George. *A History of English Prosody from the Twelfth Century to the Present Day*. Vol. 2. London: Macmillan & Co., 1908. Pages 423–35 contain the best single analysis of Prior's prosody, especially his use of anapaests and of octosyllabics.

———. *The Peace of the Augustans: A Survey of Eighteenth Century Literature as a place of Rest and Refreshment*. London: G. Bell & Sons, 1916. An original, thoughtful, sympathetic treatment of Prior's poetry, especially as containing that true English humor that mixes laughter and tears.

Shepherd, T. B. "John Wesley and Matthew Prior." *London Quarterly and Holborn Review*, July 1937, 368–73. Cites Prior's influence on both John and Charles Wesley.

Sichel, Walter. "Matthew Prior." *Quarterly Review* 190 (October 1899):356–80. Especially detailed on Prior's diplomatic career and on his relationship to Swift, Harley, and Bolingbroke.

Spears, Monroe K. "The Intellectual Background of Matthew Prior." Ph.D. diss., Princeton University, 1941. Remains the best single treatment of Prior's intellectual milieu.

———. "Matthew Prior's Attitude toward Natural Science." *PMLA* 63 (June 1948):485–507. Interprets Prior as "a harbinger of future dissatisfactions," the first imaginative writer to perceive the new science as materialistic and deterministic and to protest against its meaning in human terms.

———. "Matthew Prior's Religion." *Philological Quarterly* 27 (April 1948):159–80. Analyzes Prior as a Fideist manqué, a tragic figure wavering between faith in an incomprehensible God and logical questioning of theological doctrines.

———. "The Meaning of Matthew Prior's *Alma*." *ELH* 13 (December 1946):266–90. A detailed analysis of *Alma* as a carefully planned, significant, and characteristic application of Pyrrhonism to contemporary thought.

———. "Some Ethical Aspects of Matthew Prior's Poetry." *Studies in Philology* 45 (October 1948):606–29. Treats Prior as a resolute pessimist in ethics, convinced of man's depravity and that the passions triumph over reason, yet unsure that they should.

Spence, Joseph. *Observations, Anecdotes, and Characters of Books and Men Collected from Conversation*. Edited by James M. Osborn. 2 vols. Oxford: Clarendon Press, 1966. Almost all of Pope's literary criticism of Prior is contained in these anecdotes.

Stebbing, William. "Two Poet-Politicians: Abraham Cowley, Matthew Prior." In *Some Verdicts of History Reviewed*. London: John Murray,

1887. The Prior portion, covering pp. 82–121, is a reworking of "Article III," *North British Review* 27 (November 1857):366–401. A detailed if somewhat condescending analysis of Prior as poet and especially as diplomat, with special attention being paid to his high reputation, because "he affords, in his history, a complete epitome of his times."

Swift, Jonathan. *Prose Works of Jonathan Swift.* Edited by Herbert Davis. Oxford: Basil Blackwell, 1939–. Vols. 7–8 are especially pertinent, containing various pieces by Swift analyzing political questions in which Prior plays a major part.

Thackeray, William Makepeace. "Prior, Gay, and Pope." In *The English Humourists of the Eighteenth Century,* edited by Derek Stanford, 110–46. London: Grey Walls Press, 1949. A spirited defense of Prior's lyrics, as Horatian, easy, rich, charmingly humorous, happy, melodious.

Thayer, Harvey Waterman. "Matthew Prior, His Relation to English *Vers de Société.*" *Sewanee Review* 10 (April 1902):181–98. Sets up standards for *vers de société* and finds that by them Prior's light verse most nearly attains this ideal—compares and contrasts his verse to that of Herrick, Carew, Landor, Praed.

Welsh, John Harlan. "The Earthen Pot: Ups and Downs of Matthew Prior." Ph.D. diss., University of California at Berkeley, 1971.

Wesley, John. "Thoughts on the Character and Writings of Mr. Prior." *Arminian Magazine* 5 (November 1782, December 1782):600–603, 660–65. A defense of Prior, as man and as poet, against Johnson's "Life" and thus against Pope through Spence; ranks Prior as equal to Pope or Dryden in natural abilities, though not as painstaking and polished—and second only to Milton. Wisest interpretation of *Alma* done in its first 200 years.

Wright, H. Bunker. "Ideal Copy and Authoritative Text: The Problem of Prior's *Poems on Several Occasions* (1718)." *Modern Philology* 49 (1952):234–41. Collates seventeen copies of *Poems on Several Occasions* and receives reports on twenty-nine additional ones.

———. "Matthew Prior and Elizabeth Singer." *Philological Quarterly* 24 (January 1945):71–82. An analysis of the not very serious courtship between Matthew Prior and Elizabeth Singer, as revealed in nine of Prior's letters to her, written 1703–4.

———. "Matthew Prior's Cloe and Lisetta." *Modern Philology* 36 (August 1938):9–23. Identifies Prior's Cloe as Anne Durham and Lisetta as Elizabeth Cox and traces the probable course of his relationship with each.

———. "Matthew Prior's Funeral." *Modern Language Notes* 57 (May 1942):341–45. Describes obsequies in detail from data preserved in

Welbeck MS. records of Prior's executors, Edward Lord Harley and Adrian Drift.

―――. "Matthew Prior's 'Welbeloved and Dear Cossen.'" *Review of English Studies* 15 (July 1939):318-23. An account, based chiefly upon the Welbeck MS., of Katharine Prior, daughter of Prior's uncle Arthur.

―――."William Jackson on Prior's Use of Montaigne." *Modern Language Review* 31 (April 1936):203-5. William Jackson of Exeter in 1798 first pointed out Prior's indebtedness to Montaigne for the central idea of *Alma,* as well as for *The Thief and the Cordelier.*

Wright, H. Bunker, and Henry C. Montgomery. "The Art Collection of a Virtuoso in Eighteenth-Century England." *Art Bulletin* 27 (September 1945):195-204. A listing, description, and evaluation of Prior's collection of paintings and sculpture, based on his own list, on inventories and appraisals made shortly after his death, and on Welbeck Catalogues.

Wukadinovic, Spiridion. *Prior in Deutschland.* In *Grazer Studien zur deutschen Philologie,* vol. 4, edited by Anton E. Schoenbach and Bernhard Seuffert. Graz: K. K. Unicweaitäts-Buchdruckerei und Verlags-Buchhandlung 'Styria.' A seventy-one-page study, chiefly tracing the direct influence of Prior on certain German poets.

Index

Abelard, Peter, 85–86, *123–26*
Abell, John, 21
Addison, Joseph, 18, 22, 26, 67, 98, 130
Adrian VI, Pope (Adrian Dedel), 107
Aglionby, William, 10
Agrippina II, 117–18
Anacreon, 16
Anne, Queen of England, 18, 20, 21, 22, 23, 24, 26, 27, 29, 31, *32–33*, 34, 44, *52–55*, 85, 98, 133
Ansley, Jane (Flanders Jane, Jane, Jinny), 11, 22, 25, *61–62*, 70
Arbuthnot, John, 35, 37, 42
Aristotle, 91
Arminian Magazine, 132
Arne, Thomas Augustine, 64, 85
Athaliah, 112
Atkins, J. W. H., 132
Atterbury, Francis, 2, 26, 61, 120

Ball, F. Elrington, 121–22
Bally, George, 89, 126
Bathurst, Allen Bathurst, first Earl, 35, 91
Bavaria, Elector of. *See* Maximilian Emmanuel
Beattie, James, 107, 115
Beaufort, Lady Margaret, Countess of Richmond and Derby, 9
Behn, Aphra, 70
Bentinck, William, first Earl of Portland, 16, 17, 19
Berkeley, Charles, Viscount Dursley, second Earl of Berkeley, 10–11, 13, 46
Bertuch, Fr. Justin, 85, 133
Bett, Henry, 132
Betterton, Thomas, 66
Bible, 7–8, 15, 25, 36, 42, 60, 68–70, 87–93, 97, 99–102, 126–28, 131, 152
Billers, 4
Bion, 77
Blaithwayt (Blathwayt), William, 14
Board of Trade and Plantations, 17–18, 19, 23
Boccaccio, Giovanni, 32
Boileau-Despréaux, Nicolas, 17, 22, 47, 48, 52–53, 55–56; "Ode Sur la Prise de Namur, Par les Armes du Roy, L'Année 1692," 50–51
Bolingbroke, Viscount. *See* St. John, Henry
Bond, Richmond P., 93
Booth, Barton, 67
Bourbons, 11
Boyce, Benjamin, 147n14
Bray, Vicar of, 107, 111–13
Bredvold, Louis I., 68, 93
Bridgeman, Charles, 39
Brooks, Harold F., 142–43n23
Brothers Club, 26–27, 30, 120
Brown, Richard G., 136n30
Browning, Robert, 118
Buckhurst, Lord. *See* Sackville, Lionel Cranfield, first Duke of Dorset
Buckingham, second Duke of. *See* Villiers, George
Burleigh, 8–9, 10
Busby, Richard, 1–2, 3, 98
Butler, James, second Duke of Ormonde, 24
Butler, Samuel, *Hudibras*, 10, *91–93*

Callimachus, 108
Cambridge University, 91. *See also* St. John's College
Carew, Thomas, 80
Carye, Antony, Viscount Falkland, 13
Caryll, John, senior, 122
Cavendishes, 2
Cecil, John, Fifth Earl of Exeter, 8–9, 10, 26, 45, 60
Charles I, King of England, 114
Charles II, King of England, 44
Charles V, Holy Roman Emperor and King of Spain, 107–10, 111–12, 114
Chaucer, Geoffrey, 30, 41, 86
"Chevy Chase," 75
Churchill, George, 60
Churchill, John, first Duke of Marlborough, *21–22*, 24, 32, *52–55*, 60, 85
Churchill, Sarah Jennings, Duchess of Marlborough, *21–22*, 24, 26
Cibber, Colley, 67
Cicero, 112

Index

Colbert, Jean Baptiste, Marquis de Torcy, 17, 28, 30, 31
Congress of Ryswick, 14
Congreve, William, 3, 18, 22, 130
Coningsby, Thomas Coningsby, Earl, 34, 38, 55
Cooper, Anthony Ashley, first Earl of Shaftesbury, 127
Corneille, Pierre, 115
Cory, William Johnson: "In Honour of Matthew Prior," 133
Cotentin, Anne-Hilarion de, Comte de Tourville, 46
Cowley, Abraham, 2, 7, 8, 44
Cowper, William, 85, 90, 92, 121, 126, 132
Cox, Elizabeth, 37
Cox, John, 37
Crabbe, George, 90
Creech, Thomas, 70
Cromwell, Oliver, 107, 114–15
Curll, Edmund, 23, 41

Dacier, André, 17
Dalrymple, John, Earl of Stair, 33
Dante, 63
d'Arconville, Thiroux, 85
Davenant, William, 96–97
de Neufville, François, duc de Villeroy, 17
De Vrigny, 48
Deborah, 112
Defoe, Daniel: "Reformation of Manners, A Satyr," 21
Dennis, John (18th century), 85
Dennis, John (19th century), 37
Descartes, René, 91
Dibben, Thomas, 52
Diderot, Denis: *Les Bijoux Indiscrets*, 92
Dionysius the Younger, Tyrant of Syracuse, 109
Dobson, Austin, 121
Dobson, William, 89, 126
Dodd, Henry Philip, 57
Donne, John, 96
Dorset, first Duke of. *See* Sackville, Lionel Cranfield, Lord Buckhurst
Dorset, sixth Earl of. *See* Sackville, Charles
Doughty, Oswald, 81, 132
Draper, J. W., 74
Drift, Adrian, 16, 35, 38, 41, 42, 121
Dryden, John, 2, 5–6, 7, 15, 44, 64, 70–71, 96–97, 98, 99, 122, 130, 131, 142n15; "Absalom and Achitophel," 45, 101; Chaucer modernization, 86; *Cleomenes*, 13, 66; *Conquest of Granada, The*, 116; *Hind and the Panther, The*, 5–6, 9, 18, 45, 71–73; Preface to *Fables Ancient and Modern*, 86; *Religio Laici*, 8; Virgil translation, 119
Dudley, Henry Bate, 64, 85
Dupplin, Viscount. *See* Hay, Thomas, eighth Earl of Kinnoull
Durham, Anne, 22–23, 27, 37, 125
Dursley, Viscount. *See* Berkeley, Charles

Egilsrud, Johan S., 147n14
Eliot, T. S., 58
Elizabeth I, Queen of England, 112
Ely, Francis, Lord Bishop of. *See* Turner, Francis
Etherege, George, 3
Eves, Charles Kenneth, 130, 135n2
Ewing, Majl, 64–65, 141
Examiner, The (Tory), 26
Exeter, fifth Earl of. *See* Cecil, John

Fairchild, Hoxie Neale, 88–89
Falkland, Viscount. *See* Carye, Antony
Fénelon, François de Salignac de La Mothe, Archbishop of Cambrai, 108
Fielding, Henry: *Amelia*, 37; *Tom Jones*, 37
Finch, Anne, Countess of Winchilsea, 132
Finch, Daniel, Earl of Nottingham, 11, 29
Flatman, Thomas, "A Thought of Death," 123
Fontenelle, Bernard le Bovier de, 17, 108
Ford, Charles, 35
Franklin, Benjamin, 123

Gafney (Gaphney), 34
Galliard, Johann Ernst, 129
Garth, Samuel, 26, 97–98, 100
Gaultier, Abbé François, 28, 33
Gay, John, 26, 35, 121
Gayton, Edmund: *Pleasant Notes upon Don Quixot*, 78
George I, King of England, 23, 32–33
Gibbon, Edward, 90
Gibbs, James, 39, 42–43
Gleim, Johann Wilhelm Ludwig, 133
Godolphin, Sidney, first Earl of, 26, 97–98
Goldsmith, Oliver, 78, 92; *The Beauties of English Poesy* (ed.), 79
Gombauld, Jean Ogier de, 58
Gosse, Edmund, 90
Götz, Johann Nikolaus, 133

Gower, Humphrey, 4, 8
Greek Anthology, 58
Grynaeus, Simon, 89, 126
Guérin, Claudine Alexandrine, Mme de Tencin, 30–31
Guiscard, Antoine de, 27, 30, 54

Hadrian, 25, 123, 126, 149n18
Hagedorn, von, Friedrich, 132
Halifax, first Earl of. *See* Montagu, Charles
Hanoverians, 54
Hapsburgs, 11
Harcourt, Simon, 141n8
Harley, Edward Harley, second Earl of Oxford, 35, 37, *38–41*, 42, 58, 62, 91, 129–30
Harley, Lady Henrietta Cavendish Holles, 38, 42
Harley, Lady Margaret Cavendish Holles, Duchess of Portland, *38–39*, 41, 107
Harley, Robert, first Earl of Oxford and Mortimer, 20, 27, *28–29*, 30, 31, 32, 33, 34, 38, 54, 120
Harley, Thomas, 33, 34
Harris, Brice, 44
Harrison, George, 2
Harrison, Katharine. *See* Prior, Katharine
Hay, Thomas, Viscount Dupplin, eighth Earl of Kinnoull, 66–67
Héloïse, 85–86, 123–26
Henri IV, King of France, 51
Herder, Johann Gottfried von, 133
Hobbes, Thomas: *Leviathan*, 5
Holbein, Hans (the younger), 61
Holmes, Oliver Wendell, 133
Homer, 95, 96, 97, *Iliad*, 34, 36, *98–100*
Horace, 2, 12–13, 21, 46, 47, 48, 49, 50, 60, 71–72, 83, 95, 96, 99, 120, 121–22, 128–29
Hughes, John, 125
Hustvedt, Sigurd Bernhard, 141

Jack, Ian, 131
James Francis Edward Stuart, 9, 16, 18–19, 20, 45
James II, King of England, 9, 10, 16, 18, 20, 44, 45–46, 51, 52
Jane (Flanders Jane, Jinny). *See* Ansley, Jane
Jereboam, 88
Jersey, Earl of. *See* Villiers, Edward
Jezebel, 112
Johnson, Esther (Stella), 26–27, 29, 31, 120
Johnson, J. W., 99, 147n8, 152n55

Johnson, Samuel, 6, 50, 67, 79, 89, 90, 92, 93, 120, 127, *131*, 132, 133; "Life of Pope," 123–24, 152; "Life of Prior," 131; *Rasselas*, 80, 89–90, 131, 152; *Vanity of Human Wishes, The*, 89–90, 131
Jones, John, 75
Jonson, Ben, 2, 80; "Ode the First. The Fourth Booke. To Venus," 129
Judith, 112
Juvenal, 5, 71

Killigrew, Thomas (the younger): *Chit-Chat*, 67
King, William, Archbishop of Dublin, 121
Kit-Cat Club, 18, 19, 66
Kleynaerts (Clenardus), Nicolas, *108–10*, 111–12, 114
Kline, Richard B., 148n17
Kneller, Godfrey, 24
Koger, James Alfred, 148n1

La Fontaine, Jean de, 21, 32
Lawry, Jon Sherman, 136n16, 140n4
Le Brun, Antoine, 58
Legg, L. G. Wickham, 148n2
Legges, 2
"Letter to Mr. Prior, A," 53
Lexington, Lady. *See* Sutton, Margaret Hungerford
Lexington, second Baron. *See* Sutton, Robert
Lewis, Erasmus, 27, *35–36*, 42
Leyden, University of, 13
Locke, John, 2, 18, 107, 110–11, 114, 151n48
Locker-Lampson, Frederick, 133
Lockier, Francis, Dean of Peterborough, 6
London Post, 64
Longleat, 10
Lords Justices of Ireland, 16, 17
Louis XIV, King of France, 9, 11, 16, 17, 19, 28, 29, 31, 33, 47, 48, 50, 51
Lucian, 108
Lucretius, 67
Luttrell, Narcissus, 14

Mack, Maynard, 56, 81
Macky, John, 23, 28
Maintenon, Françoise d'Aubigné, Marquise de, 29
Manchester, fourth Earl and first Duke of. *See* Montague, Charles
Manchester House, 3
Manley, Mary de la Rivière: *Lucius*, 67

Index

Marlborough, Duchess of. *See* Churchill, Sarah Jennings
Marlborough, first Duke of. *See* Churchill, John
Martial, 58
Martin, Burns, 133, 153n68
Martin, Thomas, 92
Mary I, Queen of England, 112
Mary II, Queen of England (wife to William III), 10, 13, 45–50, 55, 61
Mary of Modena, Queen of England (wife to James II), 16, 44
Matthews, Brander, 133
Maximilian Emmanuel, Elector of Bavaria, 31
Meleager, 58
Mennes, John, 134
Meredith, George: *Modern Love,* 24
Mesnager, Nicholas, 28–29, 33
Mézeray, François Eudes de: *Histoire de France,* 25, 69
Milton, John, 96, 132: *Lycidas,* 61
Monmouth, Duke of. *See* Scott, James
Montagu, 2
Montagu, Charles, Earl of Halifax, 3, 5–7, 9, 10–12, 15, 17, 18, 19, 20, 33, 60, 69, 71–72, 128
Montagu, George, 3
Montagu, James, 3, 19, 60, 71–72
Montagu, Mary Wortley, 85, 124, 125: "Basset-Table," 85
Montague, Charles, fourth Earl and first Duke of Manchester, 17
Montaigne, Michel Eyquem de, 93, 107, 110–11, 151n48
Montgomery, Henry C., 38
Monthly Review, 79
More, Hannah, 90
More, Thomas (16th-century English), 107, 111–13
More, Thomas (19th-century Irish), 133
Morley, John, 40, 139n76
Morton, Richard, 147n14
Moschus, 58
Motteux, Peter, 14: *Gentleman's Journal,* 12, 47
Mulgrave, third Earl of, first Duke of Buckingham and Normanby. *See* Sheffield, John
Muses Mercury, 84

Nassau, 63
Nero, 117–18
Nicoll, Allardyce, 67

Nottingham, Earl of. *See* Daniel Finch
Nut-brown Maid, 84–86

Oldfield, Anne, 26, 67
Orford, Earl of. *See* Russell, Edward
Ormonde, second Duke of. *See* Butler, James
Otway, Thomas, 3, *The Orphan,* 66–67
Ovid, 2, 24, 34, 75, 78–79, 95, 124: Metamorphoses, 98, *100–02,* 109
Oxford, first Earl of. *See* Harley, Robert
Oxford University, 91

Parnham, Caleb, 75
Percy, Elizabeth, Duchess of Somerset, 3
Pindar, 4, 20, 46, 49, 51, 55–56, 120
Plautus, 27
Pliny, *Historia Naturalis,* 76
Pope, Alexander, 25, 35, 39–40, 41, 75, 90, 91, 92, 93, 99, 107, 115, 120, 121, 122–31, 134, 152; "Adriani morientis ad Animam: The Same by Another Hand," 123, 126; Chaucer modernization, 86; "Christiani Morientis Ad Animam," 123; *Dunciad,* 71, 86, 123, 124, 130; *Eloisa to Abelard,* 85–86, 123–26; *Essay on Criticism,* 99; *Essay on Man,* 8, 42, 89, 126–28; "First Epistle of the First Book of Horace Imitated," 151n48; "First Epistle of the Second Book of Horace, Imitated, The," 151n48; "First Ode of the Fourth Book of Horace, The," 129; *Iliad* translation, 36, 97, 119; "Imitation of the Sixth Satire of the Second Book of Horace, An," 128–29; *Memoirs of . . . Martinus Scriblerus* (with others), 92; *Miscellanies* (ed. with Swift), 62; *Odyssey* translation, 97, 119; *Of the Characters of Women: An Epistle to a Lady,* 86, 124; *Rape of the Lock, The,* 58, 86, 130; *Windsor Forest,* 86, 124
Portland, Duchess of. *See* Harley, Lady Margaret Cavendish Holles
Portland, first Earl of. *See* Bentinck, William
Powys, Ambrose, 61
Powys, Thomas, 61
Praed, Winthrop Mackworth, 133
Prior, Arthur, 1–3, 5, 9
Prior, Elizabeth, 1–2
Prior, George, 1–2
Prior, Katharine (Katharine Harrison), 4, 14, 60
Prior, Matthew—Life: birth (1664), 1; childhood (1664–76), 1–3, 9; collections, 37–38; Clubs: Kit-Cats, 18, 19; Brothers,

26–27; death (1721), 42; education (c. 1673–75, 1676–83, 1683–87); At Westminster School (c. 1673–75, 1676–83), 1–3, 104; At St. John's, Cambridge (1683–87), 3–5, 7, 8, 9, 10, 14, 44, 68, 70, 104; funeral, 42–43; Houses: Down Hall, 10, 39–40, 43, 74–75, 81, 139n76; "Matt's Palace," 19, 26, 36–38, 43; Mistresses: Flanders Jane Ansley, 11, 22, 25, 61–62, 70; Elizabeth Cox, 37; Anne Durham, 22–23, 27, 37, 125; retirement, 35–42; trial before secret committee, 33–35; Professional Career: Keyton Fellow, St. John's College (1688—), 7; tutor to sons of Earl of Exeter (1688–89), 8, 45; Secretary at The Hague (1690–97), 10–16, 46; Linacre Lecturer, St. John's College (1706–10), 7, 94; Secretary to the Lords Justices, 16, 17; Secretary to the British Embassy in Paris (1697–99), 16–17; Secret diplomatic agent to Paris (1700–02), 17–18; Member of Parliament from East Grinstead (1701), 18–19; Negotiations with France (1712–15), 27–30, Commissioner of Customs, 30

WORKS:

"Ad Magistrum," 8; "Adriani Morientis ad Animam Suam. Imitated," 25, 123, 149n18; "Advice to the Painter. On the happy defeat of the Rebels in the West, and the Execution of the late Duke of Monmouth," 45; *Alma: or, The Progress of the Mind*, 7, 10, 15, 35, 36, 70, 84, 90–94, 102, 107, 108, 109, 123, 126, 132; "Another" ("To John I ow'd great Obligation"), 58; "Answer to Cloe Jealous, in the same Stile. The Author sick," 81–82; "Ballad" ("THE Crown once again"), 20, 52; "Ballad" ("THE factions that Each other claw"), 20, 52; "Better Answer, A," 81–83; *Britanicus and Junia*, 115–18; "Cantata. Set by Monsieur Galliard," 129; "Carmen Seculare, For the Year 1700. To the King," 20, 51, 55, 64; "Celia to Damon," 125; "Chameleon, The," 25; "Charity. A Paraphrase on the Thirteenth Chapter of the First Epistle to the Corinthians," 25; "Charity never faileth," 25; "Cloe Jealous," 81; "Conversation. A Tale, The," 41, 74, 89; "Crest of the Arms of the Earl of Exeter a Wheatsheaf supported by Two Lyons," 10; "Cupid and Ganymede," 75; "Daphne and Apollo," 34, 75–76, 83; "Democritus and Heraclitus," 58; *Dialogues of the Dead*, 95, 102, 107–15; ("A Dialogue between Charles the Emperor and Clenard the Grammarian," 107–10, 111–12, 114–15; "A Dialogue between Mr: John Lock and Seigneur de Montaigne," 107, 110–11, 114–15; "A Dialogue between the Vicar of Bray, and Sir Thomas More," 107, 111–13; "A Dialogue between Oliver Cromwell, and his Porter," 107, 114–15); "Dove, The," 76; "Down-Hall; A Ballad," 10, 40, 74–75, 81; "Dutch Proverb, A," 25–26; "English Ballad, On the Taking of Namur by the King of Great Britain, 1695, An," 13, 50–51; "English Padlock, An," 25, 77; "Enigma," 14; "Epigram" ("HER time with equal prudence Celia shares"), 58; "Epigram" ("LUKE Preach-ill admires what we Laymen can mean"), 59; "Epigram" ("STIL craving yet stil Roger cry'd"), 59; "Epilogue to Lucius," 67; "Epilogue to Phaedra. Spoken by Mrs. Oldfield, who acted Ismena," 26, 67–68; "Epistle, Desiring the Queen's Picture, An," 32–54; "Epistle to Fleetwood Shepherd, Esq; Burleigh, May 14, 1689, An," 9, 10; "Epistola ad Magistrum," 8; "Epitaph, An" ("INTERR'D beneath this Marble Stone"), 62–63; "Epitaph" ("MY Lord there's a Christ'ning the Officer said"), 61; "Epitaph" ("NOBLES, and Heralds by Your leave"), 25, 63; "Epitaph for Sir Thomas Powys," 61; "Epitaph on True, her Majesty's Dog, An," 47, 61; "Epitaph upon Gilbert Glanvill Bishop of Rochester, as written in Rochester Cathedral. Translated," 61; "Epitaphium Joannis Comitis Exoniae," 26, 60; *Examiner*, no. 6, 26, 54, 97–98, 100; "Extempore Invitation to the Earl of Oxford, Lord High Treasurer. 1712, An," 30; "Fable, A" ("IN AEsop's Tales an honest Wretch we find"), 20, 52; "Fable, A" ("THE Fox an Actor's Vizard found"), 26; "First Hymn of Callimachus, The," 108; "Florimel,"

Index

54; "For His Own Epitaph," 32, 63–64; "For my own Tomb-stone," 63; "For the Plan of a Fountain," 24; "Frederic & ca: From Boccace," 32; "Garland, The," 85; "Hans Carvel," 21, 78–80; "Heads for a Treatise upon Learning," 4, 102–05, 115; *Henry and Emma*, 25, 64, 84–87, 89, 93, 123–24; *Hind and the Panther Transvers'd to the Story of The Country Mouse and the City Mouse, The* 5–6, 9, 45, 71–73, 98, 128–29; *History of His Own Time*, 33; "Human Life," 58; "hymn to the Sun. Set by Dr. Purcel, and Sung before their Majesties on New-Years-Day, 1694," 13, 47, 64; "In a Window in Lord V. . . . . .s house 1696," 15; "Inter Emblemata et Carmina," 48; "Jinny the Just," 11, 25, 61–62, 89; "Journey to Copt-Hall," 10; *Ladislaus*, 115–18; "Ladle, The," 24, 74, 78–80; "Lady who offers her Looking-Glass to Venus, The," 58; "Lamentatio Davidis super Saulum & Jonathanem," 60; Latin poems, 4; "Les Estreines," 21; "Letter to J. . . . ," 70; "Letter to Monsieur Boileau Despreaux: Occasion'd by the Victory at Blenheim, 1704, A," 22, 23–24, 151n48; "Letter to the Honorable Lady Mrs: Margaret Candish Harley, A," 81; "Merchant, to secure his treasure, The," 24; "Mercury and Cupid," 76; "My Birth Day," 64–66, 97; "My noble, lovely, little Peggy," 39; "New Answer to An Argument against a Standing Army, A," 15, 51; "Observations on Homer: A Letter," 34, 98–100, 115; "Observations on Ovid's Metamorphoses," 98, 100–02, 109, 115; "Ode, An" ("THE Merchant, to secure his Treasure"), 81; "Ode, Humbly Inscrib'd to the Queen. On the Glorious Success of Her Majesty's Arms, 1706, An," 23–24, 53–54, 95–96; "Ode in Imitation of the Second Ode of the Third Book of Horace, An," 12, 46, 50; "Ode. Inscribed to the Memory of the Honble Col. George Villiers, Drowned in the River Piava, in the Country of Friuli. 1703, An," 22, 25, 60, 68; "Ode. Presented to the King, on his Majesty's Arrival in Holland, After the Queen's Death. 1695, An," 13, 49, 51, 61; "On Exodus iii.14," 7–8, 68–69, 89, 100, 126; "On Fleet: Shepheards takeing away a childs bread and butter," 9, 70; "On Mr: F. S. Killing the French K. . . ," 9, 70; "On the Coronation of the Most August Monarch K. James II, and Queen Mary. The 23rd. of April, 1685," 44; "On the taking of Huy," 13, 46–47, 50; "Opinion," 102, 105, 108, 110, 115, 126; "Orange, The," 9, 45; "Parting with Flavia," 100; "Paulo Purganti and His Wife: An Honest, but a Simple Pair," 24–25, 78–80; "Pindarique on His Majesties Birth-Day. Sung before Their Majesties at Whitehall, The Fourth of November 1690, A," 12, 46; "Predestination, A Poem," 42, 69–70, 89, 100; "Presented to the King, at his Arrival in Holland, after the Discovery of the Conspiracy 1696," 15, 51; "Prologue" ("LADIES, to YOU with pleasure we submit"), 67; "Prologue, By Sir John Falstaff" (with other members of the Kit-Cat Club), 66; "Prologue, Spoken at Court before the Queen, on Her Majesty's Birth-Day, 1704," 24; "Prologue to The Orphan," 66–67; "Protogenes and Apelles," 76–77; *Satyr on the modern Translators, A*, 4, 5, 70–71; *Satyr on the Poets: In Imitation of the Seventh Satyr of Juvenal*, 5, 71; "Seeing the Duke of Ormond's Picture, at Sir Godfrey Kneller's," 24; *Session of the Poets, A*, 7; "Simile, A" ("DEAR THOMAS, didst Thou never pop"), 25; "Simile" ("THE worthless Cypher when Alone"), 59; *Solomon on the Vanity of the World*, 15, 25, 36, 42, 68, 78, 84, 87–90, 91, 92, 93, 97, 100, 102, 126–28, 131, 152; "Song" ("HAST my Nannette my lovely Maid"), 64–65; "Song, A" ("IN vain You tell your parting Lover"), 21; "Song. Sett by Mr: Abell," 21; "Thief and the Cordelier, A Ballad, The," 77; "To a Child of Quality of Five Years Old, the Author suppos'd Forty," 21, 39, 81; "To a Lady: She refusing to continue a Dispute with me, and leaving me in the Argument," 22; "To a Young Gentleman in Love. A Tale," 24; "To Dr: F. . . . . in a Letter to Beverley disswading him from drinking Waters," 70; "To Isaac Bickerstaff commonly called the Tatler," 97; "To Mr Charles Montagu," 6–7; "To Mr. Fleetwood Shepherd," 9; "To Mr. Harley. Wounded by Guiscard. 1711," 27, 30; "To Mr: K----s Tune of the Prince's march," 9, 45–46; "To the Author of Love and Friendship: A Pastoral," 22; "To the Honourable Charles Montague, Esq;" 12, 15, 69; "True Statesmen," 32, 54; "Truth and Falshood. A Tale," 77; "Turtle and the Sparrow, The," 39, 41, 77–78; "Viceroy. A Ballad, The," 34–55; " 'Who would, says Dryden, Drink this draught of Life,' " 15; "Written at Paris, 1700. In the Beginning of Robe's Geography," 21; "Written in Imitation of a Greek Epigram," 58; "Written in the Beginning of Mezeray's History of France," 25, 69; "Written in the Nouveaux Interests des Princes de l'Europe," 25; "Written in the Year 1696" ("The Secretary"), 15

WORKS—EDITIONS:
Dialogues of the Dead and Other Works in Prose and Verse (A. R. Waller ed., 1907), 102–07; *Literary Works* (H. Bunker Wright and Monroe K. Spears ed., 1959, 1971), 117; *Poems on Several Occasions* (Edmund Curll ed., 1707), 23; *Poems on Several Occasions* (Jacob Tonson ed., 1709, 1711, 1713, 1717), 26, 36, 95; *Poems on Several Occasions* (Jacob Tonson ed., 1718), 35–36, 41, 85, 95, 119, 120, 122, 123, 124, 131

Prior, Samuel, 1
Purcell, Henry, 13, 47, 55, 64
Purpus, Eugene R., 108
Pyrrho of Elis, 87, 89, 107, 127–28

Rabelais, François, 21
Racine, Jean Baptiste: *Britannicus,* 115–17
Ralph, James, 85–86: *Sawney. An Heroic Poem,* 123
Ramsay, Allan, 133: "Robert, Richy, and Sandy," 133
Ransom, Harry, 36
Rehoboam, 88
Richards, E. A., 92–93
Robbe (Robe), Jacques, 21

Roberts, W., 38
Rochester, Bishop of. *See* Sprat, Thomas
Rochester, Earl of. *See* Wilmot, John
Rogal, Samuel J., 132
Romulus, 118
Root, Robert Kilburn, 125
Rotrou, Jean de: *Venceslas,* 115–16
Rowe, Elizabeth. *See* Singer, Elizabeth
Rowe, Nicholas, 2, 18, 26, 44
Rowe, Thomas, 22
Rower, Ronald Eugene, 140n2, 147n14
Royal Society, 16
Russell, Edward, Earl of Orford, 19, 46
Russells, 3
Rymer, Thomas, 70
Ryswick, Congress of, 14, 16
Ryswick, Treaty of, 15, 16, 51

Sackville, Charles, sixth Earl of Dorset, 2, 3, 4, 6, 9–10, 18, 19, 22, 23, 41, 44, 48, 66, 72, 95
Sackville, Lionel Cranfield, Lord Buckhurst, first Duke of Dorset, 13, 41, 66, 95
Sackvilles, 2
St. John, Henry, Viscount Bolingbroke, 30, 31, 32
St. John's College, Cambridge University, 3–5, 7, 8, 9, 10, 14, 44, 45, 68, 70, 89, 94, 104
Saintsbury, George, 127
Sappho, 16
Savage, Richard, 85–86, 123–24: *An Author To be Lett,* 41
Scaliger, Julius Caesar, 99–100
Scott, James, Duke of Monmouth, 45, 106–07
Scott, Walter, 25, 90
Second Partition Treaty, 17, 19
Sedley, Charles, 7
Seymour, Elizabeth Percy, Duchess of Somerset, 3
Shadwell, Thomas, 3, 44
Shaftesbury, first Earl of. *See* Cooper, Anthony Ashley
Shakespeare, William, *Antony and Cleopatra,* 116–17; *Hamlet,* 116; *1 Henry IV,* 66; *2 Henry IV,* 82
Shaw, Samuel, 13
Sheffield, John, third Earl of Mulgrave, first Duke of Buckingham and Normanby, 70
Shelton, Richard, 42, 91–92
Shenstone, William, 85

Index

Shepherd (or Sheppard), Fleetwood, 2, 9, 10, 70
Shrewsbury, Duke of. *See* Talbot, Charles
Singer, Elizabeth (Elizabeth Rowe), 22, 24
Smith, Edmund: *Phaedra and Hippolitus,* 67–68
Somers, John Somers, Baron, 19
Somerset, Duchess of (Elizabeth Percy Seymour). *See* Percy, Elizabeth
South Sea Bubble, 43, 122
Southey, Robert, 130–31
Spears, Monroe K., 7, 8, 34, 90, 91, 115, 128, 135n2, 150n45
Spence, Joseph, 6, 75, 122, 134
Spenser, Edmund, 54, 55, 95–96, 120, 134: *Faerie Queene,* 96
Sprat, Thomas, Bishop of Rochester, 2, 141n5
Stafford, Earl of. *See* Wentworth, Thomas, Baron Raby
Stair, Earl of. *See* Dalrymple, John
Stanyan, Abraham, 18
Stebbing, William, 140n4
Steele, Richard, 18, 26, 67
Stella. *See* Johnson, Esther
Stepney, George, 3, 10, 49
Stratford, William, 37
Struckmann, J. G., 133
Suckling, John, 7, 80, 134
Sutherland, James, 81, 86, 123
Sutton, Margaret Hungerford, Lady Lexington, 48
Sutton, Robert, second Baron Lexington, 48
Swift, Jonathan, 23, 26, 30, 32, 35–36, 38, 41, 62, 98, 120–22, 130, 134, 152n52, *Battle of the Books,* 111; "Bubble, The," 122; *Cadenus and Vanessa,* 122; *Conduct of the Allies,* 27; "Excellent New Song, Being the Intended Speech of a famous Orator against Peace, An," 29; "Fable of the Widow and Her Cat, The," 121; *History of the Four Last Years of the Queen,* 28; "Horace, Lib. 2. Sat. 6," 122; "Imitation of the Sixth Satire of the Second Book of Horace, An," 128–29; *Journal to Stella,* 26–27, 31, 120; *New Journey to Paris: Together with some Secret Transactions Between the Fr---h K--g, and an Eng---- Gentleman, A,* 28–29; "Part of the Seventh Epistle of the First Book of Horace Imitated," 122; *Proposal for Correcting . . . the English Tongue,* 27; *Rod of Sid Hamet,* 27; "To Charles Ford Esq. on his Birth-day January 31st for the Year 1722–3," 35

Talbot, Charles, Duke of Shrewsbury, 14, 17, 31, 32, 33
Tate, Nahum, 44
Tatler, 26, 65, 97, 98
Tencin, Mme de. *See* Guérin, Claudine Alexandrine
Thackeray, William Makepeace, 121, 133: *Henry Esmond,* 32
Thynne, Thomas, first Viscount Weymouth, 22
Tillotson, Geoffrey, 124, 125
Tonson, Jacob, 12, 18, 22, 23, 36, 47, 50
Torcy, Marquis de. *See* Colbert, Jean Baptiste
Tourville, Comte de. *See* Cotentin, Anne-Hilarion de
Townsend, Charles, second Viscount, 15
Trevelyan, G. M., 28
Trinity College, Cambridge, 3
Turner, Francis, Bishop of Ely, 4

Utrecht, Treaty of, 29–31, 54
Uz, Johann Peter, 133

Van Doren, Mark, 81
Vernon, James, 48
Villeroy, Duc de. *See* de Neufville, François
Villiers, George (husband to Katharine Prior), 2, 14, 22, 25, 60, 68
Villiers, George, second Duke of Buckingham(shire): *The Rehearsal,* 71–73
Villiers, Mary, 21
Villiers, Viscount Edward, Earl of Jersey, 13, 14, 15, 16, 17, 21, 22, 23
Virgil, 53, 96
Voltaire, François Marie Arouet de, 90

Waller, A. R., 102, 107
Waller, Edmund, 7, 96–97, 130
Walpole, Horace, 19, 75, 76, 77, 85, 92, 115, 134
Walpole, Robert, 19, 34
Walsh, William, 90
War of the Grand Alliance, The (The War of the League of Augsburg), 11, 14, 19, 50, 51
War of the Spanish Succession, The, 29–31
Ward, Ned, 18
Warton, Joseph, 92–93
Warton, Thomas (the younger), 85
Wentworth, Thomas, Baron Raby, Earl of Stafford, 29

Wesley, Charles, 132
Wesley, John, 85, 90, 93, 126, 132
Wesley, Samuel (the younger), 132
Westminster Abbey, 42, 119, 134
Westminster School, 1–3, 7, 8, 10, 13, 66–67, 98, 104
Weymouth, first Viscount. *See* Thynne, Thomas
Whig-Examiner, 26, 98
Wieland, Christoph Martin: *Musarion*, 132
Wilks, Robert, 67
William III, King of England, 9, 10, 13, 14, 15, 17, 18, 19–20, 21, 23, 24, 44, 45–55, 64, 107
Williams, Harold, 121
Williams, Marjorie, 85
Wilmot, John, Earl of Rochester, 7, 80
Winchilsea, Countess of. *See* Finch, Anne
Wordsworth, William, 74
Wren, Christopher, 2
Wright, H. Bunker, 7, 8, 34, 38, 39, 43, 90, 117, 125, 135n2, 138n64, 139n79, 140n87
Wukadinovic, Spiridion, 132–33
Wycherley, William, 7

3